CHINA AND AFRICA ———

CHINA AND AFRICA —————

THE NEW ERA

Daniel Large

polity

First published in 2021 by Polity Press

Polity Press
65 Bridge Street
Cambridge CB2 1UR, UK

Polity Press
101 Station Landing
Suite 300
Medford, MA 02155, USA

ISBN-13: 978-1-5095-3632-0 (hardback)
ISBN-13: 978-1-5095-3633-7 (paperback)

A catalogue record for this book is available from the British Library.
Library of Congress Cataloging-in-Publication Data

Names: Large, Daniel, author.
Title: China and Africa : the new era / Daniel Large.
Description: Cambridge, UK ; Medford, MA : Polity Press, 2021. | Series:
  China today series | Includes bibliographical references and index. |
  Summary: "A concise and up-to-date guide to one of the most crucial
  modern geopolitical relationships"-- Provided by publisher.
Identifiers: LCCN 2021006334 (print) | LCCN 2021006335 (ebook) | ISBN
  9781509536320 (hardback) | ISBN 9781509536337 (paperback) | ISBN
  9781509536344 (epub)
Subjects: LCSH: Geopolitics--China. | China--Foreign relations--Africa. |
  Africa--Foreign relations--China. | China--Politics and
  government--2002- | Africa--Politics and government--1960-
Classification: LCC DS740.5.A34 L37 2021 (print) | LCC DS740.5.A34
  (ebook) | DDC 327.5106--dc23
LC record available at https://lccn.loc.gov/2021006334
LC ebook record available at https://lccn.loc.gov/2021006335

Typeset in 11.5 on 15pt Adobe Jenson Pro
by Fakenham Prepress Solutions, Fakenham, Norfolk NR21 8NL
Printed and bound in Great Britain by CPI Group (UK) Ltd, Croydon

For further information on Polity, visit our website: politybooks.com

To Judith and Martin

Contents

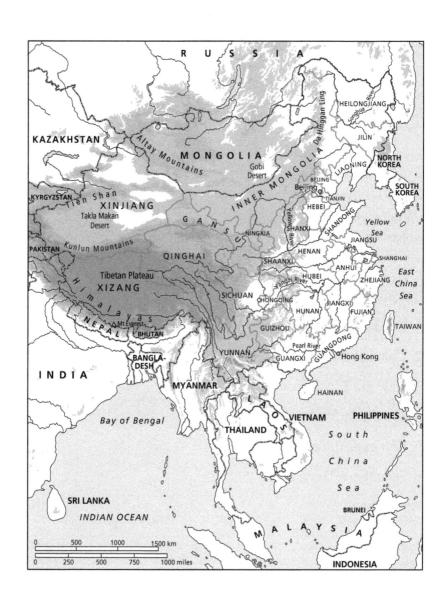

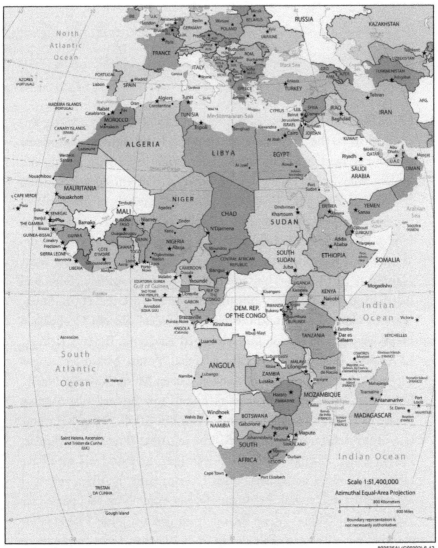

Acknowledgements

I have been intrigued by this subject since 1994–5, when I worked as an English teacher in Lishui, Zhejiang and met Ethiopian students in Nanjing, and especially since undertaking research in Kenya and Sudan from 2004, where among others I met entrepreneurs from Lishui and Zhejiang. This book relies on research in many places conducted since then; I acknowledge with great appreciation all whom I have met and learned from in the process. These include Philip Winter and John Ryle for asking 'why China?' in Athi River, near Nairobi, in April 2004. They also include Adekeye Adebajo, Seifudein Adem, Ana Alves, Kweku Ampiah, Ross Anthony, Tatiana Carayannis, Stephen Chan, Lucy Corkin, Richard Dowden, Neuma Grobbelaar, He Wenping, Jok Madut Jok, Mohaned Kaddam, Thomas Kellogg, Li Anshan, Liu Haifang, Roland Marchal, Emma Mawdsley, Angus McKee, Giles Mohan, Jamie Monson, Leben Moro, Sanusha Naidu, Shu Zhan, Elizabeth Sidiropoulos, Cobus van Staden, Julia Strauss, Jonathan Sullivan, Sun Xiaomeng, Thiik Giir Thiik, Tang Xiaoyang, Gai Thurbil, George T. Yu, Yu Ruichuan, Alex Vines, Wang Suolao, Zhang Chun, Zheng Yixiao, CEU colleagues and students who have taken my Politics of South–South Development in Africa course. I am indebted to Deborah Brautigam for her example and support since 2006, and the China–Africa Research Initiative at Johns Hopkins for granting me a Research Fellowship in 2019, when I was fortunate to work with Lina Benabdallah, and use of their graphs, in which Marie Foster kindly helped.

Special thanks are due to Julia Davies, Susan Beer and especially George Owers at Polity for their exceptional assistance, including during the COVID-19 pandemic. Posthumous thanks are due to the late Ian Taylor and his original recommendation, without which this book would never have happened. I am thankful to Thorsten Benner for his feedback on the initial proposal. I am grateful to this book's anonymous external reviewers for providing considered and very helpful feedback on the complete draft. Others read chapters and offered useful advice, including William Mangimela, Yu-Shan Wu, Lina Benabdallah and especially Yoon Jung Park. I am particularly grateful to Chris Alden, for his invaluable guidance and support; Luke Patey for his generous help and quality feedback; Ricardo Soares de Oliveira, for unfailingly exceptional assistance; and Sarah Brockmeier-Large for feedback during challenging 2020 lockdown conditions. Any remaining errors, naturally, are my responsibility. This book owes considerably to my family's support, and my biggest thanks go to Carlotta, Leo and Sarah.

Chronology

1949	Mao Zedong founds the People's Republic of China (October)
1955	Asian–African Conference is held in Bandung, Indonesia (April)
1956	Egypt becomes the first country in Africa to establish diplomatic relations with China (May)
1963–4	Zhou Enlai visits ten African countries (December–February); in Ghana, he outlines China's Eight Principles for Economic Aid and Technical Assistance to Other Countries (January)
1970–6	Construction of China's iconic TAZARA (Tanzania Zambia Railway Authority) or Freedom Railway, from Dar es Salaam on the Tanzanian coast to Zambia's Copperbelt region following an agreement signed in 1967
1971	26 African country votes help the PRC join the UN and replace Taiwan on the UN Security Council (October)
1978	Deng Xiaoping consolidates power as the top CCP leader, and 'reform and opening' is initiated
1982–3	Zhao Ziyang tours eleven African countries (December/January)
1989	Chinese military uses force to end the Tiananmen Square movement (3–4 June); Jiang Zemin becomes General Secretary of the CCP (June)

1990   Start of annual spring visit to African countries by
            China's Foreign Minister
1993   Jiang Zemin is elected President by China's National
            People's Congress; China becomes a net oil importer
1996   Jiang Zemin tours Kenya, Egypt, Ethiopia, Mali,
            Namibia and Zimbabwe
1999   China's National People's Congress approves Jiang Zemin
            as President for a second term (March); China's 'going
            global' strategy emerges
2000   Founding of the Forum on China–Africa Cooperation
            (October)
2001   China enters the World Trade Organization
2002   The African Union is founded in Durban, South Africa
            (July); Hu Jintao replaces Jiang Zemin as General
            Secretary of the CCP
2003   Hu Jintao replaces Jiang Zemin as President of the PRC;
            FOCAC II is held in Addis Ababa, Ethiopia (December)
2005   US Deputy Secretary of State Robert Zoellick urges
            China to become a 'responsible stakeholder' in global
            affairs, including in Africa (September); the first
            Confucius Institute in Africa opens at the University of
            Nairobi, Kenya (December)
2006   China issues its first African Policy (January); Hu Jintao
            visits Morocco, Nigeria and Kenya (April); the third
            ministerial and first heads of state FOCAC summit is
            held in Beijing (November)
2008   Olympic Games held in Beijing following a 'Genocide
            Olympics' campaign linking conflict in Darfur, Sudan
            with China (August); Chinese FDI to Africa peaks
            at $5.5bn after the Industrial and Commercial Bank
            of China buys 20% of the shares in Standard Bank of

South Africa; 5 Chinese oil workers are killed in Sudan (October)

2009   Hu Jintao visits Mali, Senegal, Tanzania and Mauritius (February); FOCAC IV is held in Sharm el Sheik, Egypt (November); China surpasses the US to become Africa's largest trading partner

2011   China officially becomes the world's second largest economy (February); China evacuates some 36,000 Chinese nationals from Libya by land, air and sea (February–March)

2012   New Chinese built and funded AU HQ opens in Addis Ababa (January); FOCAC V is held in Beijing (July); 18th National Party Congress approves Xi Jinping as General Secretary of the CCP and chair of the Central Military Commission (November)

2013   12th National People's Congress approves Xi Jinping as President and Li Keqiang Premier of China; Xi Jinping visits Tanzania, South Africa, and Republic of Congo (March); announcement of the BRI

2014   Collapse of global commodity prices begins; China announces it will deploy its first infantry battalion to a UN peacekeeping mission, in South Sudan (September)

2015   The AU adopts Agenda 2063 (January); Xi Jinping tells the UNGA that China will create a UN peacekeeping standby force (September); the India–Africa Forum Summit is held in New Delhi (October); China releases its second Africa policy; the second FOCAC summit and VI ministerial conference is held in Johannesburg, South Africa (December); China's counterterrorism law paves the way for future overseas security operations

2016   China officially launches the AIIB; economic growth in China falls to lowest rate in 25 years (6.9%) (January);

two Chinese UN peacekeepers are killed and others injured after fighting breaks out in Juba, capital of South Sudan (July); China hosts the G20 summit in Hangzhou (September)

2017   First BRI summit is held in Beijing (May); Kenya's Standard Gauge Railway opens (May); China's Djibouti naval base officially opens (August); China becomes the world's top importer of crude oil; the 19th CCP Congress is held; Xi Jinping Thought on Socialism with Chinese Characteristics for a New Era and the BRI are incorporated into revised CCP constitution (October)

2018   The Addis Ababa–Djibouti railway, built by two Chinese companies, opens (January); the African Continental Free Trade Area is founded (March); the China International Development Cooperation Agency is created (March); National People's Congress votes to remove two-term limit on China's presidency from the constitution (March); Xi Jinping visits Senegal, Rwanda, South Africa and Mauritius (July); FOCAC VII held in Beijing (September); China and three African members of the UNSC establish a '1+3' UNSC coordination mechanism; the Trump administration announces a new US Africa strategy (December)

2019   Second BRI summit is held in Beijing (April); anti-government and pro-democracy demonstrations in Hong Kong (June); Xinjiang becomes an international issue; the 7th Tokyo International Conference on African Development is held in Yokohama (August); celebrations mark 70th anniversary of the founding of the PRC (1 October)

2020   Outbreak of COVID-19 coronavirus in Hubei spreads globally (January); the mistreatment of Africans in

Guangzhou amid the pandemic generates wide attention (April); a China–Africa Summit on Solidarity Against COVID-19 is held (June); Hong Kong's national security law is passed (June); Zambia becomes the first African country to default on part of its debt amid looming recession (November); China marks thirty years of participation in UN peacekeeping operations

Abbreviations

ADB – African Development Bank
AfCFTA – African Continental Free Trade Area
Africa CDC – Africa Centres for Disease Control and Prevention
AIIB – Asian Infrastructure Investment Bank
ANC – African National Congress
APSA – African Peace and Security Architecture
ASEAN – Association of Southeast Asian Nations
AU – African Union
BRI – Belt and Road Initiative
BRICS – Brazil, Russia, India, China and South Africa
CARI – China–Africa Research Initiative (Johns Hopkins)
CCM – Chama Cha Mapinduzi party
CCP – Chinese Communist Party
CCTV – China Central Television
CDB – China Development Bank
CGTN – China Global Television Network
China EXIM – Export–Import Bank of China
CI – Confucius Institute
CIDCA – China International Development Cooperation Agency
CNPC – China National Petroleum Corporation
DFID – Department for International Development (UK)
DRC – Democratic Republic of Congo
EAC – East African Community
EU – European Union

FDI – Foreign Direct Investment
FOCAC – Forum on China–Africa Cooperation
FRELIMO – Frente para a Libertação de Moçambique
G20 – Group of 20
ID-CCP – International Department of the CCP
IDP – internally displaced person
IMF – International Monetary Fund
MFA – Ministry of Foreign Affairs
MINUSMA – UN Multidimensional Integrated Stabilization Mission in Mali
MOFCOM – Ministry of Commerce
MOU – Memorandum of Understanding
MPLA – Movimento Popular de Libertação de Angola
NEPAD – New Partnership for Africa's Development
NDB – New Development Bank
NGO – Non-governmental organization
OECD – Organization for Economic Cooperation and Development
PLA – People's Liberation Army
POC – Protection of Civilians
PRC – People's Republic of China
RMB – *renminbi*
SAIIA – South African Institute of International Affairs
SEZ – Special Economic Zone
SGR – Standard Gauge Railway
SOE – State-owned enterprise
SWAPO – South-West Africa People's Organization
TAZARA – Tanzanian–Zambian Railway Authority
TICAD – Tokyo International Conference on African Development
UK – United Kingdom
UNCTAD – UN Conference on Trade and Development
UNGA – UN General Assembly
UNHRC – UN Human Rights Council

UNSC – UN Security Council
UNMISS – UN Mission in South Sudan
UNOG – UN Office at Geneva
US – United States of America
WHO – World Health Organization
WTO – World Trade Organization
ZANU–PF – Zimbabwe African National Union–Patriotic Front

Tables and Boxes

TABLES

BOXES

Introduction

Two large maps of Africa and China, under the caption 'Friendship Peace Cooperation Development', stood out at an official exhibition off Tiananmen Square in November 2006. The Africa map was filled with images of smiling children, a baobab tree, a bare-chested man drumming, and hints of the ruins of an ancient civilization. That of China was filled with images of the Great Wall, Forbidden City and other civilizational achievements. At the time, the Chinese government was hosting the third Forum on China–Africa Cooperation (FOCAC) and Beijing had been carefully prepared to welcome leaders and delegations from some 48 African countries. Billboards proclaiming 'win–win cooperation' and other official slogans signalled the Chinese government's portrayal of China as a different, progressive partner of the continent. This FOCAC put China–Africa on the map of global attention, and catalysed interest in China's suddenly visible engagement with the continent. Cliché images aside, the emptiness of this map of the African continent, however, suggested ignorant paternalism at a time when relations were rapidly developing.

Much has changed since then, as has become evident in the 'New Era' of China's relations with Africa. China's New Era is the era of Xi Jinping. Since taking power as General Secretary of the Chinese Communist Party (CCP) in November 2012, and becoming state president in March 2013, Xi Jinping has presided over a transformation in China's domestic and global affairs. In 2018, at another FOCAC in Beijing, he welcomed 'African countries aboard the express train of China's development' and declared: 'No one could hold back the Chinese people or the African people as we march towards rejuvenation.' China committed financing in Africa of $60bn and a marked expansion of its investment in human capital and training. Xi Jinping reportedly met the leaders of 53 African countries for an event described by China's Foreign Minister as setting 'a new record in FOCAC history, and indeed, in all the diplomatic activities China ever hosted.'[1] Welcoming Gambia, Sao Tome and Principe, and Burkina Faso, which had previously supported Taiwan, the summit confirmed China's near total victory over Taiwan in the continent. Africa, as the President of Burkina Faso, Roch Marc Christian Kaboré said, had 'chosen China'. This FOCAC showed how established China's relations with Africa had become in Xi Jinping's New Era.

This book aims to bring the China–Africa story up to date.[2] It argues that politics defines China's New Era Africa relations most, thus challenging conventional wisdom and popular associations about China's relations with Africa, which hold that 'Chinese leaders see Africa mainly as a source of natural resources.'[3] Politics is a fluid, highly contested concept, which attracts simple definitions but defies easy characterization. Using a more expansive understanding, this book situates the politics of relations in terms of Chinese and African histories, institutional frameworks and politics, before exploring select key themes: China and Africa in global politics, evolving economic ties, the China model and African politics, Chinese–African relations, and China's expanding security engagement in the continent.

China–Africa relations have never been just about politics or economics but shifting combinations of both across different historical periods. Politics always mattered; it drove post-colonial revolutionary ties and never disappeared. Since around 1996, however, economics has been the main association between China and Africa, following the tour by China's then President Jiang Zemin of six African states that marked an inflection point 'from geopolitics to economics as the driver of ties'.[4] In 2000, President Jiang spoke of the 'all round friendship' between China and Africa. Nonetheless, economics was the foundation of a 'long-term partnership' and enhanced economic ties would do most to help China's domestic economic development while contributing to growth in African countries.[5] Since 2012, however, and Xi Jinping's leadership of China, there has been a shift towards a decisive role of politics both inside and outside China, including in its Africa relations.

Arguing that politics needs to be returned to the centre of understanding China's Africa relations today is not to suggest, simplistically, that economic ties are of secondary importance. Nor that politics can be separated from economics. Economic factors remain central to relations but are very much bound up in and determined by politics of various kinds in an evolving political economy of relations encompassing a spectrum of local to global dimensions. China's role in Africa has also always had its own politics but these have become much more prominent, deeper and widespread in the New Era. In other words, much arises from the nature of economic ties, from the diverse impacts of China within African countries, unease about China as a creditor, Chinese migration, security challenges and, ultimately, perceptions of its new power. At the same time, Chinese government officials have come to recognize how central politics is, not just for China's relations with Africa or in terms of China's global politics but also to achieving Africa's broader development goals.

What, then, is China's New Era, and what does this mean for its Africa relations? The term 'New Era' simplifies and provokes questions (what was wrong with the old one? how long can something be new?). In essence, it means the reassertion of China's party-state under Xi's leadership in Chinese domestic politics and economy. It also means a more ambitious and expansive role for China abroad, signalled in Xi's closing speech at the 18th National Congress of the CCP in November 2012, when he talked of the 'great renewal of the Chinese nation.[6] The CCP's 19th Party Congress in October 2017 was seminal in declaring the New Era and defining Xi's power. It elevated him to the core of the CCP's leadership, with no anointed successor. In his report to the Congress, Xi Jinping noted that China had 'stood up, grown rich, and is becoming strong'. The New Era would see 'China moving closer to centre stage' and this would require 'major country diplomacy with Chinese characteristics' in order to build China into a great, modern and global 'socialist power' by the mid twenty-first century.[7] The approach China had adopted after 1978, that of keeping a low profile in order to focus on domestic development, was dumped in the dustbin of history. The CCP's grand strategic goal has become the 'great rejuvenation of the Chinese nation'. Following the 19th Party Congress, the New Era refrain was incorporated into China's Africa relations. China's relations with Africa have evolved considerably to become more complex, multifaceted and consequential. Relations are continuing to evolve, in much changed and changing circumstances within China, in China's relations with 53 different African states and global politics.

During Xi Jinping's period in office, China's Africa relations have been ever more defined and shaped by politics, which extends to China's foreign policy and global politics. The prominence of Beijing's Africa engagement stands in contrast to the actual economic importance of the continent to China. Africa accounts for around 45% of China's global development aid but around 4% of China's total global trade volume in the first half of 2020, and that trade in turn was dominated by a handful of African commodity exporters.[8] Similar to trade, China's investment in Africa is not significant in the context of China's global investment, accounting for some 3.7% of total outward global investment stock in 2015. Xi Jinping's Belt and Road Initiative (or BRI) has revised Africa's former prominence in China's regional engagements by its global scope. However, for Africa, which accounted for 2.9% of world production, 2.6% of world trade and 16.3% of the world's population in 2019, China's investment and engagement means much more.[9]

The centrality of politics flows from Xi Jinping's leadership of China and the more established, far-reaching nature of Chinese engagement in Africa. Before Xi, from 1978 China's leaders after Mao prioritized economic development as the way to maintain power. By prioritizing politics, Xi Jinping has done the opposite, starting with attempting to renew the CCP's legitimacy, and reasserting its dominance over all walks of life. It was also inseparable from Xi's more ambitious foreign policy. Xi Jinping has sought to redefine China's Africa relations in his terms, including incorporating Africa more overtly into the CCP's vision for China's future centrality in world affairs. China's 53 African state allies are important in China's foreign policy and global multilateral role in this context. Since African state votes helped the People's Republic of China (PRC) enter the UN in 1971, the continent has been a significant part of China's multilateral engagement but the stakes have become higher in the New Era, which has seen more explicit promotion of the CCP's China model. In turn, China is more important in the foreign relations and global politics of many African states. Economic relations have been evolving from years of high growth rates until 2014, when global commodity prices fell. The idea that Chinese investment could propel Africa to become 'the next factory of the world' became popular.[10] Since around 2015, trade and investment have declined, debt mounted for some African states and, in 2020, the first recession in 25 years hit many African countries. China now has a more established, multidimensional and consequential presence across the continent: it is an emerged power. The importance of China within African politics on the back of its evolved economic and global role represents a major, historically unprecedented change.

In 2020, when there were celebrations to mark the 20th anniversary of FOCAC, the 2006 summit had faded into history, and China's domestic and global politics looked very different. Xi's leadership saw China become a self-declared major power with a clear sense of long-term global strategic purpose. China's relations with Africa have seen a transformation, having widened, deepened and diversified, and becoming dominated by issues like industrialization or security, which were absent in 2006. Africa is part of China's global rise, now proceeding in the context of open strategic competition with the United States of America (US). Overall, politics has become far more important, in the context of economic challenges, changing global politics and higher stakes.

Approach

Interest in China–Africa relations has grown exponentially.[11] It is expressed in ever more diverse ways, including in literature, art and film. China–Africa is an intensely mediated subject and reflects changes in the global media landscape under the impact of digital technologies and social media, which has recently become more prominent in African countries (some more than others) and in global conversations about China and Africa.[12] Chinese diplomats in Africa now use social media like Twitter to promote official views, for example, but in China, the tightly controlled media must, as Xi Jinping has said, 'love', 'protect' and serve the interest of the CCP, or be 'surnamed Party'. Like domestic issues, media coverage of Africa relations in China has to follow the official line.

China–Africa relations are often described in simplistic and sensational ways, not just by commentators but also by politicians in and outside African countries. Binary terms are commonly used, such as 'win–win development' or 'new imperialism/colonialism'; 'partner or predator'; 'saviour or monster'; 'parasitism or mutualism' etc. In addition, simple, monocausal metanarratives officially explain China's engagement as win–win development or reduce this to imperialism, dependency, or exploitation. It follows that grand causal claims frequently attend the subject; such as that China has undermined democracy or human rights, or has engaged in a deliberate strategy of entrapping African governments in debt. Such claims can place unwarranted agency in China and neglect actual African politics, multistranded external relations and forms of agency. While it is all too easy to blame the media, this influences opinion, can shape worldviews and impact policy engagements. In short, images and language matter, especially when added to personal experience in African countries. The topic of China's relations with Africa has become an information minefield. Rumours, misunderstandings, or those looking for profitable attention can manufacture myths that can take on a life of their own and fuel politics in an age where social media matters.[13] Emotive online news stories about Chinese exports of human flesh or plastic rice to Zambia, Kenya, Nigeria, Ivory Coast and Senegal, for example, have been proved false but have nonetheless continued to appear, spread disinformation and influence popular perceptions about China.

The subject of China and Africa relations has grown as an area of academic research, moving from a previously peripheral small field mainly concerned with international relations towards much more multi-disciplinary approaches.[14] African studies have grown within China. Efforts have been made to promote China-related research and education about China in an increasing number of African countries. As well as being relevant to business, this is also a very policy-oriented subject. One obvious problem with the meta-organizing tag 'China–Africa' is that this is shorthand for an increasingly diverse range of studies, conversations, media coverage, human encounters, and forms of political contestation. More than a conversation or subject of debate by spectators, this is also a meaningful, lived reality for many. China–Africa is not a subject that follows any neat, coherent narrative but has become a topic about which opinion is required and, increasingly, judgement.

Much China–Africa analysis takes development and economics as its starting point or primary interest.[15] This is essential; however, any focus on economics is insufficient when it comes to approaching China–Africa relations. This has become more readily apparent in recent years with the evolution of more complex relations that, at a minimum, combine history, economics, politics and international relations. In this way, political economy approaches seek to better locate and explore China's role beyond forms of methodological statism that ignore wider structural forces.[16] The tendency to isolate and magnify China's role has been criticized; some have argued that studies of China–Africa engagements throw broader processes like neoliberalism in Africa into starker relief. Studies utilizing a global political economy framework have thus offered reflections on the extent to which economic investment in Zambia, for example, is or can be considered 'Chinese', or reflects qualities, political relations and patterns of exploitation familiar in the global behaviour of capital.[17] This perspective recasts the Chinese role as a new chapter in global capitalist relations.[18] Such an approach, while important, risks downplaying CCP New Era Chinese characteristics and connections. In the attempt to demonstrate conformity to historical extraversion or the logic of capital, the Chinese qualities of these dynamics, even when mediated by hybrid global dynamics, can be stripped away and questions about forms of CCP-governed Chinese power avoided.

This book thus explores the interplay between political, economic and social dynamics in relations. As well as offering a deeper and broader framework, this general political economy approach helps overcome a number of problems. For instance, available data, including the accuracy of economic statistics from Chinese, African and other sources, is problematic. Even where data exist, traditional statistics like trade don't capture global value chains well. Another problem is over reliance on official Chinese foreign-policy principles. Because these are constitutive of relations, they cannot be either taken at face value or dismissed as pure hypocrisy. Much like the architect of China's economic reforms from 1978 Deng Xiaoping's emphasis on seeking 'truth from facts', examining the empirical substance of relations – what is, not what is supposed to be – enables analysis to go beyond that based on official rhetoric.

A fundamental challenge in studying China–Africa relations is the abstraction inherent in ideas about and uses of 'China' and 'Africa'. With an official population of some 1.4bn in 2019, China is a continental-sized country with 23 provinces, five autonomous regions (including Xinjiang), four municipalities, and two special administrative regions (Hong Kong and Macau). The complexity of 'China' must be always borne in mind. It also needs to be disaggregated. Although there are multiple Chinas, China has a dominant political centre controlled by the CCP party-state-military. 'Africa' can mean many things, including a place, an idea, a project, a centre or a periphery. Obviously, there are thus multiple Africas, including regions, diverse politics and economies, and some 2,140 living languages. In political terms alone, the African Union (AU) has 55 member states divided into five geographic regions.[19] This means a huge variation in the political map of the continent – and China's official interlocutors – featuring all manner of regime types, from established democracies to authoritarian regimes or conflict-afflicted states.

The 53 highly diverse African states with which China maintains diplomatic relations can be grouped into three general categories: first, states like Botswana, Benin, Ghana, Senegal, Mauritius or South Africa that have established, open and competitive democracies, even while many remain institutionally weak. A second group includes such different cases as Kenya, Uganda, Burundi, DRC or Zimbabwe, ruled by leaders with authoritarian tendencies but in contexts where there are popular opposition parties. Third, there are authoritarian governments with strong control but no qualms about holding elections, such as Cameroon, Chad or Rwanda.[20] China, by contrast, is governed by an authoritarian party-state-military system. With over 91.91m members at the end of 2019, CCP membership alone is larger than the populations of all but three African countries: Nigeria, Ethiopia and Egypt. The contrast between China's authoritarian capitalist party-state and diverse political systems in Africa is one starting point for putting relations into broad context. It also helps bring out the need to go beyond a state focus in Africa–China relations by including the diverse range of participants, such as the active role of different civil society groups or independent media in many countries in the continent.

Many books warn against generalization and then generalize; this book is no different but does not go beyond the ways in which Africa is, in its terms, part of China's foreign policy.[21] Africa may be an abstraction but is one that remains necessary to use. The main reason why both China and Africa need to be used, on top of or along with defined African countries, is because the CCP, Chinese state, corporations and others frame and approach relations in these very terms. Africa has meaning as a category in China's foreign policy, as FOCAC shows. However, China's relations with 53 individual African countries mean relations have a strong bilateral character. Likewise, China's Africa policy has a continental policy framework in theory, and 53 (or 54, if Taiwan-recognizing Eswatini, formerly Swaziland, is included) African policies in practice, and has evolved to incorporate a range of other actors and levels of politics. In China's terms, then, it makes sense to consider China–Africa, even if these should always be qualified and the difficulties of moving from particular African contexts to generalized claims recognized. Finally, this book recognizes that China's relations with Africa/African countries remains a project in the making. One way to conceptualize relations between China and Africa is as in a process of becoming, rather than something that already exists, and involving networks of agents, rather than static categories. This matters for such questions as the evolved but still evolving theme of China's 'power' in Africa.

Overview

Chapter 1 provides background to historical, political and institutional dynamics in China's changing engagement with Africa, and how different African protagonists engage with China. It first charts the main phases in relations after 1949. Second, it examines the CCP's reassertion of power within China and in its Africa relations. Despite the centralization of power around Xi Jinping, China's governing party-state-military system – and the many parts of this that maintain active Africa relations – remains fragmented. The CCP commands within China, and directs relations with African states and ruling political parties, but can struggle to exercise effective control. The Chinese government has been undertaking reforms to equip itself for major power diplomacy and better manage important parts of its Africa relations, such as development aid. Third, crucial in co-shaping relations, the diverse roles and impacts of state and non-state African protagonists exert formative influences on China's engagement. Interstate relations are formally equal but profoundly asymmetrical in reality. African states actively use external relations, including with China, for domestic political purposes. The AU, regional organizations and non-state actors, including civil society, also play important roles.

Chapter 2 examines the role and importance of Africa in China's foreign policy and global engagement, China in the foreign relations of African states and Africa in global politics, and how these relate to other external engagements in the continent. Africa's political importance for China in global terms has become more evident in the New Era. This can be seen in African state support for China's foreign policy, deepening multilateral and global governance engagement. Africa has a clear part in China's ambitions as a major power pursuing a vision of future global leadership: the continent showcases Xi's China on the global stage, supporting Beijing's claims about its progressive role in global security or development, for example, while also contributing in other ways towards China's global goals. China has become more important in the foreign-policy calculations of African states, many of which have looked to use their growing economic ties with China to try to augment their autonomy; some also have quietly sought to move away from any undue dependence on China. The politics of divergent interests extends to the question of whether the Chinese government's self-proclaimed championing of Africa in global politics is matched by commensurate political will and ability to meaningfully advance a reform agenda with and for the continent, which is itself fragmented and divided on such issues, starting with differences between states. Finally, China's New Era role in Africa can't be approached in isolation from the engagements of other external powers, in which the US stands out due to the importance of US–China global strategic competition.

Chapter 3 examines economic relations, which have been evolving from a narrow, extractive agenda to a wide-ranging engagement. It first considers trends in trade, aid and investment, showing how China matters increasingly in Africa but the continent does not have comparable economic importance to China. Second, it examines how approaches to economic development became based on an industrialization-led 'structural transformation' agenda and support the AU's Agenda 2063, an expansive vision for unity, prosperity, peace and 'transforming Africa into the global powerhouse of the future' adopted in 2015. As well as a focus on infrastructure construction and manufacturing, economic relations have seen the BRI become more central to current and future ties. Third, China's role as a holder of African debt reveals much about how relations have changed. China's response to the debt crisis facing African countries like Zambia, Angola or Kenya in 2020, in part but by no means only arising from its previous lending patterns as well as impacts of the COVID-19 pandemic, has been reshaping China–Africa relations in important ways. Finally, it argues that the idea that China can exert transformative change in economic development is a mirage in the face of the severe, intractable challenges facing African countries. These emanate not just from deep global structural constraints but the nature of African states where ruling political elites in countries like Kenya fail to seriously prioritize broad, longer-term developmental need. Further, China's economic relations with Africa are evolving in a different phase where it was less willing and able to double or triple its financing at FOCAC, with investment dropping and new emphasis on its domestic needs.

Chapter 4 examines the 'China model', which has become more salient in light of the CCP's reassertion of power within China and in foreign policy. Meaning different things at different times, this has been redefined under Xi Jinping into a form of authoritarian single-party state capitalism, characterized by extensive party-state control over political and social life, and whose economy involves a strong role of the party-state in core economic sectors together with market-based practices. The decisive New Era trend has seen Beijing more confidently and directly promote Xi's China model, understood as a set of ideas about political organization and accompanying enabling possibilities, including in technology or investment. The Chinese government still talks publicly about not imposing its model, but under Xi Jinping Beijing has been overtly promoting it and taking a more concerted, confrontational stance. China is one of various external models African states – and others – can potentially engage, but it is upheld by the Chinese government as superior. The CCP's efforts to promote its model matter, including via sustained, future oriented political party training that positions China for longer-term influence. What ultimately matters most, however, is how political elites in African states like South Africa, Ethiopia, Kenya or Nigeria understand the China model, and the ways in which these under-standings are adapted and selectively used for domestic political purposes, sometimes in conjunction with the technical capabilities offered by China or other external partners.

Chapter 5 moves to a more micro-level concern with relations between people, including Africans in China, and Chinese in African countries, and the politics this can generate. While multi-billion-dollar mega projects involving Chinese funding and corporations attract headlines – from Algeria's Great Mosque in Algiers, the largest mosque in Africa with the tallest minaret in the world, to Egypt's 'new administrative capital' city, the DRC's Grand Inga III dam, Ethiopia's Grand Renaissance Dam or Tanzania's prospective Bagamoyo port – ordinary exchanges between ordinary people and micro-dynamics matter. Often overlooked, apart from occasional moments of high political visibility, the everyday dynamics and immense diversity of such relations illustrate a complexity that simple narratives – such as those from the Chinese government about its South–South cooperation or media-fuelled stories about migrants as the vanguard of China's new empire building in Africa – struggle to convey. Three broad themes are explored. The first is Africans in China, and Chinese migration to Africa, in the context of dynamic transnational trade networks. The second considers the politics of Chinese in African countries, the various levels and ways in which migrants have become prominent, such as Chinese gold miners in Ghana, and how China and African inter-state relations can impact on Chinese communities in Africa. The third considers trends going forward: a new phase for the African population in China with tighter regulation of foreign nationals; the uncertain status of some Chinese communities in African countries; continuing mobility of those who move on; and, in contrast, signs of growing rootedness of Chinese communities in countries like Namibia.

The growing Chinese presence in Africa has also been an important contributing factor behind a new foreign-policy challenge for the Chinese government, namely protecting people as well as economic assets overseas, and was one reason why security became a defining theme in China's New Era Africa engagement. Chapter 6 examines different aspects of New Era security relations, which Xi Jinping termed a major 'pillar' of China–Africa relations in 2015. Far from being simply a defensive reaction to threat, mounting risks and vulnerability, and new realities of overseas investment protection imperatives, China's engagement has had an experimental quality in a continent that has been a testing ground for gaining overseas corporate and military experience. The very challenges different Chinese actors have faced have necessitated and enabled a more proactive military role that, as UN peacekeeping exemplifies, serves China's bilateral (gaining experience) and multilateral goals (as a self-declared responsible power contributing to global peace and security). The opening of China's first overseas naval base in Djibouti in 2017 represented a historic departure in China's foreign security policy. It was, however, one part of a multi-stranded security engagement unfolding concurrent with a reconsideration of the Chinese government's traditional approach to intervention and non-interference.[22] Under Xi Jinping, China has sought to strengthen its principle of 'non-interference' even as, in practice, this does not square the circle of a deeper role. The Chinese government maintains public opposition to non-consensual foreign intervention, but has become more accommodating of this in reality, including under the influence of shifting African approaches to intervention.

Conclusion

In just over two decades, China has gone from being a marginal, distant partner of Africa to attaining a leading position as an active participant in continental affairs, whose future importance is clear. These new trends mean more obvious disconnects between the official language of China–Africa relations and the actual realities of China's more complex and consequential role, raising concerns about the different types of China's actual, imminent and future power. China's New Era ascendancy as a leading power in Africa and a self-proclaimed major power with ambitions to global leadership has been generating stronger political reactions in some African countries, as well as support from those who regard China as the future of globalization. In this way, the different aspects of China's perceived and actual power now exert more obvious influences in relations.

The outline maps of Africa and China on display in Beijing in November 2006 should be impossible now, given how much has changed since then, including China's more conspicuous and consequential footprint in the continent and the many ways different African actors have used, benefited from and sought to shape relations in their own ways. Nonetheless, for all the official claims about friendship and development of closer ties since then, periodic episodes suggest continuing ignorance and generate new friction and politics. A far more widely seen and high-profile example than the maps on the fringe of the 2006 FOCAC came in February 2018, when the China Central Television's (CCTV) Spring Festival Gala, known as the world's 'most watched national network TV broadcast', with up to one billion viewers that year, broadcast a comedy sketch that was supposed to celebrate China–Africa relations.[23] Instead, it provoked a storm of controversy over the use of blackface by a Chinese actress, a black performer in a monkey costume and the use of tribal African dancers and female attendants from Kenya's Chinese-built railway linking Nairobi and coastal Mombasa. The sketch reproduced a narrative that was representative of China's general approach to Africa, in which China is seen as a solution to the continent's backwardness, and behind the performance was 'a consistent top-down, ego-boosting effort to see and represent China as a way for Africa to enter modernity'.[24] The 'racist and insensitive portrayals' of Africans in the sketch was criticized, and there were calls for China to 'incorporate racial awareness and sensitivity to the production of content by all its media outlets'.[25]

China–Africa relations are prone to attracting grand statements. The 1960s saw claims that 'Red China' had moved into Africa, 'a major revolutionary outpost in a Sinocentric world', and intended 'to stay there'.[26] More recently, many have argued that China can transform

African development. From the days of Maoist revolution to the 2020 COVID-19 pandemic, commentary has tended to overstate China's impact and underplay the formative influences of African protagonists. Nonetheless, today China's relations with Africa are based on long-term goals; but this is a very different China, combining with all manner of African protagonists to be more consequential than ever.

<table>
<tr><td>1</td><td>The New Era in
Context</td><td>_____</td></tr>
</table>

1   The New Era in Context

Former Tanzanian President Julius Nyerere's description of post-colonial Tanzania–China relations as the 'most unequal of equal relationships' could well be applied to relations between all African countries and China today.[1] Indeed, since 1978 this characteristic of post-colonial China–Africa relations has been accentuated by China's economic transformation. China is now the world's second largest economy, and the GDP of provinces like Zhejiang dwarf even Nigeria, Africa's largest economy. China continues to style itself as 'the largest developing country' in partnership with Africa, 'the continent with the most developing countries'. Xi Jinping's adoption of major power foreign policy, however, confirmed China's pre-eminence in an already existing de facto political hierarchy.

This chapter presents foundational context for the rest of the book. First, reviewing the history of China–Africa relations since 1949, it examines how China's New Era Africa relations follow but depart from deeper historical connections. Many 'new eras' have been declared in past China–Africa relations, but that under Xi Jinping represents a historic departure beyond its formal designation. Second, it examines the changing political and institutional framework of China's Africa engagement, emphasizing CCP reassertion under Xi Jinping since 2012 and how China's fragmented party-state-military system has been evolving as it adapts to the challenges of major power diplomacy and more complex ties with Africa. Third, it considers how African states, regional organizations, the AU and other non-state actors engage with China and co-shape relations. Rather than emphasizing China at the expense of Africa, this chapter thus introduces thematic background to both.

HISTORICAL PHASES SINCE 1949

China's official historical narratives stress the continuity of Africa relations since 1949, with phrases like 'enduring friendship', but in practice these have been episodic.[2] China's Africa relations waxed and waned after 1949 largely according to domestic Chinese politics, until the development of ties from the 1980s, and especially after 2000, saw a departure in so far as China's longer-term role was concerned. For the purposes of this book, after outlining key aspects of relations from 1949, the main focus will be on relations since around 2000.

The founding of the PRC on 1 October 1949 led to a new foreign policy under Chairman Mao Zedong. The Mao era saw politics in command of China's Africa relations. China's preoccupation with domestic affairs initially meant that it lacked the will and the means to engage meaningfully with a distant continent, much of which was still under colonial rule. At the 1955 Asian–African Conference at Bandung, China's Premier Zhou Enlai affirmed the recently formed Five Principles of Peaceful Coexistence: mutual respect of sovereignty and territorial integrity, mutual non-aggression, non-interference in each other's internal affairs, equality and mutual benefit, and peaceful coexistence. These have remained directly or indirectly foundational to how the CCP formally presents its Africa relations. Premier Zhou Enlai visited ten African countries over two months in 1963–64. In Ghana, he outlined China's 'Eight Principles for Economic Aid and Technical Assistance to other Countries'. As well as stressing equality and mutual benefit, sovereignty and non-conditionality, these defined the nature of Chinese economic aid (long-term interest-free or low-interest loans), and Beijing's intention to enhance 'self-reliance and independent economic development'. Despite domestic hardship and political convulsion, the Chinese government extended aid to African countries. It also embraced projects deemed uneconomic by Western powers but which mattered to African states. The iconic example is the Tanzania–Zambia (TAZARA) or Freedom Railway, built to connect Dar es Salaam on the Tanzanian coast and landlocked Zambia's Copperbelt region, thereby avoiding the land route through Rhodesia (now Zimbabwe) and apartheid South Africa.[3]

Under Mao Zedong, exporting revolution was a very real aspect of China's Africa relations, at least in terms of geopolitical strategy. Mao's revolutionary model inspired many in a continent emerging from or still fighting against colonial rule. Concern in the West about the growing influence of China in Africa consistently overstated the nature, extent and outcomes of Beijing's role. Revolution was prominent in China's African relations, especially from 1960 after the Sino-Soviet split, when China contended for influence not just with Taiwan or Western powers, but other communist powers as well. In practice, however, China's African relations had a more pragmatic character. Africa became the object of a concerted engagement by the Chinese government driven by a mixture of exporting revolution, self-interested strategic calculus and philanthropic purpose. Underscoring the importance of African state support at the UN, in October 1971 African votes helped the PRC enter the UN and replace Taiwan on the UN Security Council.

China's relations with Africa under Deng Xiaoping, who led China from 1978, were recalibrated away from Maoist ideology towards economic interests in keeping with Deng's reform and opening policy. Premier Zhao Ziyang toured eleven African countries in December 1982 and January 1983. The timing was significant. From 1978, China had switched from providing to also receiving aid to serve its domestic development efforts. Premier Zhao confirmed a new realism by emphasizing the effectiveness of development projects, which would preferably not require substantial investment, and declaring Four Principles of Sino-African Economic and Technological Cooperation: equality and mutual benefit; emphasis on practical results; diversity in form; and common development. These reoriented China's engagement towards a more market-based logic that would evaluate projects according to commercial viability and value, not political solidarity. This shift demonstrated how different domestic priorities, namely reform and modernization, now informed China's development-oriented foreign policy, which was guided by the maxims 'keeping a low profile' and 'biding time and hiding capabilities'.

Following the Chinese government's use of deadly force and Tiananmen bloodshed in June 1989, subsequent Western pressure on China and Taiwan's attempts to win diplomatic recognition from African states, Africa's role in China's foreign policy became more important again but economic drivers became central. After becoming a net oil importer in 1993, rapid domestic growth compelled China to look for energy supplies and other raw materials overseas. This contributed to growing ties with resource-endowed African economies like oil-rich Sudan from 1995. President Jiang Zemin visited six African countries in 1996 and framed a forward looking 'twenty-first-century' relationship. In 1997, Premier Li Peng emphasized that China's policy of providing development aid to Africa had evolved 'from aid donation to economic cooperation for mutual benefit'. In 1998, a Ministry of Defence white paper cited energy security as integral to China's overall security. The 'going global' strategy from 1999 ensured new state support for Chinese companies to expand overseas, including in Africa. Long ranked among the world's top FDI recipients, the Chinese government began actively to promote outbound investment. Chinese state-owned enterprises (SOEs) pursued resources, markets, customers and experience in African countries, as well as pathways to global markets beyond. In 2000, Beijing hosted the first China–Africa meeting of what became FOCAC. Presided over by President Jiang Zemin, it emphasized strengthening economic co-operation.

Relations gathered momentum from 2002 under Jiang's successor, Hu Jintao. The second FOCAC, held in Addis Ababa in December 2003, saw leaders, diplomats and business representatives meet and mingle. China was also developing regional engagements within its continental relations. In 2003, for example, Macau hosted the first Economic Forum for Co-operation between China and the Community of Portuguese-speaking Countries. China had created two significant policy instruments in 1994: the Export–Import Bank of China (or China EXIM) and the China Development Bank (CDB), which became more involved. The breakthrough year, 2006, began with the release of China's first ever African Policy. President Hu Jintao and Premier Wen Jiabao visited ten African countries on respective tours. In November, Beijing hosted the third ministerial FOCAC and first heads of state summit. Despite being relatively modest by subsequent standards (for instance, a $5bn China–Africa development fund), at the time China's new initiatives and financial commitments signalled ambitious intent. If the first FOCAC in 2000 passed relatively unnoticed, this summit rendered China–Africa relations visible on the world stage. A year before in Scotland, the G8 Gleneagles summit and push to 'make poverty history' captured global attention; China was upstaging that and implying Western aid to Africa might be history instead. The next FOCAC, held in Sharm el-Shaykh, Egypt, in 2009, came in the aftermath of the global financial crisis, which disrupted economic relations and renewed interest in the 'China model' as an alternative to Western politics and economics. The fifth ministerial FOCAC in Beijing in July 2012 was held in the twilight of Hu Jintao's administration. To the 50 African countries present, President Hu outlined five priority areas, including support for 'African integration' and – for the first time – a peace and security initiative.

The Hu Jintao-Wen Jiabao period saw important trends that need to be appreciated in order to understand how things changed after 2012. First, in terms of how the Chinese government managed Africa relations, power and roles broadly reflected a prioritization of economic interests. China's Ministry of Foreign Affairs (or MFA) suffered institutional decline, even while overseeing the most extensive diplomatic presence of any foreign power in Africa. By contrast, the institutional stature of the Ministry of Foreign Trade and Economic Cooperation, renamed the Ministry of Commerce (or MOFCOM) in 2003, grew as China's foreign strategy became more trade focused, including with Africa. Through its Department of Aid to Foreign Countries, MOFCOM was in charge of China's aid to Africa as part of a fragmented and poorly coordinated aid bureaucracy. Second, the number of entities involved in China's Africa relations grew significantly. With 'omnidirectional channels of influence at play', the growth of more complex decision-making reflected a process of pluralization within China.[4] During the Hu-Wen years, China had a 'strong industry, weak government' problem. China's Africa relations featured multiple actors on a multi-tier basis, featuring provinces, municipalities or local governments as well as central party and state bodies.[5] Tensions between corporate interests, such as those of China's national oil companies, and national interest became evident within a broader pattern of limits to Beijing's control. Third, tension between central policy and its ability to control SOE conduct became more apparent. Compounding this, the protection of overseas Chinese citizens and economic interests became a more prominent and challenging issue. The PLA-Navy and Air Force were used for civilian evacuation operations, notably during civil war in Libya when China's military evacuated some 36,000 Chinese by land, air and sea in 2011.

Finally, the Hu-Wen period saw China's engagement become subject to different kinds of politics within African states and beyond. In Zambia, notoriously, the former opposition leader and eventual president Michael Sata mobilized anti-China and anti-Chinese populist sentiment during his 2006 election campaign. His rhetoric against 80,000 Chinese 'invaders' and 'infestors' in Zambia was instrumental in a xenophobic campaign and contributed to sometimes violent incidents at Chinese workplaces. Sudan was another high profile example that underscored the global repercussions for China of a controversial African engagement. Following the escalation of armed rebellion in Sudan's western Darfur region in 2004, China's support for the government of Sudan brought home the risks of global reputational damage before the 2008 Beijing Olympic Games. China was accused of complicity in a genocidal conflict, culminating in a Genocide Olympics campaign.[6] Throughout, the Chinese government faced pressure to expand its engagement beyond its focus on economics. In 2005, US Deputy Secretary of State Robert Zoellick, for instance, cited Sudan as an example of China's narrowly extractive, self-interested role. More than just take oil, he argued China 'should take some responsibility for resolving Sudan's human crisis' and become a 'responsible stakeholder' in global affairs.

From 2012, starting with his priority of restoring CCP legitimacy and power in China and its foreign policy, Xi Jinping's project represented a strong reaction to the Hu-Wen decade. Xi Jinping had been involved in China's Africa relations as vice-president, having, among other things, met African foreign ministers, presidents and other leading figures from 2010, and visited Angola, South Africa and Botswana. Before becoming China's top leader, he was thus prepared to lead China's Africa relations.

XI JINPING'S CHINA AND AFRICA RELATIONS

Since 2012, the most significant change underway in China's domestic politics and foreign relations has been the reassertion of CCP control under Xi Jinping's centralized leadership, driven by the effort to ensure perpetual rule within China, better equip itself for a more ambitious global role and achieve China's rejuvenation. The 2017 19th Party Congress abolished term limits and confirmed Xi Jinping's status at the core of the CCP's Central Committee. Xi Jinping's leadership prioritized politics, specifically, attempting to renew the CCP's legitimacy and restoring its control of the state, military, business and society. In 2010, a professor in Beijing compared the CCP to God: omnipresent, but invisible.[7] Today, the CCP remains omnipresent but is visible everywhere and, as the 2017 CCP constitution stated: 'Party, government, army, society, and education; east and west, south and north, the Party leads everything.' At the apex of party, state and military institutions, Xi has sought to strengthen his power over the entire system, reversing previous attempts to institutionalize authority. He has been nicknamed the 'Chairman of Everything': general secretary of the CCP, state president and, as head of the Central Military Commission, commander in chief. His influence extends to ideology, codified as Xi Jinping Thought on Socialism with Chinese Characteristics for a New Era, and even to 'Xiplomacy'.

CCP institutions are central to China's Africa relations in terms of power and policy as well as inter-personal relations and diplomacy. The CCP Central Committee's Politburo Standing Committee is the ultimate decision-making body in Chinese politics, including foreign policy. China's Africa engagement is one among many other domestic and foreign issues that it engages. All Politburo Standing Committee members participated in Beijing's 2018 FOCAC summit, meeting African dignitaries in their dual party and state capacities. Other party organs are actively involved in China's Africa relations. Among the most important, the CCP's International Department (ID-CCP) manages ties with virtually all foreign political parties and movements. Song Tao, head of the ID-CCP and a 19th CCP Central Committee member, has been meeting African leaders, party leaders and government ministers on a regular basis. Party-to-party relations are critical because these underpin state-to-state relations, even if the CCP now engages non-ruling African political parties as well. Another important party organ is the United Front Work Department, which is in charge of strategic alliances. The CCP Central Discipline Inspection Commission has been pivotal in Xi's anti-corruption campaign within China but plays a role in Africa relations, including via scrutiny of state ministries and other bodies. It investigated the MOFCOM's management of foreign aid in 2014, for example, finding significant risks of corruption. The CCP's powerful Publicity Department is central to controlling the CCP's official message within and without China.

Under Xi Jinping, CCP leadership has been strengthened through a process of state–party integration in China's domestic politics and foreign policy. The 19th Party congress made it clear that the question of party and state separation belonged to the past. The public state sector requires both administrative and political work ('one post, two responsibilities'). Party–state integration is now part of China's constitution, legislation and regulations. Xi Jinping has overseen a pronounced strengthening of party control over the People's Liberation Army (PLA), which is the armed wing of the CCP, not a conventional state army. This has also applied to the economy and SOEs. In July 2019, Xi declared that the institutional restructuring of state–party integration was complete but measures to strengthen party control would continue, accompanied by efforts to promote ideological strengthening. The CCP has, for example, become more involved in MFA operations.[8] Xi's leadership has seen China's foreign policy evolve into 'major country diplomacy with Chinese characteristics', in which the party's role and loyalty to the party is central.[9]

Xi Jinping has been remaking China's Africa relations in his own image and, flowing from his project within China, as part of the Chinese government's global engagement and ambitions. Xi presides over the new Central Foreign Affairs Commission of the CCP Central Committee, which held its first meeting in May 2019. Since coming to power, the personal imprint of Xi in leading China's Africa relations has been notable. Xi embodies China's self-proclaimed 'diplomacy of friendship'. Xi's role fronting China's Africa relations is one role among many others, but he personifies China in its high-level dealings with African leaders and has invested, together with his wife Peng Liyuan, in an extensive, hands-on personal role; his 2018 African tour was his fourth as president, and his ninth overall. Notable in its own right, this goes far beyond the personal commitments of leaders from Europe, the US, Japan, or India.

The Belt and Road Initiative (BRI)
The global ambition of the BRI – connecting Asia, Europe, the Middle East, Africa and beyond – signalled a new phase for China's relations with Africa. Launched in 2013, the BRI is widely regarded as Xi Jinping's signature foreign-policy initiative. The BRI's importance became evident in 2017 when it was added to the CCP's constitution at the 19th Congress. In essence, while associated with large-scale infrastructure construction and buzzwords like 'connectivity', this is a multifaceted grand strategy responding to perceived US containment efforts, promoting China as a normative power, and reshaping global governance to reflect China's values, interests and status.[10] From a passing reference in FOCAC 2015, the BRI became more integrated into the FOCAC agenda in 2018; or rather, the FOCAC process and agenda was becoming more integrated into the BRI.

The BRI transcended China's different regional partnerships, including with Africa, as a strategy reorienting China's engagement to a global scale and underpinned by the intent to further extend and link China's domestic economic development in global terms. The Chinese government's activism as the architect of new institutions saw the official launch of the Asian Infrastructure and Investment Bank (AIIB) in 2016, a multilateral development bank headquartered in Beijing. While not coined by Xi Jinping, the future vision of a 'community of shared future for mankind' has become a key motif of his diplomacy and China's global engagement. Xi compared this to a Swiss army knife, or 'a Chinese-designed multifunctional tool for solving the world's problems'.[11] The Chinese government presents the concept as a superior model for global governance in politics, security, development (economic, social, technological) culture and the environment via a global network of partnerships anchored in China. In this context, China's Africa policy has been integrated into Beijing's new strategic direction framed in global terms. China's second Africa policy paper (December 2015), for example, cited the goal of working towards a 'Community of Shared Future between China and Africa'. The grand strategic goal is the rejuvenation of China.

Simply put, China is now an emerged power in Africa and this, even as it continues to evolve, represents a huge shift. Over some three decades, China has gone from being a relative outsider to a self-styled 'stakeholder', from being peripheral to highly prominent in Africa's global politics with a clear role for Africa in China's global strategy in the context of changing post-American world order. From economic relations to debt, military role and security engagement, the different aspects of China's power and perceptions of this mean greater political exposure, ambivalence and opposition of different kinds. Such issues are addressed later on but here it is necessary to outline key institutional dimensions of China's Africa engagement.

Institutional reform and adaptation
China's relations with Africa have continued to become diverse in the process of expansion, but the reassertion of the CCP's role has meant a markedly different context compared with the Hu-Wen administration. The previous relatively open public space for discussion about Africa relations has closed. The institutional landscape of entities involved in Africa relations is more crowded. The sheer number from China's side has grown significantly; for example, there

are now some 33 Chinese member departments and agencies in the Follow-Up Committee of FOCAC. While a plethora of other actors are also involved, including friendship associations, cultural bodies and education research institutions, SOEs stand out as important. These have commercial interests of their own but are also subject to CCP control. There are also different generations and types of Chinese corporations, from established SOEs like the China Civil Engineering Construction Corporation, CNPC (oil), and Sinohydro (hydropower), or companies like Huawei (telecommunications), to relative newcomer companies like Transsion, or Alibaba, which has been developing an Africa strategy of its own. The diversification of Chinese actors involved in Africa relations has continued, while the CCP's role has concurrently become more influential across the spectrum of China's engagement, from local to central government levels.

The evolution of China's Africa engagement as part of Xi Jinping's major power diplomacy has necessitated ongoing institutional reforms and adaptation, including in China's Africa relations.[12] This has seen the changing fortunes of key central state ministries. The MFA's budget, for instance, doubled in the first five years of Xi's reign. Two examples stand out. First, reforms within China's domestic security sector, notably the creation of a National Security Commission in 2013, were closely linked to its evolving overseas role. Enabling legislation, such as China's counterterrorism law (2015), paves the way for future overseas operations not just by the PLA but also the People's Armed Police. Second, in March 2018, the China International Development Cooperation Agency (CIDCA) was created in order to address the multiplying challenges induced by the huge expansion of Chinese aid since 2000 in the context of an institutional system that had remained much the same since the mid 1990s. China's emergence as global development actor, notably in Africa, had also brought enhanced interest, scrutiny and demands for cooperation with a proliferating number of external actors. CIDCA absorbed the personnel and aid coordination functions of MOFCOM's Department of Aid to Foreign Countries, and assumed the MFA's responsibility for aligning aid with foreign policy.[13] CIDCA is positioned as its own entity under China's highest government authority, the State Council, theoretically rendering it with equal standing with the MFA or MOFCOM. Stepping back from such institutional dynamics, by creating such a body, China confirmed its 'major power' elevation and the centrality of development in its engagement with Africa.

Forum on China–Africa Cooperation
FOCAC has also been evolving since 2012, becoming more institutionalized, wide-ranging and connected to wider Chinese foreign-policy engagements. FOCAC has grown from an effort to formalize ties into a major, more institutionalized and recognized venue to showcase connections, enable political dialogue, promote business and engage a wider array of sectors. Since 2000, alternating between Beijing and an African country every three years, FOCAC has become more established, with a functioning Secretariat in the MFA's Department of African Affairs, follow-up mechanisms and processes for managing relations. Originally organized principally around business and politics, FOCAC now engages a full spectrum of issue areas. FOCAC became fully incorporated into China's New Era global agenda. The 2018 FOCAC Action Plan (2019–21) clearly supported key priorities in Xi's global policy, affirming that China–Africa relations 'works to realize the two centenary goals and the Chinese dream of national rejuvenation', and further integrating the BRI into relations.

FOCAC has been a leading platform for partnerships with international actors of various kinds that have sought to become involved in China–Africa relations.[14] FOCAC anchors related China–Africa initiatives pursued at other international forums. Other mechanisms for consultations between China and Africa include meetings between African diplomats to China, triennial meetings between China's and

African Foreign Ministers at the UN General Assembly (UNGA) sidelines, as well as meetings between senior officials. Since 2018, a '1 + 3' coordination mechanism has been organized between China and the three rotating African members of the UNSC.

For all FOCAC's prominence and the media attention it receives, the extent to which FOCAC resonates within China – and indeed African countries – remains questionable. On the first day of the 2015 Johannesburg FOCAC, the only Chinese paper with anything FOCAC related on its front page was Hubei's *Dongchu Evening News* (which featured a photograph of Xi Jinping sitting between his wife and Jacob Zuma and watching the play *War Horse*). FOCAC has become a major event in Africa's international relations, but such attention and interest is not reciprocated within China. Indeed, there has been resentment fueled by perceptions of the Chinese government's aid largesse at a time of slowing growth and economic difficulty. For all the efforts made by African media delegations to publicize FOCAC, and against the backdrop of opaque mega deals, it is questionable how successful its results are in terms of popular dissemination, much less understanding. The triennial elite spectacle of FOCAC offers a misleading lens through which to evaluate ties; what happens between, around and under each FOCAC can matter more.

In China's Africa relations beyond particular countries, strenuous efforts are made to present FOCAC as a mutual endeavour between equal partners but there are major questions about how far African agency led by states shapes relations at this political level. FOCAC enables collective dialogue and action of a kind. However, it aggregates bilateral relations that, seated in one venue, amount to an African continental presence but not a policy, much less strategy, towards China. FOCAC is dominated by China, which defines its agenda, declaration and outcomes. In part this is due to the power asymmetry between China and African countries, and China's interest in advancing relations and its interests. A further contributing factor is the sheer diversity of what Africa means in practice and the challenges, apart from capacity, of formulating anything more than bilateral positions. For these reasons, it has been argued that 'Africa plays a bit-part at best' and that 'African elites attending such forums such as FOCAC can, from a particular perspective, be seen as characters reduced to beggars angling for some Chinese largesse, rather than development-conscious and certainly not "partners".'[15]

A China–Africa policy, China's African politics
Despite the centralization of personalized power concentrated in Xi Jinping, and the articulation of clear, forward-looking strategic intent, there are pronounced limits to the central Chinese government's ability to control the content of its multidimensional Africa engagement. The CCP has expanded its power, but this basic problem endures. Efforts to reform China's policy machinery, partly to enhance operational effectiveness, have involved expanding forms of collaboration with African partners of different kinds at different levels, not just in state capitals. China's security engagement, for example, now relies more on hybrid collaborations and local partnerships, constraining its ability to exert control.

One example concerns how China's party-state lacks the capacity (resources and personnel) to fully oversee the operations of Chinese SOEs in Africa. SOEs are part of China's foreign policy, with Xi Jinping having urged them to serve as unofficial ambassadors for China. Their actual conduct is more complicated. SOEs are diverse. Some collaborate with foreign corporations, like the China National Offshore Oil Corporation and French company Total in Uganda's oil sector and East African oil pipeline. SOEs undertake their own commercial diplomacy with African governments when trying to maintain existing or pursue new business opportunities. This means direct connections between Chinese corporations and African states, a further dimension of China's plural Africa engagements.[16] SOEs have proactively exploited opportunities to benefit from China's aid, for example, through tendering practices and informal cooperation with African policy-makers to ensure new requests for aid projects.[17] This points to degrees of SOE autonomy and entrepreneurial initiative. SOE entrepreneurial conduct is driven by profit-maximizing goals, meaning corporate interests can diverge from those of the Chinese state. Institutional reforms designed in part to address this characteristic commonly encounter entrenched interests. China's deficit of effective oversight mechanisms, shown by numerous corruption scandals, is compounded by often weak regulatory systems in African countries.

Facing mounting challenges of a more complex engagement, Xi Jinping and the Chinese government have doubled down on the established principles of China–Africa relations while also seeking to update these. In 2018, for example, Xi cited a 'five no' approach to China's Africa relations: 'no interference in African countries' pursuit of development paths that fit their national conditions; no interference in internal affairs; no imposition of China's will; no attachment of political strings to assistance to Africa; and no seeking of selfish political gains in investment and financing cooperation with Africa'. This was a robust attempted response to criticism of relations, from debt to China's expanding security presence.

Yet, official statements of China's intent have become far harder to square with a more complex engagement developing across a genuinely comprehensive spectrum of issues. China has a declared Africa Policy and engagement, but in reality there are multiplying de facto Chinese African policies and engagements. In many respects, this means in effect that China now operates multiple Africa policies based on individual countries and regions. In addition to China's bilateral relations with 53 African states, relations with regional African organizations and the AU, this is replicated across CCP, state, military and other actors. From SOEs to small and medium-sized enterprises and individual entrepreneurs, China's many business engagements are supposed to fall under the official policies. In reality, the divergences in conduct of these with official policy illustrate the challenges China's governing political centre has in attempting to coordinate, much less ensure conformity to the officially declared objectives and principles governing relations. China's Africa relations also involve a wider set of external partnerships, some of which, like the China–Arab States Cooperation Forum, a body that includes Egypt and Sudan as members, overlap with China's Africa relations. How far China's Africa policies in practice help understanding of anything more than overall aspirations is debatable; these matter, including for cementing shared post-colonial identity, but arguably China's political system matters more.[18]

AFRICA'S RELATIONS WITH CHINA

This section examines relations that African state and non-state actors, regional bodies and the AU maintain with China. The importance of providing this context and African perspectives on relations has been underlined by analysis of African agency in international politics in general and concerning China in particular.

African agency in relations with China is important to recognize and appreciate.[19] The term is often used but its deeper complexities – Where is agency located? Who does 'Africa' refer to? What actions constitute agency? – are not so often considered.[20] Agency has different, often overlapping uses in relation to China. One is normative, that is, a prescriptive sense of what ought to be, which risks conflating assertions that Africa *has* agency with *should have* agency. Another use has a more political rendering. China can be regarded, even valorized, as providing actual or potential space to further Africa's emancipation. A further use employs agency mainly in empirical ways. These can show positive effects; activism against the ivory trade, for example, helped place this issue on the FOCAC agenda from 2015 and the Chinese government's commitment to ending the trade. Some of the best examples of agency do not involve 'positive' ends, such as how Sudan's former President Bashir used relations with China to promote his own, violent domestic agenda. Finally, against agency, some argue instead that China's engagement is one part of the broader entrenchment of African economic dependency in context of vulnerability to and dependence on global commodity prices, rendered more important due to a failure by African states to diversify their economies successfully.[21]

There are various problems when agency is used as a frame to view China–Africa relations. Attention to African state relations with China can downplay politics within and between African states, regions and in the continent. Agency has mostly focused on African states and political elites, with insufficient attention to more diffused formations involving civil society groups, businesses, communities and citizens, as well as regional economic communities or continental actors like the AU. These are very connected; the AU–China engagement, for instance, depends on more than just the priorities of China and the AU but has also been 'shaped by on-the-ground realities in Africa', which are constantly being remade.[22] In the context of stark power asymmetries between China and 54 varied African states, the language of agency is never used for China or powerful states.

There are nonetheless many ways through which different African actors influence and shape relations in active ways. These proceed in a context where China has been attuned to the demand for economic development in African countries, and responsive to this in ways that established external powers and aid donors are not. Irrespective of the politics of China's approach to or role in African development, it retains a fundamental credibility in African countries by virtue of its domestic development, poverty reduction, and understanding of what economic development entails.[23] Examples like Beijing's support for the AU's

Agenda 2063 show that China responds to African agenda-setting, even while this can help China. At the same time, and in different ways, African states condition China's engagement across a wide array of political regime types, from democratic systems to military dictatorships. Ultimately, it is rarely a question of either agency or structural dependency but complex combinations in a global economy. Crucial to the outcomes of Chinese and other investment are thus interaction between domestic politics and China in the context of 'the relationship between domestic political economy and transnational systems of investment that shape the behaviour of African elites who broker and implement them'.[24]

African states and beyond
When fitting China in to the foreign relations and domestic politics of African states, which are diverse but share asymmetrical relations with China, a number of themes need to be noted on top of deeper historical connections.

The first concerns how ruling African political elites and states actively use external relations for domestic political purposes: regime survival is also an external affair.[25] China is the most prominent recent example in the continent but is by no means unique; for instance, political elites in Angola and Tanzania engaged the Brazilian government and companies in much the same way.[26] One enduring mechanism used by governing African elites has been termed extraversion, meaning the appropriation of resources provided by external powers in order to consolidate or concentrate domestic political authority.[27] Nigeria under President Buhari since 2015, for example, has pursued a strategy of 'economic diplomacy' based on national interests in which relations with China and other external partners are part of what Nigeria's Foreign Minister termed a 'Nigeria First Foreign Policy'. China became a controversial topic of public debate in Nigeria in 2020, over debt, infrastructure projects or the treatment of Nigerians in China, but China's importance in Nigeria's domestic and foreign policy should not be overstated. Another example is the illiberal authoritarian state agency of Rwanda, Chad or Uganda, which have instrumentalized the issue of security to successfully secure Western development assistance.[28] Among other things, this means their foreign relations can mean the continuation of domestic politics by other means (albeit the meaning and boundaries of 'domestic' and 'foreign' can be fuzzy). In this way, President Museveni of Uganda has manipulated China's engagement to suit his domestic and regional agenda but he has done the same with Western powers, including longstanding political, financial and military support from the US. Unsurprisingly, Uganda and many African states seek to avoid dependence on any single external partner and maintain diverse external relations in the pursuit of autonomy. This means China is one of many external partners for African states, albeit a more important one. China has become more important for Egypt, for example, but Cairo's relations with the US still matter.

It is very hard to set out which African states are more durably favourable towards China (as opposed to presenting variations in the intensity of their alignment across time and different issues). Indeed, China can be a factor when it comes to electoral contests. In Sierra Leone, for example, Julius Maada Bio declared that his election as president in 2018 was 'the dawn of a new era' following a campaign in which he criticized Chinese infrastructure projects as 'a sham with no economic and development benefits to the people'.[29] Relations also evolve. Angola, for example, was a key partner and pioneer for China's oil engagement and relations with the Gulf of Guinea and Lusophone Africa but this has been changing in a context of regime transition from 2017, debt and shifting external relations. The DRC's government, another example, successfully leveraged China and the IMF against each other between 2007 and 2009, securing both a major Chinese infrastructure loan and benefiting from multilateral debt relief in the process, but since then China's approach 'shifted and no longer enables the Congolese regime to leverage the Chinese presence for its own political benefit.'[30]

Some African states clearly matter more than others for China. The continental scope of Beijing's diplomatic engagement, coupled with personalized leadership diplomacy, is outwardly impressive but far from uniform in application. This is seen in how states in different regions, from Algeria and Egypt to South Africa, Senegal and Nigeria to the Republic of Congo, Ethiopia or Kenya, stand out in terms of relations with China. It is also seen in China's support for industrialization, which may be presented in continental Africa terms but rests on a handful of 'demonstration and pioneering countries', notably Ethiopia and Kenya.

Beyond state relations, competitive electoral politics and African civil society where this can operate, as well as the participation of citizens mean that a range of non-state influences operate in individual external relations. Chinese–African civil society relations demonstrate great diversity and encompass a heterogeneous range of groups, from formal non-governmental organizations (NGOs) to traditional authorities, in Ghana or South Sudan for instance. There are many critical voices and opposition to China's projects, deepening role, political effects and environmental impact. The Zimbabwe Environmental Law Association or the Law Society of Kenya, for example, have mounted legal challenges to Chinese projects. In contrast, there is also a more supportive dynamic, such as around development issues, seen in the participation of NGOs in official China–Africa cooperation.[31] Given the variation within and across African countries, this means China's engagement has to adapt to political contexts, including where civil society is independent, organized and active. China as a subject for media-influenced debate shows how it has become part of everyday politics in many African public spheres. One dimension of this has concerned the situation of Africans in China. In April 2020, the plight of Africans in Guangzhou during the COVID-19 pandemic became prominent, with many evicted from their accommodation and denied entrance to shops. This had ramifications in African countries and prompted African diplomats to make an unusual protest to China's MFA.

Regional engagements
At a basic level, a pattern of regional engagement characterizes relations and involves relations between Africa's regional economic communities and China. In north Africa, Egypt has been a pillar of China's regional and continental engagement. In west Africa, Nigeria is a giant in regional terms and has the continent's largest economy. In 2018, the Economic Community of West African States confirmed China would fund and build a new $31.6m headquarters, a surprising decision in view of Nigeria and Ghana's oil income. In east Africa, Kenya and Uganda stand out in terms of their regional role, as does Tanzania in different ways.[32] The East African Community (EAC) has more established relations with China; indeed, with southern Africa, it has been one of the most visited African regions by Chinese government delegations.[33] Eastern Africa's relations with China, however, have been driven by leaders of key individual states like Uganda, Kenya or Tanzania more than any coherent and meaningful role of the EAC itself. In the Horn of Africa, Ethiopia has been pro-China but within an approach predicated on maintaining friendships with all external powers to avoid dependence on any single one. In central Africa, the DRC has been prominent via its resource-based engagement with China and Chinese UN peacekeeping deployment. South Africa dominates the southern African region and has had close relations with Beijing but also maintains relations with other powers.

Within African states, while leaders often seek to direct relations, the ways in which China is managed vary widely and this is consistent with practical everyday challenges. Even South Africa has struggled to manage its inter-governmental China relations; since being created in 2010, the Joint Inter-Ministerial Working Group on China–South Africa Cooperation has suffered from a lack of practical implementation. China's relations with African states proceed on a formal basis but involve personalized connections; it is no accident that the birthplaces of African leaders receive greater financial flows from China when in power.[34] Within African states, debates concerning and tensions over external relations, including China, are predictable but one overlooked means by which African states conduct relations with China is through state bureaucracies. This means that in small countries like Benin bureaucrats influence negotiation outcomes in ways that can mitigate against collective state agency: in other words, the lack of coordination and competition between ministers does 'not allow for a coherent "China strategy" in the framework of infrastructure projects negotiation.'[35] Finally, African states in practice engage many Chinese entities, from policy banks, to ministries, or migrant entrepreneurs.

AU–China relations
The AU did not exist when the first FOCAC was held in 2000. As successor to the Organization of African Unity, it was established in 2002 as the key continental body. The AU's Agenda 2063 was proposed in 2013 – months before Xi Jinping proposed the BRI – and adopted in 2015 as the plan for the next fifty years under the guidance of the New Partnership for Africa's Development agency, NEPAD. It envisions Africa becoming 'a dynamic force in the international arena.'[36] The AU's role, status and importance is much debated. Despite operational and legitimacy challenges, the AU provides a degree of symbolic power and global visibility. With over 40% of member states not paying yearly contributions, the AU is highly dependent on external donor funding. In 2012, the AU Conference and Office Complex in Addis Ababa was gifted and built by China.[37]

AU–China ties have strengthened since 2012. The Chinese government established a diplomatic mission at the AU headquarters in Addis Ababa in 2015. Three years later, an AU Representative Office was established in Beijing, reportedly paid for by China. Efforts by China and the AU to coordinate policy have been made on specific issues. Notably, the AU's Agenda 2063 placed industrial strategies at the centre of African development and poverty reduction aims. In a broader sense, the AU's Agenda 2063 and FOCAC may be formally aligned but 'Africa's capacity for implementation is wanting.'[38] In theory, the AU represents – or should represent – a very important point for coordinating the continent's relations with the Chinese government. This includes the AU Development Agency – NEPAD. In practice, the extent to which the AU is meaningfully involved is questionable, and just how it manages relations with China unclear. This is consistent with how the AU operates and the challenges it faces, as documented in a 2017 report by Rwandan President Paul Kagame on rationalizing Africa's partnerships and strengthening the AU.[39] Prior to external partnerships, then, are such challenges as relations between the AU and regional African economic communities, seen when these held their first coordination meeting in July 2019.

The AU's well-known struggle to define a continental position is not particular to China.[40] The evergreen cliché 'China has an Africa policy but Africa does not have a China policy' is inherently problematic. While desirable in principle in suggesting an organized, focused effort to maximize the benefits of China relations for progressive ends, in practice this has proved impossible.[41] In contrast to China, even if this itself has myriad actors, Africa at FOCAC translates into bilateral state, AU Commission or corporate participation, each of which has different, sometimes contending interests and capacity. Each African government manages its relations with China. Beyond bilateral agreements with China, evidence that individual countries have developed policies on China in a significant, organized and strategic manner is scarce. Fragmentation, multiple regional bodies and primacy of state interests contribute to Africa's reactive 'one and the many' pattern in asymmetrical external relations, of which China is one part, meaning FOCAC is 'a case-study in how a genuinely strategic diplomatic engagement with external powers has and continues to elude Africa'.[42]

CONCLUSION

This chapter provided an overview of China–Africa relations before the New Era to provide context. China–Africa history looks very different if based on 53 (or 54) different African countries' relations with China. However, under Mao, China's relations with Africa were driven by political ambition and calculations, and featured strong ideological dimensions. The economics in command phases that followed reacted to and departed from this, starting with China's domestic politics. Under Xi, economics remain fundamental to CCP rule in China but politics and ideology have returned to the fore.

Histories matter as living influences in China–Africa relations, including China's official history, which is integral to its statecraft.[43] The CCP claim that its past conduct in Africa, especially the lack of any colonial record, is a guide to its future conduct is echoed and amplified in its statements about its global rise, which Beijing insists will be peaceful. Many rightly critique a tendency for historical forgetting in Western approaches to China–Africa, and Africa more generally, and evaluating 'China's activities on the continent as a reflection of the West's own not-so-distant histories of colonialism in Africa'.[44] At the same time, the CCP has been remarkably successful in promoting its version of the past within China and crafting a historical narrative about China's global rejuvenation under Xi's leadership. Controlling the official narrative of its African history is more challenging. This reflects the wide and deep diversity of historical experience, memories and politics in African countries encompassing, for example, a gener-ation of leaders who graduated from revolutionary training in Mao's China (such as Emmerson Mnangagwa, hailed by Xi Jinping as an 'old friend of China' after deposing Robert Mugabe to become president of Zimbabwe in 2017), and increasing numbers of African students now graduating with MBAs from Chinese universities.

The 'New Era' in China–Africa relations represents a historic departure because, in essence, China is an emerged power in the continent. Numerous challenges now stem from this underlying change, in the wider context of China's economic standing and major power status. In another sense, China's efforts to craft an identity as a different power and alternative for Africa mean that the particular kind of emerged power that China is becoming matters. China's claims to difference, which mobilize a form of historically derived exception-alism, rest on commitments to equality, reciprocity, non-interference and respect for state sovereignty, and win–win development. China continues to promote these, and style itself as an alternative promoting development autonomy and, even, contributing to a transformation in global politics conducive to advancing Africa's interests. At the same time, and in the context of the mixed identities China presents to Africa – major power, developing country, friend, competitor, agent of economic transformation, creditor – the underlying shifts in relations bring the coherence of claims to difference into question. These produce mounting tensions between Beijing's traditional principles and the new challenges in China's Africa relations.

This chapter also examined the reassertion of CCP authority and power within China and in its major power diplomacy. Continuing a pattern wherein China's Africa policies reflect its prevailing domestic politics, economy and foreign policy, this has not just been manifest within China but also in its Africa relations. From Mao to Xi, China has been depicted as a unitary state doing something to or in Africa according to a masterplan. This enables easy explanations about what, how and why China is engaging Africa, especially if the continent is similarly homogenized and stripped of agency. Closer examination of the institutional dimensions of China's Africa relations over time and under Xi Jinping shows that China's Africa policy institutions are often presented as if part of a monolithic party-state system, which over-determines coherence and underplays the diversity of actors, competing agendas and internal politics involved. By contrast, a contrary interpretation of China's Africa policy machinery as fragmented and dysfunctional can over-determine incoherence. China's Africa engagement does involve a wider, more diverse range of actors across most issue areas, and operates at multiple levels across 53 (54) African countries, but at the same time is highly orchestrated by the central CCP-state. If the 'strong industry, weak government' problem was noted during the Hu-Wen years, today the centralization of power under the CCP means an opposite trend. Since 2012, a process to recentralize and concentrate power under Xi and CCP leadership has 'increased its capacity to steer at all levels'.[45] Governance in Xi's New Era means that CCP leadership closely guides policy-making and the party ensures discipline and directs ideology.

China has an African engagement of continental scope, but regional and individual African state engagements remain foundational. The advance of politics about China within African states as part of deepening ties and China's actual and perceived rise in Africa has meant a notable part of the politicization of China reflects diverse domestic African state politics, including the role of civil society or opposition political parties. China in African state conduct has in general become more important. Long before Xi Jinping took office, however, it was well recognized that certain African countries, like Angola, were 'able to "play the China card" well'.[46]

Finally, this chapter introduced broad context behind the nature and roles of different African protagonists undertaking unequal equal relations with China. The asymmetrical nature of relations between

African states and China have become more evident, a further reason why China uses historically informed rhetoric and politics to cover manifest power imbalances. In this way, China's New African era has clarified a more basic shift: where China once positioned itself as anti-hegemonic, now a big question about its developing and future role is whether it has become an actual or potential hegemonic power.[47] Under Xi the issue of China's possible hegemony has become more salient, politicized and consequential, and is bound up in China's changing global engagement in which Africa is one notable part.

2	China and Africa in Global Politics	

Africa's political importance to China's foreign policy and global politics has become more manifest as a crucial shift in relations since 2012 and as part of the Chinese government's more ambitious global engagement. This is not a new theme; in 1971, as Mao commented, China's African friends 'carried us back in' to the UN. At the same time, Africa's importance has to be understood as relative within China's global engagement under the New Era banner of major country diplomacy with Chinese characteristics. Africa is important politically for China in global terms, but not as important as it might seem if official rhetoric is taken literally. The support of African governments is significant in China's foreign policy, engagement with existing multilateral institutions centred on the UN and creation of its own multilateral institutions. In Africa, Beijing has endeavoured to develop and showcase its credentials as a self-proclaimed 'responsible stakeholder' to the continent and the world. As Yang Jiechi, Politburo member and director of the CCP's Office of the Central Commission for Foreign Affairs, noted: in Africa 'China's international influence, appeal and shaping have been further enhanced, and it has become a recognized builder of world peace, a contributor to global development, and a defender of the international order.'[1]

The first of this chapter's three sections examines the role of African states in China's New Era foreign policy and how Beijing's active role in multilateralism and embrace of global governance demonstrates Africa's political significance for China's changing engagement in global politics. The second examines China in the foreign policies and wider global politics of African states. African states, for sound reasons based on their political interests, sought to use growing economic ties with China to try to enhance their autonomy. One noteworthy recent trend suggests continuing attempts to diversify external partners, including to offset or avoid any undue dependence on China. The final section appraises how select external powers have responded to China in Africa, using the examples of Brazil, India, Japan, the UK, France, the EU and, in particular, the US. The Trump administration's mixed signals on Africa, prominent anti-China posturing on the one hand, but a glaring lack of substance in terms of actual political or economic engagement on the other, meant that US–Africa strategy was criticized as the Africa part of America's China policy. The hardening of US policy into overt strategic rivalry with China on a global scale meant intensifying geopolitics in the continent.

AFRICA IN CHINA'S FOREIGN POLICY AND GLOBAL POLITICS

The familiar issues of Taiwan, Tibet and Japan continue in China's Africa relations. With only one diplomatic partner in the continent, Eswatini, Taiwan has been effectively eliminated from Africa in terms of diplomatic recognition. Taipei has no realistic prospect of gaining anything more than the occasional opportunistic new diplomatic friend, like the self-declared Republic of Somaliland in 2020, since the costs of not recognizing China have become too high. Likewise, African countries have become closed to Tibet. In 2017, for example, the Dalai Lama cancelled a planned visit to Botswana, whose then President Ian Khama explained that 'China engaged in intimidation', such as saying that Botswana's ambassador to Beijing might be recalled or that China would 'engage other African states to isolate Botswana'.[2]

Japan continues to represent a source of actual and potential friction for China in Africa but was overshadowed by the US.

Important new issues with global dimensions – such as the South China Sea, Xinjiang, or Hong Kong – emerged during the New Era. Beijing has sought to muster and use the support of sympathetic African state coalitions to bolster the credibility of its policy and narratives about these issues within and without China, defend against criticism, and back the Chinese government with speeches and votes in multilateral contexts. This is a sign of both Beijing's leverage, and its determination to confront and 'tell China's own story'. To this end, Chinese ambassadors in African countries have become more vocal, and proactive in terms of engaging traditional and social media, publishing newspaper articles, appearing on radio or using Twitter to promote China's views robustly and rebut criticism of China.

Beijing mobilized African governments to recognize and support its territorial claims to the South China Sea, where an accelerated program of island building and effective control was initiated after Xi Jinping took office. This included invoking the support of 'friendly countries', such as Burundi, Gambia, Niger, Lesotho, Sierra Leone, Kenya and Sudan, in its territorial dispute with the Philippines. In July 2016, the Permanent Court of Arbitration in the Hague ruled in favour of the Philippines that China's territorial claims of historic rights in the South China Sea lacked legal foundation and its actions there infringed on the Philippines' rights. Having rejected the arbitration process, Beijing rejected the ruling.

China has sought to use African government support to promote and legitimize its draconian crackdown in Xinjiang. Since 2017, over one million Uyghurs and other ethnic minorities have been detained in internment camps. China turned to Africa as a bloc and African countries for support over its hardline measures, as seen from 2019 in the context of criticism and countercriticism of Chinese state policy in Xinjiang. In July 2019, a letter to the UN High Commissioner for Human Rights signed by 22 (18 European and Western) states, including Germany, Japan, Australia and Canada, criticized China's repression in Xinjiang and called for an end to 'mass arbitrary detentions and related violations'. Not long after, a letter to the UN Human Rights Council defending China's policies and praising its 'contribution to the international human rights cause' was signed by 37 states, including Russia, North Korea, Cuba, Venezuela, Saudi Arabia, Pakistan, and 16 African countries, including Algeria, Egypt, Sudan, Somalia and Nigeria. Beijing praised the 'objectivity and fairness' of this letter, lauding it as 'a strong response to a few Western countries' groundless accusations against China'.[3]

One Chinese government tactic was that of pressuring states to exclude Xinjiang from UNSC exposure. In 2019, a US attempt to get the then UN High Commissioner for Human Rights, Zeid Ra'ad al-Hussein, to brief the UNSC about Syria was thwarted by Moscow and Beijing, due to concerns this might broach Xinjiang. The UNSC's three African representatives, Equatorial Guinea, Ethiopia and Côte d'Ivoire, abstained, the latter at the last minute and reportedly, according to its ambassador, because 'his president had received a call from Beijing instructing him to ensure the session did not happen'.[4]

Another tactic has seen the Chinese government promoting its narrative about Xinjiang in various ways. Beijing presents Xinjiang as an example of 'China's important contribution to the global fight against terrorism',[5] going beyond defensive reactions by using the international policy vocabulary of counterterrorism and deradicalization. In August 2019, China's ambassador to Nigeria published a newspaper article that, following publication of a government white paper 'Vocational Education and Training in Xinjiang', presented Xinjiang as an example of tackling extremism through vocational education.[6] In September 2019, UN Office at Geneva (UNOG) diplomats from Ethiopia, Zimbabwe, Equatorial Guinea, Mozambique, Zambia, Côte d'Ivoire, Yemen and South Africa visited Xinjiang in order to 'gain a better understanding of the region's achievements from de-radicalization to poverty reduction.'[7] Zambia's Permanent Representative to the UNOG, Martha Lungu Mwitumwa, explained how she had been deceived in Geneva during China's 3rd UN Human Rights Council universal periodic review process (November 2018 to March 2019): 'The impression I got from [what I heard] about Xinjiang in Geneva … was Xinjiang was a prison, and people were being manipulated. After seeing the situation, I don't believe what I heard in Geneva.'[8] This illustrated a battle for defining and gaining support for 'truth', undermining or discrediting the legitimacy of evidence and other submissions, following and amplifying China's official line. Equatorial Guinea's Permanent Representative to the UNOG, Lazaro Ekua Avomo, thus affirmed: 'We have seen no problems in Xinjiang, no violation of human rights or freedom of religious belief.'[9] This visit was noteworthy for the participation of South Africa's Deputy Permanent Representative to the UNOG, the parallels between apartheid and Xinjiang, and a shift from historic solidarity with oppressed people to a state solidarity of complicity in oppression.[10]

Hong Kong became a global issue in 2019, through long-running pro-democracy demonstrations and opposition to an extradition bill, and became part of China's Africa relations as Chinese diplomats sought to mobilize support for Beijing's position. Chinese diplomats campaigned against 'Western' criticism concerning the effective ending of Hong Kong's 'one country, two systems' framework, and even blamed foreigners for inciting unrest. In August 2019, for instance, China's ambassador to Uganda published an opinion article in the New Vision newspaper. Asking 'Who is the black hand meddling Hong Kong [*sic*] to her current chaos?', he cited 'interference and incitement from foreign forces', including American and Western media, insisting: 'Hong Kong affairs are China's internal affairs.'[11] On 3 October 2019, the Ugandan government issued a short media release that, almost lifting the Chinese ambassador's language, asserted: 'Hong

Kong is part of China. Hong Kong's affairs are China's domestic affairs.' China's Hong Kong security law of June 2020 took this to a new level. Of 53 countries who appeared to sign a statement supporting China at the UN Human Rights Council (UNHRC) in Geneva after the law was passed, 25 were African, including Egypt, Djibouti, Zambia, Cameroon and South Sudan (which seceded from Sudan in 2011, making its support for measures in the Hong Kong security law against secession or undermining national unification especially noteworthy). Three important African democracies, Nigeria, South Africa and Kenya, expressed no public sentiment in support of the law but neither did they openly criticize it. The impact on civil society views in Africa of China was shaping up to be quite different, in view of the enormity of the security law in overriding partial democratic freedoms and rights in Hong Kong.

The upshot is that African governments have not supported American and other attempts to condemn the Chinese government about Xinjiang at the UN, nor has there been support for democracy in Hong Kong. Support for the Chinese government on such issues, building on the established ritual of invoking non-interference and the One China principle, is a straightforward public means to enhance relations with Beijing; indeed, for some African governments, it can be used to restate domestic opposition to terrorism or separatist politics. Somalia was one state supporting China's Hong Kong security law, for example, amid efforts by Taiwan to establish diplomatic relations with Somaliland. At the same time, supporting Washington on such sensitive issues does not guarantee commensurate reward and risks Chinese investment, loans and patronage. Additionally, the stance of African governments was not unusual, sharing similarities with the Organization of Islamic Cooperation or Turkey, for example. Xi's China, however, is now more determined and better able to set the terms. Globally, few if any governments appear willing to risk jeopardizing economic relations with China by challenging Beijing over Xinjiang, Hong Kong or other issues, thereby risking retaliation. While there are risks in criticizing China over such issues, this is another asymmetrical dynamic where comparable mistakes by Chinese about Africa do not elicit the same strength of reactions. In 2017, a China Global Television Network (CGTN)–Africa report about a car bomb explosion in Mogadishu used a map depicting Somaliland as an independent state. A CGTN Twitter apology to 'followers from Somalia' insisted this was an 'honest mistake'. Any African state (or political entity like Somaliland) that committed a comparable error with Taiwan, Tibet, Xinjiang or Hong Kong would be unlikely to escape CCP censure.

Africa, China and multilateral cooperation

China is investing heavily in its multilateral engagement in established institutions and those it helped create or created. The UN has been an important arena for China's more activist foreign policy, where it has mounted a strategy of concerted engagement to demonstrate its credentials as a global power and attempt to advance its interests.[12] Engaging with the UN also allows China's different identities as a global leader/ major power on the UNSC and a developing non-Western country in the UNGA to operate. Africa has played a disproportionately prominent role in this process: key areas where Beijing styles itself as provider of global public goods, notably in development and security, relate to and derive substantially from China's role in Africa. Given that China's Africa relations involve far more than bilateral relations or FOCAC, this section considers how China relates to Africa in its multilateral engagement, using human rights and development as examples.

Most obviously, because 'Africa occupies a quarter' of UN seats, China sees numerical advantage in the votes of its 53 African state allies.[13] This is by no means unusual in historical terms, nor for other powers; the same is true for Japan, India, Brazil or Russia. As well as using African state support in its multilateral engagement in established and new international institutions, since 2018 China has coordinated with the three African countries on the UNSC. In September 2019, Wang Yi declared that if this speaks 'with one voice, their influence would ... cover the entire African continent'.[14]

African governments play a role in Beijing's efforts to expand its influence within international organizations. Chinese nationals lead a number of these, including the International Civil Aviation Organization, UN Industrial Development Organization, and the UN Department for Economic and Social Affairs, but Beijing has sought to expand its leadership of others. Despite a concerted American effort to defeat China's bid, for example, China's vice minister of Agriculture and Rural Affairs, Qu Dongyu, was elected as the new Director-General of the UN Food and Agriculture Organization in June 2019. Chinese pressure to get Qu elected was reportedly intense, and saw a Cameroonian candidate withdraw, but America's unwillingness to back the French candidate didn't help. After the election, Wang Yi said: 'From now on, there will be one more good friend of Africa in the UN agencies.'[15] Finally, increasing numbers of African states have joined new multilateral institutions created by China. By mid 2020, there were 19 African approved 'non-regional members' of the AIIB, including Egypt, Ethiopia, Madagascar, Sudan and Benin.

Human rights and development are examples of issues where African state support has become important for China. First, the Chinese government has sought African backing to promote its own agenda on human rights. Xi Jinping's foreign policy has been actively promoting the CCP's version of human rights and challenging universal democratic politics and values. In this, China has used the votes of African states at the UNHRC to advance its agenda. For China's resolution at the UNHRC on 23 March 2018, 'promoting mutually beneficial cooperation in the field of human rights', 11 of 28 states supporting China were from Africa (Angola, Burundi, Côte d'Ivoire, DRC, Egypt, Ethiopia, Kenya, Nigeria, Senegal, South Africa and Togo). The US withdrawal from the UNHRC months later only helped China. One motivation for the Chinese government is to exercise 'discursive power' via promoting its 'human rights discourse in the new era'. A central feature of this is getting its own language – such as 'community of shared destiny' or 'human rights with Chinese characteristics' – incorporated into UN resolutions. Such language also reflects underlying political priorities, as Beijing has sought to promote its own conception of human rights.[16] A 'promoting human rights through development' approach characterized Beijing's South–South Human Rights Forum in December 2017, for example or, in 2018, during the 39th session of the UN Human Rights Council, China and South Africa sponsored an event about poverty eradication and human rights, which stressed that economic development was vital to realizing human rights. Second, Africa is central to China's new role in global development. Development policy is a further area where China's global role has evolved following its domestic achievements, from experimental overseas outreach and, more recently, adoption of an ambitious and leading role in development policy. In a shift from its previous approach, China has been styling itself as a leader in global development as an area of dedicated, intentional policy, rather than the outcome of economic growth. There is power in developing other countries. China's development role in Africa partly demonstrates its power. CIDCA befits one of China's identities, that of a major power, while seeking to remain positioned as an equal Southern development partner.

The Chinese government uses Africa to reinforce claims about its contribution to global development. The CCP succeeded within China via an officially termed 'miracle of development unprecedented in human history',[17] and this is now continuing outside, predominantly in Africa. The continent is consistently cited by Chinese leaders and officials as proof of China's contribution to global public goods. For China, Africa represents a success story that can be cited as exemplifying its 'responsible stakeholder' credentials in practice via China's contribution to global development (such as the Sustainable Development Goals) and global poverty eradication. This can be used by Beijing to promote its claims to being a superior development alternative and discredit Western approaches. It uses Africa to burnish its credentials to global leadership at the level of discursive claims and formal interaction. In recent years, this has become more important in the face of a backlash against China. In development policy, China has become more influential in terms of its experience, credentials and ability to promote development and source of 'lessons', in poverty reduction for example.

Africa in China's global strategy
China's foreign policy operates according to a hierarchy of regions, in which Africa is relatively low, despite rhetoric suggesting otherwise. China–US relations are most important but Beijing's 'top priority', which is connected to its relations with Washington, is neighbourhood diplomacy. China's 'comprehensive strategic partnership of coordination for a new era' with Russia is significant, and the EU is 'also a comprehensive strategic partner'. Last are 'China and other developing countries', in which Africa is folded into Beijing's vision of 'a community of shared future'.[18] Beyond this, there is no obvious special place for Africa in general foreign-policy documents, the opposite of self-centred FOCAC statements and speeches. Distinguishing between big powers, neighbouring powers and developing countries, Chinese analysts have long regarded Africa as 'foundation of the foundations' in China's foreign policy. Africa stands out in China's global diplomacy, FOCAC being the most established regional forum outside China's neighbourhood, but the continent is now by no means the only region Beijing has sought to advance ties with. China's 'year of South–South cooperation' in 2018, for example saw Beijing hold, in

Wang Yi's words, 'collective dialogues with almost all other developing countries across the different continents'.[19]

The paradox of Africa being both central to and a relatively lower priority in China's global strategy is partly attributable to a shift since 2012 that has seen Africa's previously elevated importance for China get overtaken by other dynamics. During the expansion of China–Africa ties and China's 'going out' or 'going global' phase, the continent represented a prominent partnership, being open, receptive and willing to expand ties with a China that kept a low profile under its 'peaceful development' slogan. Today, China's trade with Latin America significantly outstrips that with Africa.[20] China's relations with the Middle East, responsible for over 40% of its oil imports, are expanding. Where once African countries were seen as the base for global exports and expansion, China expanded investment into parts of Europe and the US. The BRI's ambitions transcend Africa, meaning that the relative importance of the continent during China's 'going global' period has been superseded by China's global engagement under the BRI. This suggested that the period when Africa was a priority for China was if not over, then at least transitioning as China's role in the global South and global politics evolved.

China's African engagement played a part in influencing Beijing's adoption of the label 'responsible great power' and recent stress on using the language of global public goods, illustrating one way in which the Chinese government used Africa to assist its global rise and, in the process, was indirectly assisted by other external powers. Robert Zoellick's 2005 'responsible stakeholder' speech, for example, contributed one reputational motivation and saw China adopt this language. Global governance has been much debated within China since then, particularly from 2009, but under Xi Jinping's leadership, there has been a concerted push to engage global governance, specifically reforms that suit China's interests.

FOCAC shows a much tighter alignment of Africa to China's global strategy, folding relations into Beijing's vision while paying token lip service to AU goals. The 2015 FOCAC declaration noted a 'growing sense of common destiny' but in 2018 was titled 'Towards an Even Stronger China–Africa Community with a Shared Future'. This fusion of 'community with a shared future for mankind' and 'China–Africa community with a shared future' represented Africa's effective incorporation into China's global vision, strategy and accompanying language. If propaganda and ideology are at the core of the CCP's attempts to shape global governance, China has been successful in embedding and framing its language into the FOCAC process in its terms.

The global context appeared conducive to the Chinese government's efforts to further incorporate Africa into its vision of a global future, in which its global governance engagement is one part. Long supporting 'the democratization of International Relations', or reducing post-Cold-War American dominance, Beijing faces the challenge of global power transitions. During the Central Foreign Relations Work Conference of June 2018, Xi Jinping spoke of the 'accelerated development of multipolarization' and the importance of US–China relations.[21] One phrase widely used by Xi Jinping, officials, official documents and propaganda, that 'the world today is undergoing major changes unseen in a century', summarized the immense opportunities for China in a context of America's global role under the Trump administration. Xi Jinping has styled China as the 'stabilizing force' in the global economy, a defender of open trade and multilateralism. The CCP advertises that it is 'providing more public goods to the international community', featuring a list of global and regional multilateral platforms including FOCAC and the China–Africa Economic and Trade Expo. A disproportionate amount of the activities cited as evidence of providing global public goods, from UN peacekeeping to development aid, is Africa related. In this way, Beijing's position paper for the UNGA in 2019 styled China as 'promoter of world peace, contributor to global development, and upholder of the international order'.

Debate about whether the CCP wants to reform or transform global governance is misleadingly framed: Beijing's current focus is on reform, and managing its US relations, but its future ambition is transformation. For good reasons, China has emphasized support for an open world economy and 'better external environment for China's economic development'.[22] Xi's report to the 19th Party Congress invoked 'Chinese wisdom and a Chinese approach to solving problems facing mankind' and noted that 'China will continue to play its part as a major and responsible country, take an active part in reforming and developing the global governance system'.[23] Beijing's stated intent to be 'actively involved in global governance' is also part of the FOCAC process, notably the 2018 FOCAC declaration, where this is tied to reforms 'to make the global governance system better represent the will and interests of the majority of countries, especially developing countries.'

CHINA IN AFRICAN FOREIGN POLICIES AND GLOBAL AFFAIRS

China in the foreign relations and global politics of African states is the subject of this section. That all African states are formally friendly towards China, apart from Eswatini, says little beyond surface positions, hiding diverse approaches and changing degrees of commitments. As China's New Era has developed, Africa states seem to be more aligned on key issues in China's foreign policy and global engagement. Far from any zero-sum shift of continental allegiance, however, the reality is less deterministic and more contingent.

First, China is a more present factor in the foreign-policy activism of African states. This results in challenges for China in plausibly attempting to square its public claim to treat African countries equally with its own interests and power calculations. One illustration came when Kenya and Djibouti competed to replace South Africa in a rotating seat on the 2020–1 UNSC. Both states claimed China's support, then retracted. The Chinese government seemed to prefer Djibouti, a closer ally, even though Beijing insisted it supported 'Africans to solve African problems in an African way'. Kenya eventually won the seat in June 2020.

Second, does increased trade mean that African states become allies of China or use closer economic ties to balance China against other external powers in order to access resources and pursue autonomy? One study of African voting patterns at the UNGA and country statements in the UN General Debate showed that there were 'paradoxical effects' on the foreign-policy stances of states trading more with China: with the exception of UNGA human rights-related resolutions, increased trade with China 'leads to African states aligning more with the United States in their foreign-policy positions at the UN'. This suggests that African states engage in 'balancing behaviour with external powers whereby African elites seek to play off rival powers against one another in order to strengthen their own autonomy and maximize trade'.[24] African states align with China on human rights on the basis of similar views about national sovereignty concerns. The argument that African governments seek to leverage growing economic ties with China to enhance their autonomy makes sense. This indicates balancing behaviour organized around imperatives of internal African state politics, rather than any threat of external military intervention, underlining how such behaviour is intended to promote regime maintenance. Angola's political elite adopted such a strategy in order to maintain relations with a variety of external partners and not be dominated by China.[25] Another example is South Africa. Even though associated with China in numerous ways – foreign policy, BRICS membership, political party connections – the South African government and ruling party continues to debate how best to balance relations with BRICS partners led by China, Western partners and other East Asian allies with its own domestic interests.

Third, an emerging New Era trend suggested that some African states had evolved beyond a phase of using China to promote autonomy and were instead quietly seeking to move away from any undue dependence on China. Where previously there was interest in using China to enhance autonomy vis-à-vis established powers like the US, France or UK, or international financial institutions like the IMF, an emerging new direction could be discerned: cultivating ties with other powers to attempt to enhance leverage with China. In the late 1990s, for example, the government of Sudan was heavily reliant on China. It decided not to allow CNPC to dominate by buying the abandoned stakes of departing Canadian and European independent oil companies but instead balanced its engagement with China by attracting ONGC Videsh, the overseas arm of India's national oil company, to fill the gap. This demonstrated how agency was possible despite – indeed partly because of – dependency on China.[26] Following President Bashir's overthrow in April 2019, Sudan maintained good relations with China and repositioned itself as having strategic value under the BRI. It also sought to restart ties with the US, enhance relations with the EU and reconnect with Russia. Another example, Angola, became very close to China under longstanding former president dos Santos who ruled until 2017 but, more recently, under his successor João Lourenço, the Angolan government has maintained pro-China rhetoric but sought to renew relations with Western powers. A familiar theme in post-colonial African history, China is likely to experience more of such strategies. When situated in the context of deeper debate within more democratic African countries with active civil society, such pressures can only grow stronger.

The context facing African states as their New Era relations with China evolve had come to be framed by China as a shift to being a 'major' global power, in which the Chinese government began more blatantly to wield economic clout in pursuit of political goals. Such examples as Australia provide stark demonstration effects about

China's use of economic coercion to punish political transgressions. China's denunciation of Australia's 'series of wrong moves' in late 2020 – from criticizing China on core interests like Taiwan, Hong Kong and Xinjiang, to accusing China of 'infiltration' operations, banning Huawei and ZTE from its 5G network or advocating an independent inquiry into the origins of COVID-19 – was clearly signalling a message beyond Australia.[27] This high-profile example of the threat and use of economic coercion was clearly not lost on African states. Even if China's adversarial relations with Australia meant that there were potential future economic benefits for some African countries – for instance, given that iron is Australia's top export to China, Guinea might benefit from increased iron ore exports to China (including from the Simandou mine, a joint venture between Chinalco, a Chinese mining SOE, and the Anglo-Australian multinational RioTinto) – the example did not seem conducive to dispelling disquiet over how China's growing economic stature in African countries might be converted in political terms in the future. However, African states lack meaningful alternatives: even if they went against Beijing, there are no other external powers with the same economic means and willingness to cooperate that might render such action viable, rewarding and sustainable. Explicitly offending Beijing would stand little chance of being affordable via other sources. Not just China's neighbours, but African states, civil society and citizens understand that, even if this is still emerging and evolving, China's power is a new reality. There were thus parallels between the different contexts of China's neighbourhood strategy and its strategy with more geographically distant Africa. In its regional neighbourhood, Xi Jinping's China has moved beyond simple engagement and now employs 'more proactive efforts to manage regional order and promote an integrated region under Chinese leadership'. Xi Jinping's neighbourhood strategy thus ultimately 'rests on an asymmetric bargain: respect China's core interests in exchange for benevolence'.[28]

Africa's friend in deed?

Although the Chinese government's foreign-policy rhetoric and FOCAC statements make much of global reform, the actual willingness and ability of China to meaningfully advance a reform agenda with and for Africa is very questionable. China's favoured language of friendship with Africa, African countries and peoples, which successfully conflates and confuses interstate and interpersonal relations, is overlaid onto much harder dilemmas of interest, as well as complex politics. China and Africa have long stated, as the Beijing Declaration of the Forum on China–Africa Cooperation 2000 put it, that 'a just and equitable new international political and economic order is indispensable for the democratization of international relations and for the effective participation of developing countries in the international process of decision-making'. Similarly, the BRICS make grand statements of aspirational intent about global reform; the 2018 10th BRICS Summit Johannesburg Declaration, for example, cited 'a fair, just, equitable, democratic and representative international order'. The example of UNSC reform, which FOCAC declarations invoke following AU precedents, demonstrates a deficit of action, matching rhetoric and the difference between formal expressions of commitment to UNSC reform, and the challenges of undertaking this in practice.[29]

Xi Jinping has sought to perform the formal role of exercising global leadership on behalf of Africa, as seen in the G20 where this overlaps with China's global objectives. In 2016, the China-hosted G20 summit in Hangzhou saw Africa receive more attention than in previous such events. Within the overall theme of development, as Xi stated, 'for the first time, cooperation is being carried out to support African countries and LDCs in their industrialization'.[30] China used its convening power to invite Chad (on behalf of the AU), Egypt and Senegal, meaning that three of the five developing countries present were African. The Leaders' Communique expressed support for 'industrialization in developing countries, especially those in Africa' and advanced a

G20 Initiative 'Supporting Industrialization in Africa and LDCs to strengthen their inclusive growth and development potential'. At the June 2019 G20 Summit in Osaka, the China–Africa Leaders' Meeting between Xi Jinping and South African president Cyril Ramaphosa, Egyptian president Abdel Fattah al-Sisi (as AU chair), and Senegal's president Macky Sall (co-chair of FOCAC), and UN Secretary General António Guterres, saw China's leader convey proposals for 'building a closer community with a shared future between China and African countries'. These included a call for more international support for African development, illustrating China's adopted leadership role on development in the continent.

Beijing presents itself as a global leader for Africa but faces questions about the extent of its political will behind such a position. Longstanding questions about what in practice the Chinese government can and will do to advance African interests, which are not always clear in the face of multiple competing agendas, became more pressing due to China's more active global role and ambitious agenda under Xi Jinping, especially given US foreign policy under the Trump administration. In part, these questions flow from the obvious discrepancies between the fluent rhetorical idealism in China's official policy documents and actual realpolitik calculations and transactional relationships. The decisive shift, however, has been China's more high-profile global role on the back of its economic development, which has raised expectations as a result. Nonetheless, does China actually stand up for and advance African global interests or just talk about doing so? Within many parts of the continent, there is a generally positive faith that China can advance African geopolitical interests as part of a project to advance a more multipolar (less Western) world. That being said, scepticism abounds about the extent of Beijing's political will and practical commitment to advancing Africa's global interests. Beijing's ultimate ambivalence about UNSC reform but overt strong support for the authority of the UNSC, for example, seems to entail an unstated preference for a continuation of the status quo. Beijing talks about 'democratizing international relations' as more than merely code for reducing US power but seems to prefer to protect its elite, veto power status, indirectly assisted by the fiercely contested politics within Africa concerning which African state or states might join such a reformed UNSC.

CHINA, AFRICA AND OTHER EXTERNAL POWERS

China's New Era Africa relations have brought into closer focus the evolving engagements of other external powers in the continent. Reacting to news coverage about China in Africa, Chinese officials used simultaneously to complain and explain that 'we are not alone'. With Africa, China is indeed not acting in a vacuum and any singular spotlight on Beijing risks detracting from inter-relations with multiple other powers. China's ascendancy in Africa has also been formatively influenced by other external powers. China's New Era in the continent, however, has seen a more confident change in the Chinese government's approach from a type of lower profile listening and learning mode to a more assertive, confrontational and ambitious role flowing from the CCP's objectives for China and its role in global politics.

China's Africa relations involve other external powers, and the ways in which this theme has evolved since the 1990s needs to be appreciated before more recent dynamics are considered. More than any single external factor, China has been responsible for a remarkable turnaround in external perceptions, interest and engagement in the African continent. Following the 1990s, a phase of awakening and adaptation to the arrival of a 'new' power between 2000 and 2008 saw efforts to shape and socialize China's trajectory, mostly centred on 'development' cooperation and US-led calls on Beijing to become a 'responsible stakeholder'. Development donors of the Organization for

Economic Cooperation and Development (OECD) sought to promote the convergence of China's principles and practices with OECD norms on aid, alongside common interests around counterterrorism. The period 2008–15, following the global financial crisis, saw greater recognition and acceptance of China's role, more targeted efforts to influence this on behalf of Western powers (around corporate social responsibility, for instance), and the advent of more competitive dynamics, as seen with US policy on Africa. From 2010, the expanded BRICS including South Africa added impetus to non-Western engagement. China's influence and example boosted investor confidence, helping to reframe Africa as a rising continent of commercial opportunity. Where OECD countries had sought to shape China according to its principles, notably around development aid, interest in how China's domestic experience might be used in Africa grew. Efforts to teach or preach to China were superseded by efforts to learn from China's development approach and find innovative ways to collaborate instead. Since around the 2015 FOCAC, more competitive politics have been emerging. There has been greater acceptance that, as Xi Jinping's New Era shows, the ideal of engagement premised on China's convergence was an illusion. There was a functional convergence of interests between China, other external powers, African states and the AU around issues like conflict, stabilization and political order but since 2017 intensifying strategic competition between the US and China meant new geopolitical dynamics in Africa.

Many countries have sought to rejuvenate or start partnerships with Africa, notably Turkey, which had increased the number of its embassies in the continent from twelve to forty-two by 2020, as well as Iran, Saudi Arabia or Russia, which held an Africa summit in Sochi in October 2019. The following section, however, considers China's relations with Brazil and India, before looking at Japan, the UK, France, the EU and the US.

China and Southern powers

Brazil's ascendancy in Africa was driven by former president Luiz Inácio Lula da Silva, for whom South–South cooperation was central to his geopolitical ambition of enhancing Brazil's global status and promoting multilateral reform. As president between 2003 and 2010, he visited 27 African countries in twelve trips. His period in office saw an attempt to institutionalize relations, expanding Brazil's diplomatic presence, organizing the Africa South America Summit and reviving the India, Brazil, South Africa dialogue forum. His successor, Dilma Rousseff, continued in his path but political turmoil and economic recession contributed to a fall in trade in 2016.[31] The election of Jair Bolsonaro as president in 2018 meant a sharp relegation of Africa relations to military and commercial contacts, and a strong critique of his predecessor's South–South diplomacy. While a vocal critic of China, and aligning with the US, Bolsonaro pursued pragmatic relations with Beijing, including hosting a BRICS meeting in Brazil in November 2019. China's interest in aligning the BRI with Brazilian development remained but was tested by more fractious relations.

The government of India sought to rejuvenate its relations with Africa under Narendra Modi, who became prime minister in 2014. New Delhi hosted the third, most ambitious India–Africa Forum Summit in October 2015.[32] All African countries were invited to a grand event intended, as Modi put it, to 'launch a new era of India–Africa partnership'. The 2015 summit, touted as the 'largest such gathering of African countries outside the continent, outdoing similar summits that China and the US have held', sought to showcase India's global role under Modi.[33] Competition with China was present in India's Africa engagement, albeit with less public attention by China. Intensified tensions between China and India, seen in a fatal border skirmish of 2020, added a further dimension. The extent to which India was a genuine rival to China in Africa, however, was questionable. As well as common interest and areas of corporate cooperation in Africa, this was seen in the basic reality of China's far bigger economic importance. If India could not match China's financial means, it did have comparative advantages like a prevailing trade surplus with numerous African countries or being outside the politics of debt. Other advantages included linguistic, cultural or historical connections, notably through the Indian diaspora in Africa, which Modi attempted to engage but in practice did not easily translate or cohere with the government of India's objectives. India also styled itself as the world's largest democracy in an effort to capitalize on its political credentials and pursued rival ventures, notably the Asia–Africa Growth Corridor involving Japan and African countries.[34] Proposed at the 2017 meeting of the Asian Development Bank in Gujarat, this promoted 'a free and open Indo-Pacific region' and, inevitably, was seen as a BRI alternative, but remained dormant. Nonetheless, the government of India appeared intent on further expanding relations over the longer term. This was seen in July 2019 when India's finance minister announced that eighteen new diplomatic missions would be opened across Africa. It was also seen in reforms, such as to the Indian Development and Economic Assistance Scheme, and continuing interest in military engagement, such as plans to develop a naval base in the Seychelles as part of efforts to promote cooperation among Indian Ocean countries. In late 2020, 'vaccine diplomacy' emerged as a further area of Indian interest in Africa. Overall, India added additional options to African governments seeking to diversify external relations.

China and Northern powers
Japan has a long history of development aid in Africa, including since the first Tokyo International Conference on African Development (TICAD) in 1993. Operating within the OECD development assistance framework, Tokyo did so in a low-profile manner and downplayed talk of competition with China in Africa. China's rise in Africa inevitably meant an extension of Tokyo–Beijing politics onto

African settings and galvanized Japan's engagement. TICAD was held for the first time in an African country, Kenya, in 2016. In August 2019, proclaiming that TICAD was 'reborn', Prime Minister Shinzo Abe was keen to stress that Japan's relations with Africa had begun a new era.[35] Part of this involves an attempted reorientation of Japan's engagement with Africa towards business, a response to recognition of economic possibility, domestic economic imperatives and the example of Chinese corporations. Tokyo's 'new' Africa outreach sought to carefully but clearly differentiate Japan vis-à-vis China, emphasizing the superior advantages of Japan's approach, such as promoting 'quality infrastructure' or the rule of law. Following Shinzo Abe's departure in September 2020, Japan looked set to remain engaged. Foreign Minister Toshimitsu Motegi toured Tunisia, Mozambique, South Africa and Mauritius in December 2020, with Japan looking ahead to the next TICAD in Tunisia in 2022.

Starting before the 2006 FOCAC, the United Kingdom (UK) was one of the first Western governments to attempt to engage with China in Africa. Initial ad hoc contacts evolved into a more institutionalized dialogue process and efforts to undertake trilateral development cooperation. Africa featured prominently in the work of the former Department for International Development (DFID), but Britain's relations with China always also mattered. London withdrew its development aid presence in China and courted Chinese investment. China's example in Africa stimulated interest in the business potential of the continent, re-linking aid with trade, and refocusing development on economic growth. A 2017 DFID strategy document, for instance, cited China as proof that 'Economic growth is essential for overcoming poverty and for allowing human potential to flourish.'[36] Following the 2016 EU membership referendum, the UK government attempted to woo Africa on the basis of a post-EU 'global Britain' engagement. London's courtship featured slogans, visits and posturing – Theresa May became the first prime minister for thirty years to visit Nairobi in

August 2018 and spoke of the UK being 'the number one G7 investor in Africa by 2022' – but little substance in practice. Her replacement, Boris Johnson, had a divisive record on Africa (once writing that 'The problem is not that we were once in charge, but that we are not in charge anymore').[37] His leadership continued in much the same vein, talking up prospects and hosting a UK–Africa Investment Summit in January 2020. With London preoccupied with Brexit, and its newly created Foreign, Commonwealth and Development Office tasked with a post-Brexit policy with Africa when the domestic challenges of the COVID-19 pandemic were pressing, what meaningful substance there would be in future Africa relations remained to be seen.

France's waning influence in West Africa has provided a point of contrast with China's push, centred on Senegal, to deepen its engagement in the region. China has displaced France as the top exporter to most of France's former colonies. This economic shift has also seen new commercial collaboration between French and Chinese businesses, with French companies forming new commercial partnerships or, like Societe Generale, promoting China–Africa business.[38] Following his election in 2017, French President Emmanuel Macron positioned Africa as a key part of France's foreign relations and sought to reset these by declaring that 'La Françafrique', a strategy of military, political and commercial influence over its former colonies, was over. In 2017, Macron became the first French president to visit English-speaking Ghana in sixty years, where he listened awkwardly to President Nana Akufo-Addo speak about the need for Africa's 'own propulsion' and to escape a 'mindset of dependency', a mindset about 'what can France do for us?' Such criticism of France, as part of a call for Africa to get its houses in order, meant that Macron's own lectures to Africa about the dangers of China to sovereignty missed the mark. In 2019, Macron visited Ethiopia, Kenya and Djibouti, where he was received at the new Chinese-built presidential palace. Efforts to advance a Franco-Chinese partnership in Africa did not always succeed but, rejecting the idea that France and China were strategic rivals, Macron focused on development cooperation. With France's military engagement with Africa standing out among EU states, he also sought Chinese support for the regional G5 Sahel Joint Force (Burkina Faso, Chad, Mali, Mauritania and Niger) combating terrorism in West Africa. Beijing has provided limited but increasing support to the G5 Sahel Joint Force, emphasizing capacity building and counter-terrorism training as it attempts to contribute while maintaining its relative independence.

The EU's engagement with China on Africa has transitioned from a transformative normative ambition to an engagement tempered with greater realism vis-à-vis Xi Jinping's China. Africa was mentioned in a joint EU–China policy statement for the first time at the ninth EU–China Summit in September 2006. The EU's affirmation of 'the principles of good governance and human rights', and China's emphasis on its five principles of peaceful coexistence, including non-interference, illustrated how far apart both sides were. Nonetheless, interest was expressed in dialogue and 'practical cooperation on the ground in partnership with the African side [sic]'. The EU's internal debate reflected differences between those wanting to more pragmatically 'engage China', and those pushing a more ambitious, principled and transformative agenda. Rather than adapt EU policies to Chinese and African preferences, EU policy-makers sought to shape their behaviour and 'make them more similar to that of the EU', and rather than approaching China and Africa as equal partners, instead 'expected them to comply with European demands'.[39] As Brussels–Beijing relations became more strained, the prospects for cooperating on development in Africa appeared to be waning. In March 2019, a European Commission report described China as simultaneously a cooperation and negotiating partner, economic competitor and 'a systemic rival promoting alternative models of governance'.[40] The 21st EU–China Summit in Brussels in 2019 saw convergence around the low-hanging fruit of cooperation on peace and security in Africa. By June 2020, the EU–China Strategic Dialogue briefly noted mention of cooperation in Africa on issues concerning the economic consequences of the COVID-19 pandemic. This reflected a further deterioration of relations when Beijing was making efforts to target the EU as part of its attacks on the failings of Western democracy. At the same time, EU relations with Africa were evolving and, despite the symbolism of Ursula von der Leyen visiting Addis Ababa on her first overseas visit as president of European Commission in December 2019, not proceeding smoothly. In March 2020, the EU proposed that 'a new comprehensive EU strategy with Africa' could be built on five partnerships: 'green transition and energy', 'digital transformation', 'sustainable growth and jobs', 'peace and governance', and 'migration and mobility'.[41] However, this was derailed after an EU–AU summit scheduled for October 2020 and a 'mini-summit' scheduled for December 2020 failed to happen in the context of the COVID-19 pandemic and other disagreements.

Washington's approach to China in Africa went from engaging to confronting China as a strategic competitor. In 2005, Robert Zoellick's famous call on China to become a 'responsible stakeholder' in global affairs cited Sudan as an example of China's narrowly extractive, self-interested role and argued that, more than just take oil, China 'should take some responsibility for resolving Sudan's human crisis'. In 2007 an Africa–China–US trilateral dialogue reported that there was 'no strategic conflict' and 'no zero-sum dynamic' between the US and China in Africa.[42] In 2008, President George W. Bush repeated this line, saying 'I don't view Africa as zero-sum for China and the United States'. US officials encouraged China 'to do more in Africa', albeit in coordination with Washington, IFIs and other major donors, and cited infrastructure and business as providing 'positive results for the African people [sic]'.[43] The Obama administration vocalized concern about China's role in the continent. In June 2011, Secretary of State Hillary Clinton said in Lusaka: 'We don't want to see a new colonialism in Africa'. Later, in Dakar, she affirmed that the US would 'stand up for democracy and universal human rights, even when it might be easier or more profitable to look the other way, to keep the resources flowing'.[44] President Obama made promoting governance central to his approach to Africa. Despite lofty rhetoric ('strong institutions, not strong men') and some exceptions like health or counterterrorism, Africa was essentially marginal in US foreign policy. Washington pivoted towards China as a strategic priority. US relations with China came to influence views on its role in Africa, which became a sub-set of the wider China engagement paradigm. When this came crashing down during Xi Jinping's reign, views of China's role in Africa were similarly affected, and the continent became another front for critiquing China.

Under the Trump administration, US views on China hardened into overt confrontation, which was translated into the US government's Africa engagement. The US approach to China in Africa under President Trump was initially marked by rhetorical condemnation of China's lending practices. Speaking at Camp Lemonnier in Djibouti, for example, in March 2018 the then Secretary of State Rex Tillerson warned African countries to 'not forfeit any elements of your sovereignty as you enter into such arrangements with China'. In December 2018, the Trump administration's new Africa strategy was unveiled by John Bolton, the then National Security Advisor. Aspirations to improve the investment climate, private sector or increased economic engagement to protect US national security interests (and 'safeguard the economic independence of Africa') were floated, but Bolton was explicit in stating that the US aimed to counter the 'predatory' practices of China and Russia. Both, he argued, are 'deliberately and aggressively targeting their investments in the region to gain a competitive advantage over the United States'.[45]

This represented a new engagement in formal terms but, in reality, Africa was not and has not been a priority for the US, except where

China is concerned. America's Africa strategy demonstrated notable similarities with China's rhetoric (such as shared use of phrases like 'African solutions to African problems', 'investing in Africans, not just Africa', or peace and security). In October 2018, Trump signed the Better Utilization of Investments Leading to Development (BUILD) Act into law and established a new federal agency, the US International Development Finance Corporation, which indicates interest in enhancing commercial ties. For all such rhetorical bluster and potentially significant new initiatives, Africa was a low-level concern and simply not a priority. There was concern that America was not even competing with China in Africa. Mike McCaul, the lead Republican in Congress's Foreign Affairs Committee, contrasted China's 'all government approach' in dealing with Africa with an over-burdened US–Africa Command, saying: 'in Africa, we are losing'.[46] With the BRI, 'they [the Chinese] are taking over African nations without a shot fired ... we're not there, we're not competing in Africa, and if we're not there, if we're not competing, we lose'.[47]

US engagement gave distinctly mixed signals. On the one hand, there were strong statements of intent. Promising a more strategic, and 'very aggressive posture', in May 2019 US Assistant Secretary of State for African Affairs, Tibor Nagy, told a US House of Representatives Committee on Foreign Affairs hearing that America was 'weaponizing our embassies to confront the Chinese across a whole range of issues, most prominently the commercial one because ... the Africans tell us over and over and over again they would much rather deal with US businesses than the Chinese but they've been dealing with the Chinese because the Americans haven't been at the door'.[48] On the other hand, actual engagement was far removed from such proclamations. US political engagement was sharply reduced, conspicuously low-level and featured harmful, punitive measures against African countries (such as briefly sanctioning South African steel or taking away African Growth and Opportunity Act privileges for Rwanda and Cameroon). It was also marked by contradictions, such as banning immigration from Nigeria when supposedly seeking to advance economic ties with the country to counter China and Russia.

For good reasons, then, the Trump administration's Africa strategy was popularly derided as 'the African component of America's China policy'. The 2018 US National Defence Strategy designated China a strategic competitor in global terms and China's 'predatory actions' in Africa were framed as 'sub-components of broader Chinese strategic initiatives', including the BRI.[49] If Washington's Africa policy was a component of its China policy, it faced pronounced political limits in the face of China's more established position across the continent. This became apparent over the Trump administration's efforts to target the technology company Huawei, including in Africa, for example. Huawei had been established for over two decades in Africa (since 1998), profiting more from services and equipment than phone sales. Up to 70% of Africa's digital infrastructure has been reportedly built by Huawei with Chinese loans and grants. The US–China struggle over 5G failed to widely resonate, especially in a context where establishing and extending internet provision is a basic priority for many. One argument favouring Huawei in Africa thus rested on the importance of internet connectivity, not network security. Not long after Trump's executive order against Huawei, in late May 2019 Huawei and the AU signed a three-year agreement strengthening their partnership in broadband, the Internet of Things, cloud computing, 5G and artificial intelligence. At the June 2019 G20 summit, South Africa's President Ramaphosa pledged support for Huawei. In February 2020, US Secretary of State Mike Pompeo warned Africa to be 'wary of authoritarian regimes and their empty promises' and argued that economic partnership with the US was the path to 'true liberation'. He subsequently intensified criticism of China over its lending practices and COVID-19 diplomacy. Such messaging made sense in terms of US politics and the Trump administration but evoked the Acholi saying: 'A roaring lion does not catch any prey. Overall, Bolton's Africa Strategy set the tone for US efforts to confront and counter China.

China's diplomatic strategy with the US in Africa involved sharp criticism of the Trump administration, coupled with strong support for Xi Jinping's New Era agenda for world affairs, but also benefited from the nature of US engagement. China's former ambassador to South Africa, Lin Songtian, criticized Trump's trade war with China for undermining global economic stability and threatening multilateral trade and 'rule-based world order'. In contrast to America's 'complete unilateralism, protectionism and extreme individualism' under Trump, FOCAC would 'embrace a new era of win–win co-operation for common development'.[50] In September 2019, advertorials in South African newspapers by Ambassador Lin criticized America's 'wilful and bullying acts', inviting it to 'enter the new era at an early date so as to strive for win–win cooperation and common development with other countries in the world'.[51] Less directly, China was assisted by the Trump administration's wider approach to global affairs, including on multilateralism, which gifted Beijing diplomatic benefits, as seen in the US withdrawal from the WHO or opposition to the Nigerian candidate for World Trade Organization (WTO) director general. The election of a new US president in November 2020 set the stage for a potential new engagement by America with Africa but, in view of how domestic pressures were dominating, just how far this would or could go in terms of responding effectively to China was in the balance.

CONCLUSION

Arguing that Africa's political importance for China has become more clearly significant in the New Era, this chapter examined the evolving place and role of African states in China's foreign policy and global multilateral engagement. Just as Africa is a prominent example for those critical of China's rise in global affairs, so it plays a prominent part in Beijing's efforts to promote a positive narrative of its major power diplomacy, mobilize support and repudiate criticism. This signals Africa's importance to the immaterial goals of China's rise and how the Chinese government not only pursues interests or power, but also craves status, recognition and a milieu in which it feels comfortable.[52] A further theme was China in the foreign relations of African states. By considering how other external powers have been responding to China as part of their own evolving Africa engagements, it argued that China needs to be understood not just in narrow terms of its own engagement but in relation to others.

In the face of mounting US–China geopolitical rivalry, one optimistic hope was that Africa could avoid a return to a 'new type of Cold War' revolving around US–China relations. It appeared unlikely that the continent could avoid being caught up in US–China competition going forward, regardless of who governed Washington and Beijing, given that China–US rivalry has become a defining part of global politics. African countries may have to choose or play their cards carefully, using opportunities other powers present.

Considering China–Africa relations narrowly risks overstating the continent's importance in Beijing's global politics. This has changed over time. For all Beijing's hype, use of Africa to promote claims about being a responsible global power and inflated rhetoric about Africa's growing importance in world affairs, the continent is a relatively low priority in China's foreign policy and global politics, despite the impressive personal investment in relations by China's leadership. This is dominated by the US. Africa played a key role in China's 'going global' strategy but has now become a less pivotal part of China's global economic engagement in the BRI era. China's trade with Latin America far exceeds that with Africa, for example, and it has been relying more on Middle Eastern oil imports. Africa, however, retains its significance in supporting China's foreign policy on traditional concerns like Taiwan, Tibet or Japan, more recent issues like Xinjiang, Hong Kong, or China's multilateral engagement and vision of its future world role. By and large African states are open to and outwardly supportive of China, while prioritizing their own interests and seeking to maximize these actively. Intensifying US–China strategic competition renders the geopolitical context of China's relations with African countries uncertain.

Looking forward, Africa's relative importance may well change, as seen with technology, markets and political allies. One aspect of China's rivalry with America concerned future standards in technology and connectivity. However, the contrast between China's role within and importance to African countries, and Africa's significance to China, was striking: China's economic and political footprint in Africa is real and growing, but Africa in China's domestic and foreign policy is much less pronounced. As the next chapter considers, this pattern is also seen in terms of key aspects of economic relations.

New Era Economics ────────────

China's domestic economic transformation has been central to the Chinese economic advance in Africa and continues to importantly influence China–Africa economics in the New Era. It took just three decades for China to advance from being a poor country to the world's second-largest economy that now, even if China is a middle-income country, exerts major influence in the global economy. China's economic growth entailed a growing demand for commodity imports and new overseas markets in the 1990s, contributing to a convergence of interests with African countries, some well endowed with resources but without the capital and infrastructure, as well as political will, to develop. Another, later convergence happened in the context of the AU's Agenda 2063's stress on accelerated industrialization as critical for economic development and poverty reduction in Africa. Economic changes within China, notably rising labour costs, industrial overcapacity and the BRI, contributed to an opportunity identified for Africa and China to benefit from a new phase in relations. For example, Helen Hai, the CEO of the Made in Africa Initiative, championed the idea that 'Africa should follow China's development model and aim to become a light-manufacturing hub.'[1] Such transformative prescriptions and claims concerning the potential for African countries to benefit from China's changing growth model have been strong on aspiration but weak on political and practical efficacy. African countries, heterogeneous as these are, remain structurally subordinate in the global economy and continue to face the challenges not just of economic growth but of achieving inclusive human development as well. For some, China represents Africa's best chance of escaping historic constraints on economic development; others instead point out that economic growth is not the same as development, and that China is essentially continuing a historic process of underdevelopment by entrenching a new dependency.[2]

This chapter examines four general but key themes in 'New Era' economic relations. It first looks at trade, aid, investment, and how Africa is a market for a diversifying range of Chinese business.[3] Trade remains concentrated in a handful of African countries and, while China's importance in Africa's global trade has been rising, the continent has a significantly less important position in China's global trade. China has become a major investor in Africa, although Africa accounts for a proportionally small part of global Chinese investment. A more diverse range of Chinese businesses have been engaging in more varied economic sectors in Africa. CNPC exemplified China's 'going global' engagement in Africa over a decade before Xi Jinping's New Era, but the likes of Transsion or Alibaba exemplify a shift towards communications, technology and e-commerce. Second, since 2015, the guiding framework in China's approach to economic development in Africa has been termed 'structural transformation', which is premised on an effort to connect industrial development in Africa with China's industrial upgrading. Infrastructure construction and manufacturing have been important parts of this. The BRI initiated a formal new chapter in economic relations, with African countries joining a global initiative transcending the China–Africa framework of economic relations. Third, China as a holder of African debt became one of the most high-profile economic issues. Debt had been a challenge before 2020, but the COVID-19 pandemic tipped the balance into a crisis for a number of African countries. As the largest bilateral holder of African debt, China's response to the debt issue, in part arising from its lending patterns, has been reshaping its relations

with Africa in important ways, including through the political consequences of economic dependence, real or perceived, on Beijing. Finally,
this chapter argues that the idea that China can exert transformative
change in economic development is a mirage in the face of the severe,
intractable challenges facing African countries. These emanate not just
from deep global structural constraints but also the nature of African
states and the failure of ruling elites, such as in the example of Kenya,
to seriously prioritize broad, longer-term development.

TRADE, AID AND INVESTMENT

Much of the last two decades of China–Africa economic relations
was characterized by growing trade. Starting from a relatively low
base, China–Africa trade grew rapidly, with an annual growth rate of
over 40% between 2004 and 2009 but decreased after the 2008 global
financial crisis (see Table 1). Overall trade went from a then record of
just over $10bn in 2000 to $222bn in 2014. The high-growth years
were driven by a 'super cycle' between 2003 and 2013, underpinned by
China's role in driving global commodity demand and high prices. A
major factor was China's imports of raw commodities from resource-
endowed African countries, underlining the importance of countries
like oil-rich Angola to China's energy and resource needs at the time.
Chinese demand reflected domestic growth, role in global production
and trade. From 2014 to 2015, however, weak commodity prices
meant a steep fall in the value of African exports to China, and trade
deficits. From $170bn in 2017, total import and export trade volume
with Africa reached $208.7bn in 2019.

In this context, five themes regarding macro China–Africa trade
patterns are worth noting. First, China–Africa trade is dominated
by a few commodity-rich African exporters and South Africa, which
has a more mixed economy. At a minimum, there are 'resource-
intensive' and 'non-resource-intensive' African countries. The former

Table 1. China–Africa Trade, 2002–2019

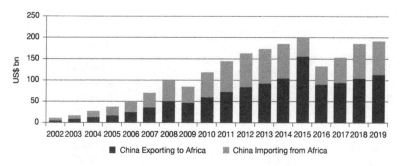

Source: Johns Hopkins University SAIS China–Africa Research Initiative 2020, using UN COMTRADE

group of 24 countries is particularly exposed to global commodity price fluctuations. The concentration of China–Africa trade reflects the importance of commodity-rich African exporters in overall trade figures. In 2018, over half of all China's imports from the continent came from just two African countries, South Africa (28%) and Angola (26%) followed by the Republic of Congo (7%).[4] Macro China–Africa trade figures, however, only provide a general indicator of economic relations between China and the continent.

Second, there is a pronounced asymmetry between China's growing importance in Africa's global trade and the continent's continuing minor position in China's global trade. This is symptomatic of China's status as an industrial superpower and Africa's subordinate position in the global economy. Africa has the lowest regional share of world exports, which declined from 3.5% in 2008 to 2.5% in 2018.[5] The continent accounted for just 2.7% of global trade in 2017.[6] In a global context, the role of China in Africa's trade has become more important. In 2018, China accounted for 16% of Africa's imports, this figure having been 4% in 2001; and around 15% of Africa's exports were destined for China, this figure having been 3% in 2001. Conversely,

Table 2. China Imports from Africa: Top 10 Countries, 2019 (US$mn unadjusted)

Rank	Country	Total
1	Angola	23308.30
2	South Africa	9595.42
3	Republic of Congo	5934.47
4	Libya	4765.67
5	Gabon	4612.51
6	DRC	4436.61
7	Zambia	3298.46
8	Nigeria	2652.14
9	Ghana	2543.92
10	Guinea	2504.86
Overall Africa total		78,683.32 (78.68bn)

Table 3. China Exports to Africa: Top 10 Countries, 2019 (US$mn unadjusted)

Rank	Country	Total
1	Nigeria	16634.07
2	South Africa	16560.93
3	Egypt	12217.15
4	Algeria	6945.57
5	Kenya	4984.58
6	Ghana	4906.97
7	Morocco	4030.06
8	Liberia	3909.85
9	Tanzania	3814.73
10	Libya	2452.89
Overall Africa total		113050.93 (113.05bn)

Source: CARI via UN COMTRADE

Africa represents a very small share of China's global trade, about 3.5% of Chinese exports and 4% of imports into China in 2015.[7] In the first half of 2020, Africa accounted for some 4% of China's total global trade volume.[8]

Third, despite complementary trade patterns with African commodity exporters in particular, the Chinese economic engagement in Africa is also competitive and can have negative impacts. Studies have shown that the increased import penetration by Chinese products on the continent may have had negative effects on African producers and intra-African trade. The impact of Chinese trade on production and employment in South Africa between 1992 and 2020, for example, resulted in a 5% lower output in 2010 and a reduction of around 8% in manufacturing employment.[9] Others suggest that this might have nudged some domestic producers to innovate.[10] Low-cost Chinese imports have been a particular concern for African textile sectors, with countries like Madagascar and Mauritius, which export textiles or other manufactured goods, being comparatively worse off in terms of trade effects, contributing to fears that Chinese imports crowd out African manufacturers.[11]

Fourth, the direction of Africa's external trade has been changing but its composition has not. Africa's external economic relations have been moving away from traditional partners in Europe and the US, towards India and especially China. In Senegal, for example, France has been emasculated in trade terms, with China being the top source of imports, followed by Nigeria and India. At the same time, Africa's outward trade in general and with China in particular remains dominated by primary commodity exports, especially oil and mineral products. Overtaking the US to become the world's largest oil importer in 2017, China became Africa's largest buyer of crude oil. China, India and the Asia–Pacific region accounted for 20% of African oil exports in 2003, but 50% by 2019, with the Chinese market essentially replacing the US (with Europe buying some 40% of African crude exports).[12] In turn, African economies import manufactured products from China. The proportion of manufactured goods, as with food and agricultural products, has been growing, but this has been much less as a proportion of trade compared with that of primary commodities. Around 70% of sub-Saharan Africa's exports to China involve commodities, especially oil, minerals and metals, while about 20% of the region's imports are from China, in which consumer goods count for 45%.[13]

For resource-rich African economies, this means continuing commodity dependence and vulnerability to global price fluctuations. Between 2014 and 2015, for instance, the value of African petroleum exports to China dropped 50% (from $53.1bn to $27.5bn) almost entirely due to falling prices, rather than fewer barrels exported (the quantity exported decreased by just 5%).[14] In practice, Africa's deepening interdependence with China applies more to African commodity exporters, for whom the waning of the China–driven commodity cycle since 2014 has had particular impacts. Prior to 2020, slowing global demand associated with US–China trade friction meant weaker Chinese demand for Africa's commodity exports. Nigeria, South Africa and Angola were already struggling with weak growth and investment as well as declining oil and industrial metals prices, before the 2020 pandemic made things much worse by causing a sharp commodity price downturn.

Finally, most African countries have a trade deficit with China. In 2018, China's highest trade surplus was with Nigeria (exports to Nigeria exceeded imports from Nigeria by $12bn), Egypt ($10bn), Algeria ($7bn) and Kenya ($5bn). South Africa, China's most important economic partner in the continent, is a notable example of the trade deficit issue. In 1990, China was South Africa's 18th import partner and 34th as export destination but since 2009 has been the country's top trade partner (for both imports and exports). South Africa's trade deficit with China appeared to mean imports were almost twice as high as exports but differences in data reporting meant uncertainty.

According to Chinese customs data, South Africa has a trade surplus with China (of $18bn in 2019); but South African Revenue Service data indicates that South Africa operates a trade deficit with China. Regardless, the trade imbalance is often cited and politicized and the structure of trade is clear.[15] South Africa mainly exported low value-added commodities to China, and mainly imported high value-added manufactured products. China, in turn, has a trade deficit with only fifteen African countries, mainly its major trading partners such as Angola, South Africa or the DRC.[16] This means only fifteen countries exported more products to China than imported from China.

Aid and investment

Officially, China's financial resources for foreign aid mostly comprise grants and interest-free loans (from China's state finances) and concessional loans (from China EXIM).[17] Detailed statistics are not available but, according to official figures, between 2013 and 2018 Africa received 45% of China's foreign aid, a decrease on the period 2010–12 when it received 51.8%. Between 2013 and 2018, 48.52% of China's global aid was in the form of concessional loans, 47.3% in grants and 4.18% in interest-free loans.[18] Chinese investment and aid used to be often bundled together, but it has been a long time since that was true.[19]

The context for Chinese investment in Africa is the continent's marginal position in terms of global investment. In 2019 Africa accounted for some 2.6% of global inward FDI stock. FDI flows to Africa totalled $45bn in 2019 (compared with $389bn to East and Southeast Asia), a decline since 2017.[20] In this context, two points stand out: first, China has become a major investor but is not currently the top investor in the continent, and second, although Africa does not represent a sizeable proportion of global Chinese FDI, Chinese investment in African countries matters.

First, despite popular perceptions to the contrary and although its expansion has been very noteworthy, China has become a major investor but not yet the top investor in Africa. Annual Chinese FDI flows to Africa have increased significantly from a low base of US$75m in 2003 to $2.7bn in 2019.[21] When China is compared to other foreign investors in Africa, the lack of accurate data is a problem. FDI statistics also may capture financial flows but may underestimate actual investment. One analysis using Eurostat statistics, which discounted FDI from the Netherlands (for tax reasons rendering FDI not Dutch per se), showed that France had the largest stock of FDI in Africa (€46bn) in 2018 and China ranked second (€41bn).[22] Other rankings place China lower.[23] One clear trend, however, has seen Chinese FDI flows to Africa exceed those from the US since 2014.

Second, while Chinese investment in African countries matters, the continent does not represent a sizeable proportion of China's total global outward investment stock. In comparative terms, Africa is behind other regions when it comes to Chinese FDI outflows. These peaked in 2016. China's investment in the US and Europe has since fallen. Africa, however, accounted for just 3.7% of China's total outward global investment stock in 2015 (the bulk of Chinese investment then officially going to Hong Kong; by comparison, Africa constituted only 1.4% of US global FDI stock).[24] In other words, China's FDI in 2016 'in all of Africa was equal to 14.1% of the amount China invested in the US, and the same as the amount China invested in Germany'.[25]

Within Africa, Chinese FDI is uneven and concentrated in a small number of countries and sectors. In 2019, the top recipients of Chinese FDI flows were the DRC, Angola, Ethiopia, South Africa and Mauritius.

Fuelled by high-profile investments in Sudan, Angola or the DRC, the idea that Chinese investment is dominated by extractives became popular but is out of date. FDI to the major recipients of Chinese investment, resource-rich DRC, Nigeria, South Africa, Sudan and Zambia has been decreasing compared to other countries, with an increase in Chinese FDI in manufacturing in Ethiopia and other

Table 4. Chinese FDI Flows to African Countries: Top 10 Recipients in 2019 (US$mn, unadjusted)

1	DRC	930.96
2	Angola	383.24
3	Ethiopia	375.3
4	South Africa	338.91
5	Mauritius	185.89
6	Niger	178.36
7	Zambia	143.39
8	Uganda	143.22
9	Nigeria	123.27
10	Tanzania	115.58
	Total (all African countries)	2704.39 (2.70bn)

Source: Johns Hopkins University SAIS China–Africa Research Initiative (The Statistical Bulletin of China's Outward Foreign Direct Investment, MOFCOM)

non-resource sectors, alongside a continuing focus on construction and mining. Construction has been the largest sector of Chinese FDI stock to date, accounting for 31% of China's FDI stock to Africa in 2019 and reflecting the continuing importance to Chinese firms of African real estate and infrastructure. Mining was the second highest sector in Chinese FDI stock (25% in 2019), followed by manufacturing (13%).[26] Rising numbers of Chinese firms were investing in Africa: beyond high-value resource sectors, a growing source of FDI was from smaller and medium-sized enterprises. There were also new Chinese provincial investment promotion initiatives, such as the China–Africa Economic and Trade Expo in Changsha in June 2019, and the China–Africa Private Sector Cooperation Program. One emerging area of economic exchange concerned so-called private Chinese companies looking to expand investment and business in Africa, including in the prospective post-pandemic context.

African markets: business opportunities

There has been a huge expansion in the number and nature of Chinese companies doing business in African countries, testifying to their attractiveness as markets. If there were 'more than 800 Chinese state-owned firms' in 2006, a recent estimate was that there were 'more than 10,000 Chinese-owned firms operating in Africa today'.[27] Chinese enterprises span a widening range of sectors, from services, pharmaceuticals, forestry, food processing, furniture and agriculture, where Chinese investments in farming are relatively low compared to other sectors. This expansion has meant a diversification beyond extractives and construction, sectors in which the bigger Chinese SOEs are active. The construction boom in the African continent, however, including residential and infrastructure investments, served to attract numerous Chinese contractors, primarily SOEs. Trade with Africa may form a very small share of China's global trade, but Africa accounts for a significant share (nearly one third in 2015) of the value of global contracts in which Chinese companies engage.[28] Chinese contractors accounted for almost 60% of contract revenues in Africa's construction market for the leading 250 international contractors by 2017 (having accounting for 15% in 2004). Indeed, while these can be interlinked, the value of Chinese construction projects and contract revenues surpassed the flows and even stocks of Chinese FDI to Africa, reaching nearly US$45bn compared with US$3.1bn in FDI flows and some US$20bn of FDI stocks in 2013.[29] Between 2015 and 2019, however, there was a consecutive decline in the gross annual revenues of Chinese companies' construction and engineering projects in Africa. In 2019, five countries – Algeria, Nigeria, Kenya, Egypt and Angola – accounted for 46% of all Chinese construction project gross annual revenues in Africa.[30]

From the 1990s, China's national oil companies like CNPC were foremost in Beijing's 'going global' strategy; however, more recently, different companies like Transsion, Alibaba, or those in financial services such as China UnionPay, have been prominent in corporate engagements around communications, technology, services and data, not crude oil. Africa is a growing market in telecoms, digital commerce and financial technology (fintech). Chinese corporations like CNPC formerly looked to gain experience in African countries in order to break into more lucrative markets in Europe and North America, but in recent years Chinese companies have demonstrated profit opportunities in African markets. Transsion, notably, is the top-selling phone manufacturer in Africa via its three main brands: Tecno, Itel and Infinix.[31] The company has focused on African consumer markets and is well known for competitive pricing and tailored designs like longer battery life or keyboards for African languages. The leading music streaming service in Africa, Boomplay, is owned by Transsion-Netease. Fintech is a new growth area. The financial services corporation China UnionPay, for instance, has been expanding in Africa, largely through a partnership with Standard Bank, predominantly catering to overseas Chinese and African businesses trading with China.

China's trade, aid and investment in Africa show the stark imbalances that have existed, and still exist in economic relations between China and its 53 different African country partners, but partly in response to the structural economic challenges facing African countries, the basis of an aspirational transformative economic agenda in China–Africa relations emerged after 2012. Termed 'structural transformation', this was styled by the AU, African governments and the Chinese government as supporting the AU's Agenda 2063 vision (and later the UN's Agenda 2030). The meaning of 'structural transformation' has varied but in the African context 'implies a relative decline of low-productivity agriculture and low value-added extractive activities, and a relative increase in manufacturing and high-productivity services'.[32]

STRUCTURAL TRANSFORMATION

Structural transformation became a more overt, public part of relations in 2015. It had been discussed before. Citing the need to 'innovate on pragmatic cooperation', for instance, Premier Li Keqiang argued in May 2014 that cooperation should not be limited to 'energy, resources and infrastructure' but expanded to include 'industrialization, urbanization, agricultural modernization', and more. In January 2015, China and the AU agreed to develop continental transport infrastructure, including high-speed rail, road, aviation, ports and other projects to support industrialization. Later in 2015, the Johannesburg FOCAC summit fleshed out detail and guidance around structural transformation. China promised $10bn towards a China–Africa Industrial Capacity Cooperation Investment Fund. In 2016, under China's influence, the G20 committed to help African industrialization, and the UNGA proclaimed that 2016–25 would be Africa's Third Industrial Development Decade.

The Chinese government's championing of structural transformation follows the AU's vision, and in part responded to African concerns and critical reactions to the competitive aspects of economic relations, but also emanates from its domestic experience and self-interested reasons related to changes in China's economy. Since around 2008, rising production and labour costs coupled with environmental regulation helped incentivize Chinese companies to relocate to places with lower production costs outside China. It also contributed to a conjunction of China's industrial upgrading involving overseas production and Africa's industrial development. Chinese manufacturing investment in African countries was viewed as capable of generating economic spillovers and technology transfers to help develop local manufacturing and contribute towards structural economic change.[33] Just as China did in the 1980s, the argument was that African countries could seize the opportunities offered by the relocation of labour-intensive industries from China to catalyse their own structural change. Two leading Chinese economists argued that 'African countries ... can grow as dynamically as the East Asian countries because, fundamentally, all successful countries started their structural transformation from light manufacturing.'[34] This represents the ideal of 'co-transformation', meaning that it 'serves both Africa's industrial development and China's industrial upgrading.'[35]

The structural transformation vision is often framed by the Chinese government in continental 'Africa' terms, as in FOCAC, but in practice has evolved in a more targeted, restricted manner. China maintains a continental approach to economic development but in reality this has become more focused and refined. As the then head of the MFA's Department of African Affairs observed in June 2016, the 'new era' brought 'new thinking and new measures.'[36] In this way, the pursuit of 'intensive development' in the context of immense diversity in Africa would entail a more targeted strategy based on 'helping demonstration and pioneering countries for capacity cooperation' such as Ethiopia or Kenya.

Infrastructure development

'Africa's re-enchantment with big infrastructure' came in the context of a decade of sustained economic growth, rediscovered interest in regional integration, new technologies and neoliberal governance, and involved a fixation with 'the transformative potentialities of infrastructure.'[37] China is a major financier of infrastructure in Africa. Chinese infrastructure commitments grew at an average annual rate of 16% from 2012 to 2015.[38] In 2018, Chinese commitments to infrastructure in the continent ($25.7bn) were second to African national governments ($37.5bn) but greater than the combined total of the Infrastructure Consortium for Africa ($20.2bn), whose members include bilateral donors of G7 countries and Russia, South Africa, multilateral agencies like the African Development Bank (ADB) and World Bank, and African institutions like the AU Commission as observers.[39]

A further shift involves the evolution of established finance mechanisms, particularly China's infrastructure-for-resources deals. The blueprint for these has been attributed to China EXIM bank's major concessional credit line to Angola in 2004, following the end of its civil war in 2002, which was to be repaid with the proceeds of oil sales from Sonangol, Angola's national oil company. This gave rise to the 'Angola model', though the mechanism drew on China's previous domestic experience.[40] This model sought to minimize lending risks, support the expansion of Chinese SOEs into African markets, and ensure long-term supply and collateral access to resource assets.[41] Resources for infrastructure arrangements were neither new nor the only model but became associated with China's engagement and a key instrument of state-sponsored corporate support for Chinese SOEs to 'go global'. The 'old' infrastructure-for-resources Angola Model came into disrepute, being associated with a number of issues like corruption. It worked when oil prices and Chinese demand were high, and China had fewer supply options. Angola's role as a key supplier of oil to China diminished, as China diversified its oil supply and oil prices dropped. Other Chinese-financed projects have not lived up to their economic promise. 'Feasibility' is now a key word, referring to the challenge of financing operations to avoid creating a debt burden for any partner country and ensure loan repayment. As well as risk mitigation, the issue of debt is also spurring attempts to find new financing models. These included efforts to develop alternative, more sustainable financing mechanisms, such as public–private partnerships. New arrangements termed 'China–Africa swaps' sought to involve more diverse partners than the previous emphasis on government deals, including the private sector or SOEs, to spread risk and debt; and while resources would still underpin deals, the way in which this was arranged was different in how these were sold.[42] Ghana's 2018 bauxite for infrastructure deal, for example, created a new parastatal organization charged with selling the bauxite on the open market and then repaying the Chinese.

Manufacturing

The proportion of manufacturing in China's FDI stock in Africa has remained relatively low – around 13.2% in 2017 – despite wide interest in establishing special economic zones (SEZs) in a number of African countries. There have been attempts to boost manufacturing as part of the structural transformation agenda and efforts to evolve economic ties. From 2015, the China Africa Fund for Industrial Cooperation, for example, had a mandate to promote manufacturing investment from China to Africa but mostly supported familiar mining, power or infrastructure areas. Nonetheless, there has been top Chinese leadership support for manufacturing linked to industry. In July 2018, for example, Xi Jinping promised to make Senegal's industrialization a priority and support the Emerging Senegal Plan, which features a new industrial park near Dakar. Ethiopia has been foremost in efforts to showcase the potential of Chinese manufacturing in Africa, and opened various new industrial parks.

One report in 2017 estimated that 12% of Africa's industrial production – some US$500bn a year – is already handled by Chinese firms.[43] Chinese factories in Africa countries predominantly serve domestic markets. Transsion, for example, opened a factory manufacturing phone handsets in Addis Ababa in 2011 and employs some 1,800 Ethiopians in its three local plants producing around 1m units annually.[44] Chinese companies have also been able to take advantage of African countries' preferential market access to the EU and the US.[45] Senegal, for example, benefits from US trade preferences for quota and duty free entry, including for textiles and apparel, meaning companies like C&H Garments, which also operates in Rwanda and Ethiopia, can benefit. Manufacturing is far from being restricted to official cooperation initiatives and, outside official policy, represents a dynamic area of Chinese business. In Kenya and Tanzania, for instance, Chinese investments in manufacturing and agriculture were dominated by private, migrant entrepreneurs, who have mainly been driven by market considerations, such as production cost and market proximity, rather than government incentives in home or host country.[46]

Attracting wide interest due to their role in China's domestic development after 1978, the Chinese government and others have promoted SEZs in Africa. With a variety of forms, so far these have been less important than commonly credited. The Chinese government's lead role in economic cooperation over SEZs has evolved in the face of similar initiatives by SOEs and private enterprises. Only four (in Egypt, Nigeria, Zambia and Ethiopia) of 25 SEZs in Africa were approved by MOFCOM as national-level parks, thus eligible for central government support, meaning most are funded by local governments or Chinese corporations, such as shoe manufacturer Huajian's light-industry park in Ethiopia, and the Anhui Foreign Economic Construction Group's Manga–Mungassa Economic Zone in Mozambique.[47] In addition, there were other signs of an evolving Chinese government role amid provincial level Chinese outreach. The Ethiopian–Hunan Industrial Park in Adama, some 100km south of Addis Ababa and not far from the Ethiopia–Djibouti Railway, was inaugurated in October 2018 with an investment of nearly US$350m. Owned by the Changsha Economic Development Zone, with the Ethiopian government as a partner, this was styled as 'the first provincial-level sample development zone to promote construction in Africa.'[48]

Africa in the BRI
The BRI has become a foremost part of China's expansion in the continent as part of a strategic global engagement. The potential for joining the BRI's vision with the emphasis on industrial cooperation in China–Africa relations and AU priorities had been noted earlier by Chinese economists. In 2015, for example, one cited the 'transfer of labor intensive industries' from China to Africa and complementary infrastructure construction as 'core tasks' in incorporating Africa into

the scheme.[49] The sheer ambition of the BRI, which Xi Jinping labelled 'the project of the century', generated hype and a momentum of its own in Africa and around the world to the point where the BRI was 'the most talked about and least defined buzzword of this decade'.[50] As well as addressing domestic economic challenges like industrial overcapacity within China, and supporting the 'Made in China 2025' industrial strategy, one way to think of the intention behind the BRI is that it represents an unprecedented attempt by China to jump from being 'a big country with global influence' to a 'comprehensive global power'.[51] By 2020, the BRI's future was uncertain in the context of the Chinese government's changing approach to domestic growth and economic management, as well as challenges of implementation, but it remained integral to China's longer-term development strategy.

Beyond official surface BRI talk, the experience in Africa has been very diverse, reflecting the different range of projects and circumstances.[52] In its African context, the BRI was initially focused on East Africa. The Ethiopian and Kenyan prime ministers attended the first BRI Forum in Beijing in 2017 (together with ministerial-level representation from Egypt and Tunisia). The BRI added additional 'economic corridor' projects including the Suez Canal Economic Zone, the 'North–South Passage Cairo–Capetown Pass-way' and the Addis Ababa–Djibouti economic corridor, that were presented as advancing the structural transformation agenda in Africa. As an important part of the BRI, the Digital Silk Road involved expanding cooperation in building digital infrastructure like fibre optic cable and telecommunication networks, e-commerce and mobile payment deals or smart cities, as well as promoting associated Chinese standards in emerging technology like 5G. By 2020, the BRI had been extended to include countries from around the continent, with some 44 African countries and the AU signing BRI deals.

By 2020, the BRI had already contributed other effects on China's economic relations with Africa in the context of Beijing's evolving geoeconomic engagement, such as diversifying its sources of oil, timber or other resources that had dominated Chinese trade and investment in Africa. Facing a more challenging global environment, two issues influencing its future direction in Africa became apparent. The first involved security concerns. Mali's accession to the BRI in July 2019 and military coup in August 2020 underscored the centrality of security and political instability to the BRI's future prospects in the Sahel region, and beyond. The second issue concerned changes in Chinese financing for the BRI and debt. The BRI was evolving through experience in a pattern of adjustment and a major slowdown in the implementation of BRI projects. In 2019, overseas energy financing by the CDB and China EXIM was at its lowest level since 2008 with loans advanced for only three projects, worth US$3.2bn, including hydropower projects in Guinea and Nigeria.[53] China's overseas lending declined in 2019, partly due to political stress in the CDB and a corruption scandal involving its former president, although by how much was disputed. Regardless, this fall in funding came when criticism that China was burdening poorer countries with unsustainable debts was growing.

Further questions about the BRI in Africa were generated in 2020 due to the salience of the debt issue in the continent. One major effect of the COVID-19 pandemic-induced economic shocks and higher costs it generated was to tip the balance of certain African countries into debt. The 2020 debt crisis applied to some African countries more than others. In November 2020, Zambia became the first African country to default part of its debt following the start of the COVID-19 crisis. The onset of debt distress for some African countries, including those where BRI projects were being undertaken or planned, heightened uncertainty about future investment prospects and confirmed, as the next section now considers, China's status as a very prominent bilateral creditor in Africa.

CHINA AS CREDITOR

Finance has emerged as an expanding area of cooperation. This section examines the build up to and nature of the debt crisis that became manifest in 2020, but the subject of finance also needs to consider the entry and expansion of Chinese banking in African countries and China's promotion of the use of its currency, the *renminbi* (RMB) on the continent. The latter is used by China in order to deepen relations with African countries and promote the strategic goal of RMB internationalization. Part of China's 13th Five-Year Plan (2016–20), this internationalization seeks to promote China's economic influence by strengthening use of the RMB (the eighth most traded currency) and weaken the US dollar's dominance. An increasing number of countries in Africa have signed currency-related agreements with China. In 2018, a meeting of fourteen African countries in Harare, including Angola, Mozambique, Zambia, Kenya and Zimbabwe, discussed adopting the RMB as one of their reserve currencies. In June 2019, Vice Commerce Minister Qian Keming said that eight African countries, including South Africa, Ghana, Mauritius, Nigeria and Zimbabwe had included the RMB in their foreign reserves, enabling liabilities to be repaid in China's currency and exports to China.[54] China and Zambia established RMB clearing arrangements. China has signed bilateral currency swap agreements with South Africa, Egypt, Morocco and Nigeria, which provide RMB liquidity, and African current liquidity to China. The Central Bank of Nigeria and the People's Bank of China signed a three-year Currency Swap Agreement in April 2018 worth ¥16bn (around US$2.5bn), which allows trade in the lira and RMB (without the US dollar). In a context of US–China trade friction and the BRI, China was endeavouring to add substance to the notion of 'de-dollarizing' the world.[55]

Debt became salient in China's relations with Africa from 2017. The idea of 'debt trap diplomacy' – that the Chinese government was engaging in a strategy of deliberate predatory lending to enmesh countries in debt and extract concessions – made waves after being adopted by the Trump administration in 2017. Despite becoming widespread, the idea lacked supporting evidence.[56] In Africa, and in a context of various multilateral and bilateral lenders as well as private Eurobond finance, only Zambia, Djibouti and the DRC could attribute most of their debt to China. For other African countries, China is one of many creditors. Even if empirical support was lacking, however, the theme resonated due to wide concern about how China might convert its economic position into political influence. EU governments, among others, seemed genuinely concerned at China's use of debt to exert political influence, and that Bretton Woods institutions might have to bail African governments out.[57] The geopolitics of China's 'debt trap diplomacy' continued. By removing agency and responsibility from African governments, the narrative almost absolved them of accountability for their borrowing behaviour.[58]

The path to the 2020 debt crisis had been laid over the past two decades of financing. China's policy banks, led by the CBD and China EXIM, advanced US$53.4bn in concessional loans and credit lines to 43 African countries between 2000 and 2011, much of it to capital-scarce countries and the most earmarked to pay Chinese companies to build infrastructure projects through engineering, procurement and construction project contracting in those same countries.[59]

This trend gained momentum after 2012. Africa's debt to China increased sharply up to US$143bn by 2017 (representing roughly 22.9% of China's total external loans and 20.6% of Africa's entire external debt).[60] The collapse of commodity prices in 2014 meant real pressure on African commodity exporters and other countries that were indirectly affected as well. One impact, some years before 2020, was that a number of African governments struggled to repay debts from infrastructure spending. For Ethiopia and Kenya, both of which took out large commercial loans to pay for new standard gauge railway

Table 5. Chinese Loan Commitments to Africa, 2000–2018

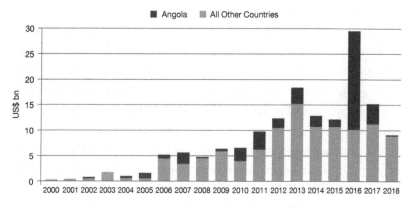

Source: Deborah Brautigam, Jyhjong Hwang, Jordan Link and Kevin Acker, 'Chinese loans to Africa database' (Washington, DC: China–Africa Research Initiative, Johns Hopkins University School of Advanced International Studies, 2020)

Table 6. Chinese Loan Commitments to Africa by Lender, 2000–2018

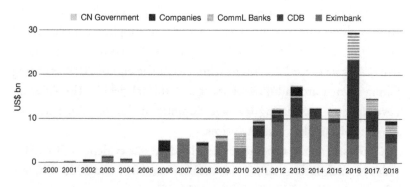

Source: Deborah Brautigam, Jyhjong Hwang, Jordan Link and Kevin Acker, 'Chinese loans to Africa database' (Washington, DC: China–Africa Research Initiative, Johns Hopkins University School of Advanced International Studies, 2020)

projects, loan repayment became a source of pressure on foreign reserves. The composition of debt meant that China – understood as the government, policy banks and SOEs – was the largest bilateral creditor with around 17% of Africa's external debt.[61] Multilateral institutions, such as the World Bank, and private lenders held about one third each, meaning that Ethiopia, Nigeria and Kenya, for example, were paying more to private creditors than to the Chinese government and policy banks.

China's track record of debt forgiveness saw it cancel at least $3.4bn of debt, and restructure or refinance approximately $15bn of debt in Africa between 2000 and 2019.[62] Much of this was to clear old debts from the 1980s and 1990s but entailed the cancellation of zero-interest loans (94 cases in 40 countries between 2000 and 2019), as opposed to the restructuring or refinancing of loans. Some African countries that borrowed significant amounts from China managed to renegotiate a portion of their loans. For example, in 2018, after deferring debt payments on its Standard Gauge Railway loans for one year, Ethiopia successfully renegotiated its $3.3bn loan to thirty years, double the length of time from the original agreement. Approximately one third of all Chinese lending in Africa went as oil-backed loans to Angola alone, due to its importance as an oil supplier; between 2000 and 2017, it received $43bn in Chinese loans.[63] According to its central bank, Angola owed $22.4bn to China as of the end of 2019, meaning China owned around 45% of its total external debt.[64] The Angolan government's negotiating leverage diminished due to China diversifying its oil supplies and low prices.

China's changing appetite for new lending was evident in FOCAC's reduced pledges for grants and loans between 2015 and 2018. Chinese officials signalled clear awareness of risks. Beijing appeared to become more cautious about providing new large loans; Kenya and Ethiopia struggled to secure additional China EXIM bank finance for railway project extensions. Chinese analysts noted concern about the rising overall debt burden in African countries, and increasing debt vulner-ability.[65] In 2019, Xi Jinping told the second BRI Forum that China would push for sustainable financing to ease debt burdens and commit itself to 'transparency and clean governance'. While such measures were being communicated, on the ground in Zimbabwe, for example, the Chinese government was employing new techniques to manage debt and attempt to prevent losing money to corruption and out of concern about Zimbabwe's ability to repay its outstanding debt. For all the Chinese leadership insistence that there were 'no strings attached', measures undertaken before 2020 included withholding further money and compliance monitoring by Chinese officials in Zimbabwe, where the placement of Chinese officials in ministries and parastatal offices caused friction within elements of the ruling Zimbabwe African National Union–Patriotic Front (ZANU–PF) party.[66]

A reckoning with debt had thus been on the cards some time before 2020. Scholars had noted the risk that large infrastructure-for-resources loans might push countries like Angola into a new debt cycle.[67] Before 2020, the coming decade was shaping up to be 'a period of concentrated demand on African debtors to start servicing the principal to China'.[68] Indebtedness to China, moreover, was by no means the only factor. Between 2008 and 2018, total external debt for sub-Saharan Africa increased by nearly 150% to $583bn, according to World Bank data. Average public debt increased between 2010 and 2018 by 40% to 59% of GDP.[69] In December 2019, the IMF reported that almost half of 54 African countries were near or at 'distressed' debt levels. Such accounts were disputed, however, with arguments that the debt-to-GDP ratio was manageable and that borrowing was essential to build infrastructure.

Debt relief

Outside China, debt relief to affected African states became a major issue during the COVID-19 pandemic but had been subject to political controversy before the pandemic. In various African countries, mounting concern had been expressed at debt in general, but China's role invariably served as a prominent lightning rod for grievances. The topic of Chinese debt had become politically fraught in a number of African countries, where it was linked among other things to concerns about sovereignty.[70] In Uganda in 2018, for instance, a leaked letter by finance minister Matia Kasaija to President Museveni noted that 'Given what is happening in our peer countries as regards to China debt, we strongly believe we should protect our assets from possible takeover.' One opposition MP, Ssemujju Ibrahim Nganda, was even blunter: 'We are fighting to become a colony of China ... And Museveni is entrapped. The things he wants to do, he thinks he can only do them with China.'[71] In August 2019, the Parliamentary Committee on National Economy reported that Uganda was not generating sufficient revenue to pay back its debts, with expenditure on debt servicing rising by 129% in 2017/2018. The largest chunk of Uganda's total debt repayments (42.45%) went to PTA Bank, the financial arm of COMESA, followed by China EXIM (18.72%).

Already a major issue in Uganda and elsewhere, the politics of debt was intensified by the COVID-19 pandemic. Pressure on China went beyond debt per se. It extended to demands for Chinese financing to help address the economic consequences of the pandemic. Former Nigerian education minister Obiageli Ezekwesili argued that China should pay reparations to Africa for its COVID-19 failures. In response, the Chinese embassy in Nigeria called on her to 'stop letting herself dance to other's tune, stop attacking and blaming China for nothing'.[72] Efforts to respond saw China participate in the G20 Debt Service Suspension Initiative for Poorest Countries process and mount a bilateral process of its own. As part of the G20 process, agreed on 15 April 2020, China recognized that G20 countries, including itself, would suspend principal repayments and interest payments from May until the end of 2020.[73] Notably, the G20 pledge did not cover commercial loans with sovereign guarantees. China's own process saw Xi Jinping announce at the 73rd World Health Assembly in May 2020 that China would provide '$2 billion over two years to help with COVID-19 response and with the economic and social development in affected countries, especially developing countries'. This suggested an indirect, alternative means of addressing debt relief. In June 2020, Xi Jinping told the China–Africa Summit on Solidarity Against COVID-19 that China would 'cancel the debt of relevant African countries in the form of interest-free government loans that are due to mature by the end of 2020'. This sounded much better than it actually was: interest-free loans have been cancelled frequently and are a small part of China's foreign development assistance (under 5% of China's lending to Africa between 2000 and 2018).[74] Concessional loans form the bulk of China's foreign aid and, with non-concessional loans, are normally rescheduled, not written off. Although Xi Jinping directed Chinese financial institutions to undertake 'friendly negotiations' with African countries on commercial-based sovereign credits, it seemed that distressed loans disbursed on relatively commercial terms by the CDB and China EXIM bank were excluded from the debt standstill deal.

In contrast to the prominence of 'debt' in Africa and the West, in China debt relief did not receive extensive media attention. Disgruntlement at perceived government largesse surfaced periodically, including in Chinese social media, contributing to caution by Chinese officials about openly discussing China's foreign aid. From March 2020, however, risk alerts by Sinosure, which underwrites many CDB and China EXIM loans mainly in relation to political risks related to non-payment or default, showed how the issue was gaining traction.[75]

Overall, 2020 demonstrated that the Chinese government did not seem keen to mount decisive action to resolve debt. The mechanics of African debt management within the Chinese government appeared to be one factor in this, with multiple Chinese creditors translating into separate negotiations. Debt cancellation and restructuring was undertaken on a loan-by-loan basis. Despite pressure on China to change its approach, and indications of, for example, China EXIM bank support for the G20 Debt Service Suspension Initiative, it seemed bilateral negotiations leading to restructuring or refinancing lay ahead.[76] China seemed intent on providing some form of debt relief, but blanket forgiveness was not countenanced. It could be that Beijing will opt for a politically directed course of action calculated and designed to ensure continuation of effective working relations; such a political calculus, however, would go against ingrained market logic and need for return on investments. However, with the politicization of debt compounding various prior grievances, there was a real need to address this beyond inter-state fixes and as part of a longer-term future economic strategy.

THE MIRAGE OF ECONOMIC TRANSFORMATION

Even before structural transformation became salient under AU direction and Chinese sponsorship, the idea that China could 'transform Africa' was promoted: weak African state capacity or corrupt regimes would be swept up in a tide of entrepreneurial dynamism, and China could serve as 'a model and motor' of twenty-first-century success; moreover, China's 'transformative impact' in Africa could 'turn out to be far larger than that of Japan in Asia'.[77] Counter arguments held that China essentially replicates Africa's historic economic relations with the outside world, thereby developing its underdevelopment and reproducing entrenched patterns of dependency.[78] Both perspectives were aired during the commodity-boom before 2014, when China contributed to economic growth as well as deindustrialization and underdevelopment in African countries. For all the talk of transformation, which reprised attempts to accelerate economic modernization in post-colonial Africa, actual change was limited, despite signs of promise and potential anchored less in faith in economic salvation from without and more intra-African avenues.

Even before the economic stress of 2020, the vision of transformative economic change was highly questionable. The idea that 'Made in China' could shift to 'Made in Africa' was confronted with the reality of a continent as dependent on agriculture as it was four decades ago, and as dependent on resource exports as when Jiang Zemin toured six African countries in 1996. It also ran against the trend of deindustrialization; manufacturing accounted for 10.4% of sub-Saharan GDP in 2018, having been 18.1% in 1981. The idea and fanfare of structural transformation displaced attention to competitive dynamics of China's multifaceted economic relations with African countries via its narrative of transformation; while present, this overshadowed better suited alternative priorities for many countries in rural, agriculture reform (crucial in China's own domestic reforms from 1978).

As seen, the structural transformation agenda has applied best and most in practice to a small number of African countries and only a few, like Ethiopia or Ghana, have managed limited diversification. In 2020, the official First Continental Report on the Implementation of Agenda 2063 after a decade noted 'slow progress' on the goal of 'transformed economies and job creation'.[79] Actual industrial Chinese 'offshoring' to African countries was limited, such as Chinese manufacturing in Ethiopia. China's industrial upgrading concentrated instead on offshoring to neighbouring countries. The prospect of automation, the Digital Silk Road and the 4th Industrial Revolution raised questions over the vaunted lower potential labour costs in African countries (and employment generation needs more generally). The Chinese government did not want to remain the factory of the world and looked more towards the service sector.

The 2020 COVID-19 pandemic, compounded by US–China geopolitical confrontation, meant that the challenges of economic development, much less transformation, were even greater. As well as a commodity price collapse, numerous Chinese-funded projects such as in Nigeria, Zambia, Zimbabwe, Algeria and Egypt were paused due to COVID-19, as debt servicing became a pressing economic question in relations. Key trends in China's engagement, namely reduced lending and changing approach to investment and political risk, pre-dated but were confirmed by the pandemic. Geopolitical dynamics also intruded. Reduced economic growth in China appeared set to continue and, combined with domestic pressure to prioritize health care in China and not direct aid overseas, further constrained overseas lending and investment. The notion of 'dual circulation' became a focal point of China's future economic strategy, predicated on ensuring 'development security' under CCP rule by ensuring China's economy was less exposed to external vulnerabilities. China's 14th Five-Year Plan (2021–5) focuses on domestic demand and emphasizes technological self-sufficiency amid China's ongoing techno-trade conflict with the US. China is projected to slow its international engagement over the next few years and its role as a driver of global growth recede, meaning Angola, Kenya, Ethiopia, Ecuador, Ghana and South Africa 'could struggle to find alternative international sources for funding, investment and trade to sustain their economic growth'.[80]

The structural constraints facing transformation had deepened and become more challenging. Some argued that latecomer Africa countries could chart their own development paths, for instance by leapfrogging traditional, carbon-intensive methods via green industrialization, or regional integration and regional trade value chains as key steps towards Africa competing globally.[81] The constraints on such proposals, however, were severe and rooted in Africa's subordinate position in the global economy. On its own, China's economic engagement did not offer the prospect of breaking the historic constraints faced by commodity-dependent African economies. The global context, including American and European farm subsidies, means trade terms remained unfavourable for Africa, especially commodity exporters dependent on fluctuating prices. Despite the range of African country experiences, even the greater integration into global value chains of some African countries, like Nigeria or Ethiopia, was 'not leading to an increase in the share of higher-value activities in its export structure'.[82]

Approached alternatively, however, industrialization formed part of a broader intra-African reform agenda that represented a more realistic basis for working towards development, rather than economic growth without broader human development and poverty reduction. The African Continental Free Trade Agreement (AfCFTA) was due to officially begin in 2021, boosted by Nigeria's participation. It offered the prospect of increasing intra-African trade, which was approximately 15.2% between 2015 and 2017 (compared with 67% in Europe, 61% in Asia, 47% in America and 7% in Oceana).[83]

Politics continued to represent a fundamental challenge to Africa's structural transformation and, in particular, the vital role of a developmental state 'to the process of accelerated economic growth and transformation of any country'.[84] Kenya, and the long-running saga of its Standard Gauge Railway (SGR), exemplified such problems.[85] The SGR, Kenya's biggest infrastructure project since independence, was intended to connect the port of Mombasa with Nairobi, and Kenya with Uganda and other states in the region. It was also supposed to showcase the BRI and Kenya's Vision 2030, a plan to become a middle-income country by 2030. A $3.8bn contract between the China Road and Bridge Corporation and the Kenyan government, mostly funded by China EXIM (85%) over fifteen years, was expedited following dubious feasibility studies and bypassing procurement laws. Mired in controversy over environmental impact, labour relations, or corruption during construction, its financial viability has been in doubt. Regional neighbours, led by Uganda, have been reluctant to join the network.[86] Criticism about the SGR has been directed at both China, due to lending policies that encourage over-priced, unnecessary large infrastructure projects, and Kenya, because of corrupt elites uninterested in long-term development. This 'flagship' BRI project turned into a capital-intensive enterprise threatening 'to leave Kenya with a loss-making and expensive white elephant'.[87]

The politics of African states remained in various ways fundamental to future development prospects, even allowing for global dynamics and structural constraints. Chinese officials also identified political challenges facing development cooperation, from weak law and regulation, to the 'frequent change of ruling parties in some African countries', the lack of stability or policy continuity, and power of trade unions, as well as security risks.[88] Such security risks became evident when the Ethiopian government, one of the most prominent examples of structural transformation and top recipient of Chinese investment in the first half of 2020, mounted a military campaign against Ethiopia's northern Tigray region in November. This followed fighting between federal troops and forces of the former ruling party, the Tigray People's Liberation Front, after major differences concerning the composition of Ethiopia's federal government. Overall, in their China relations and more generally, however, the ability of African states to improve the terms of their economic relations was highly constrained. Angola and Zambia, for example, showed that more power rests with African rentier states when commodity prices are high but, when prices fall, more power rests with China and other external partners. The upshot is that 'the power of African elites has been confined to bargaining rather than structural change'.[89]

CONCLUSION

This chapter examined key themes in the economics of China's New Era Africa engagement. China has become Africa's top single trade partner, bilateral creditor, major investor and sponsor of structural transformation. From undersea internet cables to launching satellites,

China's multidimensional influence is now such that the language and reference points of economic development and business imaginations have been evolving; Tanzania's potential port development, Bagamoyo, for example, was labelled 'the new Shenzhen', and Jack Ma's role in his foundation's Africa Business Hero TV competition, won in 2020 by Chebet Lesan of BrightGreen Renewable Energy, in Kenya, offered a new business role model.

The first theme examined trade, aid and investment in the context of diversifying and deepening Chinese economic ties, which have been taking relations beyond the previous trade focus. A more diverse Chinese business engagement has been emerging and expanding. More than a decade before Xi Jinping took power, CNPC exemplified China's 'going global' engagement. Now the likes of Transsion, Alibaba's ambitions for Africa or efforts of its affiliate Ant Financial exemplify a shift towards communications, technology, e-infrastructure and e-commerce. With the prospect of more business in a post-pandemic world, other sectors looked set to expand. For example, the enhanced position of 'agricultural modernization' at FOCAC 2018 signalled that agriculture would become more prominent again, as confirmed with the first Forum on China–Africa Cooperation in Agriculture, held in December 2019 in Sanya, Hainan, China.

Second, the China–Africa economic development agenda is more wide ranging and ambitious. China championed industrialization partly to repurpose its economic relations in self-interested, forward-looking ways. As the framework guiding China–Africa economic engagement has evolved, however, the challenges of matching declared intent and actual delivery became clear some time before the COVID-19 induced disruptions of 2020. China's 'New Era' focus on industrialization within the terms of the AU's Agenda 2063 followed comparable historic attempts in Africa. Much rides on whether or not this latest attempt can, unlike its historical precursors, be meaningfully realized: if the desired industrial upgrading is not achieved, the familiar dominance of resource exchanges will remain a default setting in many African countries.[90] Instead of transformative change, under-development could end up being reinforced. By 2020, the prospects for Africa's Third Industrial Development Decade were poor. By galvanizing calls for African countries to forge alternative paths, and more effectively use China in the process, the unintended conse-quences pointed towards the potential of strengthening intra-African approaches and links, even if major political barriers remained.

Third, debt became a defining, highly political and globally visible issue. This posed more severe challenges in some African countries more than others, as Zambia showed. The new debt crisis showed the extent to which China has become a deeply involved and more exposed protagonist. Its familiar opacity and debt forgiveness methods, which brought political credit when these involved insubstantial zero-interest loans or were used to critique Western powers, have reached their limits.

Many, including the Chinese government, argued that the answer to debt was economic growth. Following years of exponential commodity-driven growth, however, China and Africa economic relations were adapting to slower growth within China, and the Chinese government's changing domestic economic strategy in the context of US–China trade and technological competition. For all the economic growth in African countries, during the boom years until 2014 and since, the extent to which there has been broader, inclusive and sustainable devel-opment and durable poverty reduction was exposed by the COVID-19 pandemic, which exacerbated the progressive developmental agenda.

An emerging new architecture of trade links on a wider African–Asian basis indicated future directions for African economic ties involving but going beyond China. This involved a trend whereby African states were looking beyond China to other partners in order to pursue diversification of economic relations. In 2020, as an example of an effort to pursue relations with Asian states beyond China,

South Africa became a signatory to the Association of Southeast Asian Nations' (ASEAN) Treaty of Amity and Cooperation, joining two other African states, Egypt and Morocco. This was expected to promote trade ties. Second, with ASEAN creating a single trade bloc incorporating China, South Korea, Japan, Australia, New Zealand into a new Regional Comprehensive Economic Partnership agreed in November 2020, one future prospect involved links between the AfCFTA and ASEAN. Third, and more present on policy radar, was newfound interest in linking the AfCFTA and the BRI. This was an incipient stage for an ambitious continental project that will take years to develop; signing the agreement into existence was the easy part. Furthermore, the presumed harmony of interests between the AfCFTA and the BRI was questionable in view of potential issues of competition.

The prominence of China in African countries' development agenda was not solely due to economics. China's – and Chinese – deepening economic interactions in Africa were generating a proliferating range of challenges and complications. The common denominator was politics, ranging from micro-scale responses to competition between Chinese entrepreneurs to more macro structural issues like trade deficits, loans or dependency concerns. The expansion of a more diverse Chinese business engagement across the continent, together with Chinese migration, also meant that security became a more prominent concern for the Chinese government. This raised dilemmas about protecting overseas interests, further underscoring the nature and extent of China's more established position. China's engagement extended significantly beyond infrastructure projects and embraced a full range of governance and legal measures, enhancing investment environments or enhancing law enforcement capacity. Given the Chinese government's embrace of capacity building and the importance of sound institutions in managing its economic ties with African state counterparts, the former cliché that Beijing only did the hardware (infrastructure) and the West did software (governance) of African development was clearly outmoded. Like China's economic approach to its African relations, Beijing's political engagement was undergoing a process of adaption and evolution, which could be clearly seen in debate around the changing China model and African politics.

4 | Xi's China Model, African Politics

Under Xi Jinping, the CCP has more confidently promoted a New Era version of the China model, a form of authoritarian single-party state capitalism, in order to strengthen China–Africa relations and promote its foreign policy amid geopolitical competition and change. This represents a departure from China's previous approach and, while a notable feature in China's Africa relations, applies to developing countries more generally. In 2017, for example, while discussing 'major power diplomacy', Foreign Minister Wang Yi proclaimed that the China model 'can provide a new path for all developing countries to modernization'.[1] In the Chinese government's relations with African countries, the determinative factor remains not so much any 'export' by the CCP of ideas about its model so much as how African protagonists understand, adapt and selectively import and apply these in African politics. Recent analysis and policy debates, in the US for instance, has tended to emphasize Beijing's intent, or export of influence, with recent departures exploring deeper questions about ideas, inter-personal relations and power.[2] African politics, however, ultimately continues to be the most important shaping factor.[3]

This chapter is structured into three parts. The first puts the politics of the China model, which has meant different things at different times, into context.[4] The second considers how the politics of the China model has evolved under Xi Jinping, and why and how Beijing has been promoting this in direct and indirect ways, such as through education, training, media and political party training. The third part considers the China model in terms of African politics and what is actually involved in terms of political practice, not ascription or hype. For all Beijing's intentions and efforts to promote its approach, the actual ways in which this is understood, adapted and used in African countries are most consequential and, in the process, reveal limits to the CCP's ability to export its model in its terms. Recent geopolitical posturing about competing models in Africa detracts attention from more challenging, harder to fathom questions concerning the processes by which 'the China model' is selectively understood, used and revised by different involved protagonists according to domestic African country imperatives. Placing African politics first, and locating the China model as subject and subordinate to changing domestic African politics, provides a sounder basis for considering actual dynamics and questions about impact.

CHINA MODELS IN CONTEXT

The prominence of the Xi Jinping model in China's current Africa relations can convey the impression that this is a new phenomenon but interest in learning from – and following – 'the China model' has been a recurring feature of post-colonial Africa's relations with China. Foundational to current relations is the Maoist example of anti-colonial emancipation and egalitarian socialist development, which was influential in military, economic and political terms in certain African countries. In Tanzania, most famously, President Julius Nyerere's agricultural collectivization program was inspired by his understanding of China. Beijing exported its version of communist revolution as an integral part of its foreign policy and global strategy. This saw Mao's China position itself not just as an alternative to American capitalism, but to Soviet communism and Taiwan, generating possibilities for African countries to benefit from competing external powers.

The Maoist model was inspirational for some, controversial for others. In 1963, for instance, noting how China 'enchants many leading figures in African politics that they want to make it their model', one Ghanaian analyst compared his actual experience of living in China to Maoist rhetoric. Pointing out the difference between proclaimed equality and actual social inequality, he suggested: 'An important lesson for Africa to learn from China is the folly of the craze for prestige for its own sake.'[5] Just as current claims about 'the China model' often highlight and glorify select aspects, while downplaying, ignoring or excluding others, commonly propagated and received ideas about Mao's model were frequently at odds with China's real-life domestic experience. The Maoist example also shows that the idea of China exporting a model to African countries never translated easily into practice. The Maoist era may seem distant today, but Xi Jinping has resurrected aspects for his own power purposes and brought ideology back into Chinese politics.

After Mao, China under Deng Xiaoping's leadership provided a more compelling and enduring example of economic reform and development. Rooted in pragmatic experimentalism, this entailed a process of 'directed improvisation', a combination of state direction, experiment and uncertainty concerning outcomes.[6] When Ghana's then leader, Jerry Rawlings, visited Beijing in September 1985, Deng Xiaoping advised: 'Please don't copy our model. If there is any experience on our part, it is to formulate policies in light of one's own national conditions.'[7] This is often cited as proof of China's aversion to being the source of learning or provider of lessons to African countries but reflected a particular moment and phase of China's experimental opening to ideas about what might work in economic development. As seen, some that did work in China, like special economic zones, were later exported to African countries.

China's economic development and rising world profile under Hu Jintao was accompanied by a search for a revised China model. A major debate concerned the supposed contrast between the Washington Consensus, originally a list of ten policy recommendations that became synonymous with neoliberal ideology, and the Beijing Consensus, which in essence was a heavier, state-led development model.[8] The Beijing Consensus proved attractive partly because its cheerleaders portrayed China as a counter to the Washington Consensus and liberalism more generally.[9] It showed how debate about 'the China model' often reflects interpretations based on other interests and agendas. Coined outside China, the Beijing Consensus in practice shared much in common with the original Washington Consensus. Furthermore, it was hard to compare across time, and the single model of Chinese development that became associated with the Beijing Consensus contrasted with emergence of multiple models within China.[10] In April 2006, Hu Jintao told Nigeria's parliament in Abuja that China supported 'diversified models of development' but under Xi Jinping there have been major changes regarding the China model.

CHINA'S NEW ERA MODEL

Under Xi Jinping, the China model has many manifestations, from national politics down to New Era civic values of individual Chinese citizens, but in essence it is a form of authoritarian single-party state capitalism characterized by extensive party-state control over political and social life, including the media, internet, and education, and whose economy involves a strong role of the party-state in core economic sectors as well as market-based practices.[11] Integral to this Xi-era China model, on top of Xi Jinping Thought, are sophisticated high-tech methods of political control backed up by a national security state.[12] Deng Xiaoping accepted that there were risks to being open to foreign capital and ideas but argued these were useful and could be controlled, saying: 'Open the windows, breathe the fresh air and at the same time fight the flies and insects.' In contrast, Xi Jinping has firmly closed China's windows. Moreover, the Chinese government is promoting its own proto-global cyber governance system based on state-controlled cyber-sovereignty.

Under Xi Jinping, and CCP leadership, Beijing has been more confident, overt and direct in promoting China's model, to Africa and the world, but has continued to officially maintain that it does not seek to 'export' any model. The difference between promoting and exporting can be debated. Xi Jinping has been very clear, however, about the superiority of China's system, that it is worth emulating and that promoting it can help not just China's foreign policy and economic interests but address global challenges as well. At the CCP's 19th Congress in 2017, he stated: 'The China model for a better social governance system offers a new option for other countries and nations who want to speed up their development while preserving their independence.'[13]

China's leadership has repeatedly insisted that it does not export the China model. At the 2017 BRI Forum, for instance, Xi Jinping said: 'we are ready to share practices of development with other countries, but we have no intention to interfere in other countries' internal affairs, export our own social system and model of development, or impose our own will on others.'[14] In 2018, Xi Jinping affirmed that China would not 'import' foreign models of development, 'export' China's model or 'ask other countries to copy the Chinese practice.'[15] As the Chinese government's white paper 'China and the World in the New Era' similarly asserted in 2019, China 'does not "import" foreign models, nor "export" the Chinese model, and will never require other countries to replicate its practices.'[16] Such an argument is made in order to render this compatible with its rhetoric about 'a new type of international relations', support for sovereignty and non-interference. By rejecting the notion of any universal model, moreover, the Chinese government also seeks to undermine multi-party liberal democracy, arguing that there can be development without democracy and that 'there is no universal model of development'.[17] Integral to the Chinese government's approach is a paradoxical rejection of 'universal models' in favour of its model that it promotes on a universal basis, based on the sacrosanct power of individual states not the rights of individuals.

China's leadership went from downplaying to promoting the Xi Jinping incarnation of the China model, which has become central to Beijing's relations with and role within Africa. This was communicated by Xi Jinping himself, such as when, in December 2018, he argued: 'Forty years of practice has fully proved that China's development has provided successful experiences and shown bright prospects for the majority of developing countries to modernize.'[18] China's domestic poverty reduction record is one aspect of its foreign policy, with Xi Jinping having pledged to end extreme poverty in China by 2020 ahead of the CCP's centenary in 2021.[19] Showing how the content of the China model has been changing, some in China argue that Xi's model is different to the state-led model supported by market forces, which helped reduce poverty to a major degree after 1978. Xi has prioritized a party-led and dominated state approach, with a more circumscribed and controlled role for market forces.[20]

The Chinese government argues that its experience of development is better suited to African countries and that it has a more informed understanding of what development requires.[21] This is a positive claim made in China's own terms. It is also made in critical comparative reference to 'the West's' failure to contribute significant development gains in Africa. Another argument is based on outputs, that China's authoritarian political system delivers better results than Western liberal democracies. Finally, China presents itself as not just a model but also an enabler of economic development. In this sense, the BRI has been a vehicle for Xi Jinping to spread the CCP's model in the world.[22] The geopolitical ambition behind the BRI is to legitimize the CCP's model of state capitalism and political authoritarianism in the world.[23]

Why is Beijing promoting the China model?

The promotion of Xi's China model is rooted in domestic politics and efforts to mobilize CCP legitimacy within China. Promoting the China model, and receiving vocal support from a host of African allies in the process, can be used to bolster domestic legitimacy by demonstrating to a domestic audience China's success under CCP leadership and why this should be replicated by other governments. It signals that the CCP's political system is positively regarded and praised, and its attractiveness proved by efforts to learn from or replicate it in African countries.

Linked to, but going beyond domestic politics, other drivers can be identified. First, promoting the China model can help promote not just the Chinese government's political interests but also economic ones. For example, Chinese companies can sell technology used to support and enable the model. Second, the China model is used in attempts to promote China's soft power, informed by strategic calculations and harder forms of interest and power. By putting people-to-people relations at the centre of its Africa relations, through funded training programmes for instance, the CCP seeks to promote 'Chinese know-how and expert knowledge' to developing African countries interested in learning about China's experience with development. This means that 'one mechanism through which Chinese norms are diffused is through China's investments in human resource development and professionalization trainings in the developing world'.[24] Third, as part of Beijing's foreign policy, promoting the CCP's model affirms China's identity as a major global power. The Chinese government still asserts its developing country status but promoting the China model helps bolster its major power credentials and vision of world order. Fourth, the China model is used to enhance China's reputation and position against adversaries, especially the US. The CCP uses the Xi Jinping incarnation of the China model to critique the failed 'Western model' in Africa. In talking up the benefits of the China model, which is now promoted as part of the BRI, Beijing's global development blueprint and reform agenda, the CCP also critiques 'the West' and any claims to universal values and human rights. One dynamic thus involves contending external models in Africa driven by political agendas, in which China asserts the superiority of its own model, most importantly over that of the US.

Under Xi Jinping's leadership, China's new era of Africa relations involves a battle of ideas in the wider context of strategic and ideological competition with the US. Xi's China model competes with others, seeks to affirm its superiority, and promote interests threatened by the US. One example came in an August 2019 newspaper article by China's ambassador to Uganda, Zheng Zhuqiang, which criticized 'foreign forces' for 'making irresponsible remarks on the internal affairs of Uganda' concerning a story claiming that Huawei helped the Ugandan government 'spy on opposition politicians'. Pointing to the US implicitly, he stated that 'the black hand of these foreign forces does not stop at one place ... and their disgraceful behaviours of interfering with other countries' internal affairs go on endlessly.'[25] The US, in turn, sought to mobilize what former US Secretary of State, Rex Tillerson, described to the AU in February 2018 as 'an American model of development', based on 'sustainable growth that bolsters institutions, strengthens rule of law, and builds the capacity of African countries to stand on their own two feet'. He criticized 'China's approach, which encourages dependency using opaque contracts, predatory loan practices, and corrupt deals that mire nations in debt and undercut their sovereignty, denying them their long-term, self-sustaining growth.'[26] As seen, this became a quotidian part of US public diplomacy on China in Africa under the Trump administration. Amid such geopolitical competition, in a global context where, from 2020, Beijing used the COVID-19 pandemic to further argue that Western liberal democracy was dysfunctional in contrast to the CCP's successful response to the virus, promoting aspects of China's approach forms part of Beijing's efforts to reform global governance in its own image and interests. This involves the China model's being expanded to the global level and applied to global politics.

Overall, Beijing's efforts to promote the China model are driven by a combination of defensive reasons to protect the CCP from criticism, as well as more proactive efforts to promote China's values and interests in Africa and around the world, which also serve to defend and enhance the CCP's grip on power in China. At a time of widespread efforts to promote Xi Jinping Thought, this is seen in a number of areas.

Promoting the China model in practice
If public statements by China's leadership take care not to suggest any imposition of its approach to politics, the thrust of practical efforts to promote the CCP's China model, as a bundle of influences driven by interests, provides more convincing evidence of concerted, strategic and focused intent. There are numerous ways and channels through which different parts of China's government, led by the CCP, seeks to promote its approach in Africa. As seen, one involves efforts to promote China's model through participation in international institutions and regimes. The December 2019 South–South Human Rights Forum in Beijing was one example of Beijing showcasing the benefits of its authoritarian system as the basis for delivering development. In terms of China–Africa relations, four areas stand out: education, training, media and political party training.

First, education is central in CCP efforts to promote its China model and, in the process, gain longer-term influence. A familiar historical theme, the role of education has been considerably enhanced in recent years. China has been attracting increasing numbers of foreign students, including from Africa. Between 2003 and 2018, the number of African students in higher education in China increased by nearly 4,500% (from around 1,793 African students in 2003, to 81,562 in 2018, according to China's Ministry of Education).[27] In

2018, FOCAC nearly doubled the number of Chinese government fellowships from the 30,000 announced in 2015 to 50,000, as well as training 1,000 African leaders, an impressive outward indication of the importance attached to this (even if little is known about how this is implemented). By doing so, China provides education across a range of categories, from technical experts to government officials, journalists or scholars; in other words, 'the African political, economic, and social elites and opinion leaders that will shape the future of the continent and its relations with China'.[28]

Educational links include research exchanges and funding. Since around 2010, the Chinese government has been emerging as the provider of research funding for African researchers. One goal is to enhance research on Africa within China, partly to promote a 'Chinese Brand' of research but also to exert greater control by holding the discourse of 'China–Africa relations in China's hands'.[29] In short, following a history elsewhere of building up academic area studies to support foreign policy, including in the US, knowledge is power. One aspect of this is ensuring that university research and teaching on China in countries like South Africa conforms to CCP approval.

Educational links also include increasing numbers of Confucius Institutes (CIs) in Africa. In contrast with the recent trend of closing CIs in North America and Europe, more CIs have been opening in the African continent. The first CI was established at the University of Nairobi, Kenya in December 2005 and by 2020, there were 61 in 46 African countries.[30] (By comparison, there were some 180 Alliance Française centres in Africa in 2018.)[31] Funded by the Chinese government, CIs were run by Hanban, under supervision of China's Ministry of Education (before it became the Centre for Language Education and Cooperation in 2020). Despite wide variations, CIs in African countries 'share a main goal of portraying the strengths and appeal of China's culture and traditions' and, through their teaching curricula, 'diffuse and normalize the Chinese regime's party line and its official stance on sensitive topics like China's human rights record, Taiwan, minority rights, and the Hong Kong separatist movement.'[32]

Second, and related, training has been central. China's training programs now target and involve a wide range of African participants, from government officials, to high-ranking military personnel, journalists or teachers, as well as university students. At the 2018 FOCAC, Xi Jinping announced that China's professional training in Africa would expand with a series of vocational training workshops, or Luban workshops, intended 'to provide vocational training for young Africans' leading to suitable jobs and improved living conditions.[33] This announcement was followed by the launch of the first Luban Workshop in Africa in March 2019, a partnership of the Tianjin Railway Technical and Vocational College and Djibouti's Industrial and Commercial School.

The related expansion of the Chinese government's capacity building programs in Africa has been marked since 2018; previously, the language of 'capacity building' was not overtly present. The 2015 FOCAC committed government scholarships and training but in 2018 the Chinese government elevated capacity building as part of an effort to strengthen exchanges of development experiences and development planning cooperation. Over the past decade Chinese government capacity building programs, particularly training programs for African officials and young leaders, have 'morphed into a systematic campaign to promote China's development achievements, development models, and bilateral cooperation.'[34] FOCAC 2018 committed to support the construction of an Institute for Capacity Development alongside the African Capacity Building Foundation in Harare, Zimbabwe, an AU specialized agency, 'reflecting Chinese assessments of how to tackle governance deficits in Africa by fostering a broad range of policy and operational skills for delivering public goods.'[35]

A second area involves different types of media, old and new, and has been unfolding as part of a global CCP push to 'tell China's story' in order to advance China's 'discourse power'. One notable departure has seen China's diplomats in African countries defend and promote Chinese government positions on social media (often via platforms, like Twitter, that are banned in China). China's former ambassador to South Africa, Lin Songtian, for example, became renowned for his outspoken views and role pioneering a confrontational style of public messaging, notably on Twitter, subsequently taken up by other diplomats. Social media is seen as important in a global information battle, with China's MFA adopting a more direct and combative approach to public communication.

China has made concerted efforts to promote its state media in Africa: China Radio International, which has operated in Nairobi since 2006 and now broadcasts in Kiswahili to some 100m listeners in eastern and central Africa; China Global Television Network (CGTN, formerly CCTV-9), which opened its Africa headquarters in 2012 in Nairobi; and the *China Daily* newspaper, which started printing a weekly Africa edition in 2012. China's state-run news agency Xinhua opened a purpose-built Africa headquarters also in Nairobi in 2019. State-backed Chinese investors have purchased stakes in South Africa's Independent Media and other African media companies. Chinese government propaganda is channelled into more mainstream African media in different ways: via sponsored features, news feeds of Xinhua content, publishing Chinese-produced content as locally generated news,[36] or sponsoring journalist trips to China to attempt to cultivate better ties.

China's state media has a comparatively small presence and viewership compared to established foreign outlets like the BBC or CNN; one study, for instance, estimated CGTN news content reached 2–8% of elite audiences in Kenya, Nigeria and South Africa.[37] China's media footprint may be growing, albeit in relative terms and not consistently across the continent, but how far this translates into growing influence is questionable. One study of audiences in Kenya, Nigeria and South Africa found that direct exposure to Chinese media such as CGTN Africa, CRI or the African edition of the *China Daily* was marginal, with multiple layers of resistance to engaging with content produced by news organizations linked to the CCP and Chinese government. This stemmed from deep-rooted beliefs that journalists should play a watchdog role in society, such as scrutiny of Kenya's SGR by local journalists, which is at odds with how journalism is seen and practised by most journalists working for Chinese state-owned media. It was also linked to a credibility gap facing Chinese state media, arising from the dominance of official narratives and ideological messages, the often defensive approach to rebutting what it deems to be Western media misrepresentation of China's role in Africa, filtering out of negative news or avoiding sensitive topics like Hong Kong.[38]

The challenges facing China's traditional state media in Africa contrast with the rapid growth of digital technology and internet-enabled media. China's state media have struggled to break into the traditional news industry, but Chinese private companies are capturing new opportunities to expand media soft power and business. Central to this is the changing way in which many in African countries access news. In Botswana, for example, the number of people using social media (Facebook, Twitter or WhatsApp) for daily news doubled between 2014 and 2019 to reach some 34% of the population.[39] Internet use in Africa has been growing at a rapid pace.[40] More Africans are using the internet for news and information with expanded mobile access, with social media already serving as the staple source of news and information for many. Chinese companies were quick to realize the potential of mobile news and develop successful innovative news platforms amid advances in mobile internet technology. These include entertainment mediums like Vskit ('the African version of TikTok') created by the Chinese company Transsnet (a joint venture between

NetEase and Transsion). The demographic profile of younger users undoubtedly helps but the wider context is the ongoing development of African mobile internet (from mobile payments to music streaming, short video social networking, or online games).

In this context, the longstanding role and established position of Huawei and other Chinese companies in providing training to African civil servants and building digital infrastructure in African countries has been important. The Nigerian government, for example, has a partnership with Huawei to offer ICT training. As well as giving rise to concern about how this can be used by authoritarian leaders in Africa, the CCP's model of media control offers a complementary demonstration effect, not just in terms of obvious control of traditional media but, more important, future digital forms. In January 2019, all seven of China's Politburo Standing Committee members attended a meeting on media convergence in the digital age, which was part of a project to remake China's state-dominated media system to enable the CCP to use digital methods to control the ideological sphere.[41]

Third, the CCP seeks to promote its model through political party exchanges and cadre training, a highly significant area of active, future-oriented engagement predicated on personal relations and networked connections.[42] Xi Jinping's New Era has seen a more overtly ideological approach to political party training, involving a central role for the ID-CCP. Indicating how important party-to-party relations are, the ID-CCP is active in maintaining personal connections with a wide range of African political party leaders and members.[43] This means that CCP relations with African political parties, rulers and politicians have become one of the most important parts of China–Africa relations. Party-to-party relations is a means to promote the Chinese government's foreign-policy interests and support its global strategy but is also a means of promoting authoritarian learning and diffusion.[44]

Box 1. ANC–CCP Party Relations

The African National Congress (ANC) is a preeminent political partner for the CCP in Africa. Since 1994, it has been the ruling party in South Africa, a country with regional, continental and global significance, and political party relations have been central to South Africa's relations with China. Political ties had a deep history prior to the establishment of diplomatic ties in 1998.[45] Important party connections thus long pre-dated Xi Jinping's leadership of China. While visiting China in 2008, for example, Jacob Zuma proposed that the CCP provide leadership training to the ANC, after which there was an agreement in 2010 to send members of its National Executive Committee to Beijing for training and to enable government officials to undertake training with counterpart ministries in China.

Jacob Zuma had cultivated relations with China before becoming President of South Africa but during his leadership (2009 to February 2018) the CCP became the ANC's best friend. It also saw the intrusion of party politics as a form of personal enrichment into bilateral state relations, as evidenced in numerous corruption scandals.

The ID-CCP has met frequently with the ANC, which ranked 10th out of the CCP's twenty most important partners between 2002 and 2017 in terms of the total number of contacts (Sudan's National Congress party ranking 7th).[46] It also maintains strong ties with the South African Communist Party. Political party training has been a key area of ANC–CCP cooperation. One ANC participant on a 2015 tour of China explained how the party's 'delegation was lectured on, among others, building and managing party structures, understanding communism and a market-oriented economy, and running state-owned enterprises.[47] CCP–ANC relations span different levels of party structures, from training of provincial-level cadres to senior leadership exchanges that involve overlapping party and state roles. How far such exchanges and party training has actually been utilized in practice is unclear (as is whether seeing is believing for other such African visitors). The ANC, however, has also sought to establish a political party training school of its own in South Africa. In 2007, the party's 52nd National Conference in Polokwane declared that this would 'be modelled on the China Executive Leadership Academy Pudong' but little progress has been made in establishing a physical school.

The ANC's foreign-policy positions have been consistently pro-China. A 2015 discussion document by the ANC's National General Council declared that China's economic trajectory was 'a leading example of the triumph of humanity over adversity. The exemplary role of the collective leadership of the Communist Party of China in this regard should be a guiding lodestar of our own struggle.'[48]

The institutional weaknesses of the Jacob Zuma administration and backlash against state capture opened up space for other political parties, which China has not appeared keen to engage. The Democratic Alliance, South Africa's second largest party, challenged the ANC, including on foreign policy and China relations. For example, it criticized the ANC government for refusing to grant the Dalai Lama a visa to visit in 2014. When Solly Msimanga, a Democratic Alliance party member and mayor of Tshwane, visited Taiwan in December 2016 on a business trip, he was criticized by the South African government's Department for International Relations and Cooperation, Chinese associations in the country and the ANC's Tshwane caucus, who labelled his trip 'treason.'[49] (It later emerged that the

Minister of the Department of Trade and Industry, Rob Davis, had undertaken a similar trip in 2014.) The Economic Freedom Fighters, a more radical party led by former ANC Youth League member Julius Malema, criticized China's relations with South Africa and accused the Chinese government of neo-colonialism. How far such anti-China sentiment reflects a real or more pragmatic, opportunist critique of the CCP for its close ties with and support for the ANC, as opposed to Pan-Africanist ideology or xenophobic tendencies, was unclear.

ANC–CCP relations advanced under Jacob Zuma's successor, Cyril Ramaphosa, but faced mounting challenges. Prior to being elected ANC president in December 2017, and becoming South Africa's president in February 2018, Ramaphosa had longstanding and high connections with the CCP. Before South Africa's 2019 general election, the ANC made enhanced efforts to promote ties with the CCP, including lessons about managing public relations, party discipline and loyalty.[50] Despite Ramaphosa's efforts to consolidate domestic reform and manage economic distress within South Africa, and promote relations with external partners including China, his government confronted deepening problems. The long-running example of power generation, for example, and the difficulties of reforming public electricity utility company Eskom, were so challenging that in 2019 the CDB reportedly withheld disbursement of loan funds due to concern that construction of agreed projects would not materialize. Former Chinese ambassador Lin Songtian said that South Africa could only attract Chinese investment if it revived its stagnant economy, renovated infrastructure and guaranteed the governance of state-owned enterprises. In other words, 'the South Africa–China relationship also has its boundaries'.[51]

Political exchanges under the FOCAC process, which now span a wider and deeper range of high-level forums, exchanges between leaders, legislatures, local governments as well as political parties, involve important training aspects. Political party training workshops can be viewed as instruments of influence but are also 'productive of power'.[52] These have a number of roles: generating opportunities for networking, diffusing norms by marketing Chinese expertise, and bearing 'a cultural influence and power', particularly those trainings held in China that, before the interruption of the COVID-19 pandemic, featured tours of Chinese cities in different provinces, underscoring China's domestic economic success and indirectly its political system.[53] The CCP's China Executive Leadership Academy Pudong is at the forefront of such exchanges and training programs. In May 2019, for instance, following the re-election of President Macky Sall in February, this held a program for Senegal's ruling Alliance for the Republic party on 'Governance Capacity-Building and National Development'. Or in June 2019, a Tunisian delegation featuring participants from its six ministries and Central Bank participated in a 'China Development Experience Workshop' featuring Xi Jinping Thought.

Four themes concerning the evolution of such political training stand out. The first concerns a change from the CCP's former preference for dealing exclusively with African ruling parties to also maintaining relations with opposition parties, albeit maintaining an emphasis on incumbent parties. This was brought about via experience and pragmatic, necessary adaptation to political realities. The CCP previously only worked with incumbent ruling parties, but now engages with a much wider array of opposition parties and even civil society groups, as part of a deepening and broadening of connections brought about by experience of multi-party African politics, political transitions and the need for a less rigid approach.[54] Secondly, a defining aspect of political cooperation with regard to training and education is its forward-looking investment in younger generations of future

African leaders. The Chinese government pays particular attention to providing training for younger generations of future elites, such as through the African Political Party Leaders training program under the Sino-Africa Young Political Leaders Forum. At the 2018 FOCAC, the number of 'young Africans' to be invited to China was increased to 2,000. Given that this is intended to socialize and shape future political preferences, the impacts remain to be seen but such efforts represent a systematic, deliberate attempt to expose African political parties to China's experience, the CCP's New Era governing methods and cultivate networks of connections.[55]

Third, the CCP's support for political training extends beyond China. In July 2018, for example, a ground-breaking ceremony was held for the Julius Nyerere Leadership School in Kibaha, not far from Dar es Salaam. With financial support from the Chinese government, this was founded by six African political parties: the CCM (Chama Cha Mapinduzi, Tanzania), the ANC, FRELIMO (Mozambique), MPLA (Angola), SWAPO (Namibia) and ZANU–PF. Xi Jinping sent a message of congratulation. Song Tao, head of the ID-CCP, spoke at the ceremony, as did Tanzania's President and CCM chairman John Magufuli, whose party has held power since 1961 and who declared: 'There is no alternative to the CCM' and that it will be 'in power forever, for eternity'.[56]

Finally, political exchanges are officially part of what the 2018 FOCAC Action Plan termed enhancing 'experience sharing on state governance' but the extent to which such sharing has been two-way in practice is minimal. Such unidirectional sharing also characterizes China's professional trainings and the lack of African counterparts to CIs.[57]

The idea and language of promoting or 'exporting' conveys the ways in which China tries to spread its model across borders and around the world. It is less able, however, to capture and convey the multifaceted ways this happens in practice, which involve much more than sending ideas, capabilities or technology abroad.

THE CHINA MODEL IN AFRICAN POLITICS

Questions concerning the CCP's export of its model, and the intentions behind this, receive wide attention, tied as this is to the Chinese government's major power ambitions, and show how debate about models has been dominated across time by one-way interest in the China model. Much, if not most, coverage has involved what African countries should, could or can learn from China. The China model has to be understood from the CCP's perspective, but this is insufficient in the face of immense variation in political circumstances of African states and their relations with China and other powers, which also seek to promote political models of their own.

African countries, historically and today, are often represented as or assumed to be somehow uniquely susceptible to CCP ideological influence.[58] The abolition of term limits on Xi Jinping's leadership, for instance, was seen as a potential catalyst for the rolling back of democratic gains in Africa. While rightly pointing to an enabling example, this overemphasized external influence.[59] Such an approach betrays a failure to understand ways in which politics in Africa operates and responds to foreign influence. African states have established ways of dealing with external powers, of which China is the most prominent latest, in order to use material or moral external resources for domestic political purposes.[60] China's approach to politics in Africa is distinctive in going with, not against, the grain; that is, formally accepting and not seeking to change politics via political conditionalities or other means. Nonetheless, this does not mean it is not susceptible to extraverted strategies.

The China model is much hyped. Its allure, based on the insights into economic development it supposedly contains, extends beyond many African states to include other states outside the continent as well as international organizations like the UN Development Programme (UNDP), for example, who have sought to identify, adapt and apply China's development lessons learning for Africa. Nonetheless, the response to China of influential African governments and policy-makers suggests that some, at least, see it as much more than just another external source of technical assistance and development lessons. Instead, and amplified by Beijing, one perspective is that seeking to emulate China 'will not only have a transformative impact on Africa but it will further a larger emancipatory agenda for the continent as well.'[61] There is an affinity between some authoritarian African regimes and the CCP model, including its critique of multi-party politics. Some African leaders, such as Rwanda's President Paul Kagame, have criticized the imposition of 'Western democracy' in Africa. Others similarly criticize this and claim that representative liberal democracy is Western, such as in Uganda, where President Yoweri Museveni presides over a 'no-party' polity controlled by his National Resistance Movement. However, there are strong counter arguments, including how democracy is related to economic development: 'African countries which genuinely pursued democracy, such as Mauritius, Botswana, Cape Verde, and recently Seychelles, have achieved higher growth levels, have industrialized quicker, and have had more sustained peace.'[62] Empirical evidence shows that democracy leads to development in Africa, not just in terms of growth but public services, including in rural contexts in Ghana and Botswana for example.[63]

Importing models
The China model is shorthand for a more complex set of deeper political dynamics, which go beyond any narrow, benign developmental associations. As such, and superficially, the China model is frequently invoked in order to attempt to legitimate domestic political choices. In Nigeria, for example, China is invoked in diverse ways

and, according to one writer, 'provides our politicians with a ready and idealized example of a "benevolent dictatorship", one that they can call up to substantiate their insidious agenda for Nigeria.'[64] In one case, the Comptroller General of the Nigeria Customs Service justified closing Nigeria's land borders in 2019 to counteract illegal trade by saying: 'We must eat and drink Nigeria. Even China closed its borders to the whole world for 40 years and today it is considered a great nation. Don't you want to be a great Nigeria?'[65] Most significantly, what exerts the greatest influence is the manner by which African political protagonists import their understandings of the China model in their way according to their needs, and as one aspect of a broader set of extraverted external relations. Sudan's former ruling National Congress party, for instance, cited the China model and a 'Sino-Sudanese model of development' as elite discourse, and shared a common belief in the power of transformative mega infrastructure such as dams and authoritarian single-party government. However, it also adroitly incorporated Chinese investment into its domestic and foreign-policy agenda. Chinese assistance empowered the regime and helped it maintain power amid multiple conflicts, with Beijing acting as a friendly shield for Khartoum in the international arena, but the centre of gravity lay with the government of Sudan. In Sudan or other cases like Ethiopia, rather than citing a list of policies derived from China's example, a deeper issue concerns governing 'elites' perceptions of the domesticability of the Chinese example.'[66]

Xi Jinping's China model is one of many external models in Africa, meaning that Chinese influence and engagement is part of what in practice are hybrid influences. President Paul Kagame, reelected with 99% of the vote in Rwanda in August 2017, has thus cited Singapore or South Korea, together with China, as examples of models he finds inspiring. Ethiopia's former leader, Meles Zenawi, who favoured South Korea and Taiwan as examples of developmental states that successfully subverted neoliberal dogma, saw China as challenging American dominance to make space for development policy alternatives. For him, the challenge of Ethiopia's development was primarily a political one: 'It is the politics of the state that unlocks development.'[67] After Meles' death, Ethiopia remained an example of an approach seeking to harness and adapt aspects of different external models for domestic purposes. After gaining power in 2018, Prime Minister Abiy Ahmed endeavoured to decrease Ethiopia's dependence on China by courting Western investment and support, including from the IMF. From November 2020, the Ethiopian government's war (with Eritrean support) against the Tigray region served as a reminder of the role of violence in politics, and at a time of increasing civilian suffering, displacement and death, Ethiopia's former foreign minister and ambassador to China, Seyoum Mesfin, was amongst those killed.

Prior to questions about the import of the China model, the sheer practical challenges can be neglected, including those that inhere to the attempted transfer of any external model in any given African institutional set up. Importing processes are shaped by understanding and need, often a historical basis of 'China has lessons for Africa' approaches.

For many African states, the surface attraction of the China model fades when scrutinized; it is not a coherent and transferable set of policy prescriptions. Underlying the actual political relations falling under the China model are a variety of power relations between and among political elites. Political relationships embedded in China connections offer a range of direct and less direct benefits, including measures that can bolster patronage. In December 2019, for example, Nigeria's President Muhammadu Buhari ceremonially inaugurated construction of a new university in his hometown, Daura, Katsina State. Funded by the China Civil Engineering Construction Corporation, this is intended to train Nigerian railway engineers in operating an expanding network of Chinese-built rail lines in Nigeria, following a 2018 agreement between the company and Nigeria's Transport Minister to provide two new universities in Nigeria.

Actual 'importing' processes can also take the form of selective assistance, such as the technological transfer of new capabilities, facilitated by political connections but carried out by Chinese companies. In Uganda, such a linkage of preferred modes of order, resources and transfer of technical knowhow is undoubtedly assisted by common affinity between the government and China, seen in 2017 for example, when the China National Electronics Import and Export Corporation agreed to help Uganda's Communications Commission, Ministry of Internal Affairs and police combat 'cybercrime'. This does not necessarily show the success of the China model so much as further evidence of the diversified strategy of attracting resources for regime maintenance and economic opportunity.

The China model is about much more than narrow economic development; the relations it rests on can have developmental uses but, potentially, friendship with China offers a range of other benefits. The China model provides a point of reference and menu of choice for African states and ruling parties. This is seen in the ways in which internet shutdowns in Africa, following China's example during violence in the capital of Xinjiang in July 2009, have gone from being regarded as extreme and rare, to being a more established and frequently used part of politics. In 2019, for example, there were at least 25 incidents of internet shutdowns in 14 African countries, including Algeria (6 cases), Ethiopia (4), Sudan (3), Benin (2) as well as Cameroon, Zimbabwe, Liberia, Mauritania, Gabon, Eritrea, Chad, Egypt, DRC and Malawi.[68] This is also seen in interest in China's influence on cybersecurity laws in Tanzania and Zimbabwe, and as a role model for regulating social media, as in Nigeria, where the President's wife Aisha Buhari infamously explained her support for a 'Social Media Bill' by saying, 'If China can control over 1.3 billion people on social media, I see no reason why Nigeria cannot attempt controlling only 180 million people.[69] It is also seen in the enabling technology for surveillance that Chinese companies like ZTE, Hikvision or CloudWalk Technology can provide, the latter signing a deal in 2018 with Zimbabwe to provide facial recognition software. The 2020 COVID-19 pandemic stimulated new opportunities for exporting surveillance technologies for, in the first instance, disease monitoring. Beijing's model of internet control based on cyber sovereignty is attractive, including the ability to switch off the internet as an ever more important government tactic by some African governments.[70] In other words, demand by African governments for such assistance is crucial, and means other non-Chinese companies are involved, but the results reflect the specific political circumstances of the African state involved.[71]

Model problems: The primacy of African politics
The China model, as promoted in idealized form, downplays or overlooks entirely the costs within China. These include the environmental impacts of resource-intensive and more recent consumption-fuelled growth (China has 60 of the world's 100 most polluted cities, for instance). In addition, a common misconception is that China's remarkable economic development and poverty reduction record since 1978 happened because of its one-party system. It was not 'one-party dominance per se that has magically brought development to China' but instead such factors as 'pragmatic foreign learning, evidence-based policy, determinedly pursuing growth, human capital development and reasonable meritocracy'.[72] What these, and other issues, mean is that at the same time as Xi Jinping's China promotes its model to Africa and the world, there are mounting questions about its actual efficacy and deeper political implications within China. The CCP's mismanagement of the outbreak of COVID-19 initially triggered strong criticism of the authoritarian political system within China, and even calls for Xi Jinping to step down. The CCP moved

rapidly to silence critics, re-establish control and promote claims about the superiority of its response compared to Western countries.

The politics of the China model – and China more generally – in democratic African states is often first and foremost about their domestic politics. China is attractive to such states for the benefits it can bring, such as infrastructure, which can be used for domestic electoral purposes. At a more basic level of politics than any necessarily direct or indirect China model connection, China's prominence, financial capability and ability to mobilize money and infrastructure construction contractors rapidly mean it inevitably gets caught up in electoral politics and the competing strategies of politicians promising dividends if elected or re-elected. In Senegal, for example, where Xi Jinping visited in July 2018, incumbent President Macky Sall lauded major infrastructure projects during elections in 2019 as part of his 'Emerging Senegal' plan. China is invoked in positive terms by such political leaders, who harness it as a provider of external resources in order to pursue their domestic political goals.

When it comes to more controversial dynamics, it is not necessarily 'China' per se, or only China, that can become the object of political contestation within African states, democratic or otherwise. Although China is involved, and can be heavily criticized, it is not necessarily the main target in domestic politics. The politicization of China, in some African countries more than others, involves African elites but also partly derives from political pluralism and the strength of civil society.

Kenya is one example. During the construction of Kenya's Chinese-funded and built SGR, there were widespread grievances about different aspects of the project, from land confiscation and poor compensation, to lack of employment opportunities for Kenyans and corruption arising from an expensive project caught up in clientalistic politics. One political dynamic ensuring that the SGR was a controversial project was the mobilization of political grievances against President Uhuru Kenyatta's government. During Kenya's 2017 presidential election, the SGR was criticized by opposition politicians but praised by the government, who used the railway as proof of its ability to deliver.[73] In addition, the Jubilee Party invited Chinese officials to election events and sourced branded T-shirts from a factory in China. The politics of the SGR continued after the election, with concerns about its economic viability, that the loan agreement for the railway threatened Kenya's sovereignty by reportedly containing the port of Mombasa as loan collateral, and indebtedness to China. In June 2020, a Court of Appeals verdict found that Kenya Railways' contract with the China Roads and Bridges Corporation, the SOE that built the railway, was illegal for failing to follow procurement laws. In this never-ending saga, the Kenyan musician, King Kaka (Kennedy Ombima) released a massively popular song Wajinga Nyinyi (You Fools) in December 2019 containing the line 'Karibu [welcome] to Kenya, the Republic of China.' Much more than any comment on Chinese neo-colonialism, in reality this song is a critique of Kenyan politicians and Kenyan voters for corruption, incompetent leadership, toxic tribal politics and other social ills.[74] From this perspective, the Jubilee Government's 'mortgaging' of Kenya to China is indicative above all of Kenyan political failure in which China is implicated but not primarily responsible for.

Zimbabwe offers insights into the deeper politics of relations with China, and the need to separate the China model from more important tensions between ostensible 'all weather' partners. Under its former long-time president Robert Mugabe, and facing external pressure and isolation, Zimbabwe's 2003 'Look East' policy effectively evolved into a narrower 'Look China' policy. Since then, and beyond shows of surface solidarity, relations have demonstrated tensions deriving from Zimbabwe's entrenched kleptocracy. When he became president in November 2017 following Mugabe's fall, Emmerson Mnangagwa proclaimed: 'Zimbabwe is open for business.' Many praised Mnangagwa as Zimbabwe's Deng Xiaoping: pragmatic, reform minded and able to succeed in a new era. Visiting China in April 2018, Mnangagwa and Xi Jinping declared 'a new chapter' in relations, despite underlying tensions emanating from Zimbabwe's imploding economy, debt and corrupt ruling party-state. One illustration of public discord came in December 2019 following a 2020 budget statement by Finance Minister Mthuli Ncube listing China's aid at $3.6m out of a total of $194m from bilateral donors. China's embassy in Harare issued a forthright public correction stating China's 'actual bilateral support provided to Zimbabwe' was $136.8m between January and September 2019. Pointedly noting that this excluded other forms of bilateral support, it called on the Zimbabwean government to 'accurately reflect its actual situation'.[75] No such clear figures were provided in 2020, however, when China's embassy and government faced questions about Zimbabwe's debt to China. Tensions were also created as a result of Mnangagwa's efforts to cultivate relations with other external powers, notably the US, where he attempted to get sanctions first imposed in 2003 (including on Mugabe and Mnangagwa) lifted.

The issue of China featured conspicuously in Zimbabwe's July 2018 elections. The manifesto of the opposition Movement for Democratic Change Alliance committed Zimbabwe to becoming a 'democratic developmental state', and its leader, Nelson Chamisa, criticized the ZANU–PF government for 'asset-stripping' through deals with China and other partners, promising to revisit the terms of such deals if elected to broaden benefits beyond elites. Media reporting over Chinese business ventures sparked further controversy. In September 2020, an article by journalist Tawanda Majoni suggested that the Chinese government had pressured Mnangagwa to allow the return of Anjin Investments Ltd, a joint venture between the Anhui Foreign Economic Construction (Group) Co., Ltd and a company formed by Zimbabwean military interests that had been expelled in 2016. This provoked a forceful rebuke by the Chinese embassy, deemed 'ominous' by the Zimbabwe Union of Journalists. Finally, Chinese investment in

Zimbabwe has been a leading subject for civil society activism. At a time of wide concern about unsustainable foreign investment, there was public outrage at news that two Chinese mining companies had been granted permission to begin coal exploration in the Hwange National Park, Zimbabwe's largest game reserve. This resulted in a September 2020 government ban on mining in national parks. The Zimbabwe Environmental Law Association sought clarity about what this meant, and also mounted legal action against the government concerning opaque foreign investment. One example was the controversial $3bn Sengwa coal power plant, an initiative led by Zimbabwean Rio Energy Limited working with the China Gezhouba Group Corporation and seeking Industrial and Commercial Bank of China funding.

Before Robert Mugabe was ousted from power in November 2017, the man who spearheaded this transition, army chief General Constantino Chiwenga, was visiting Beijing and seems to have informed his Chinese interlocutors of what would happen.[76] This generated much speculation about China's role in the power transfer. By 2020, speculation continued about China's role in the politics of Zimbabwean governing elite and possible preferences over its future under Emmerson Mnangagwa or his younger vice-president, the former army chief Constantino Chiwenga.[77] Much about the inner workings of ZANU–PF are unknown but it was clear that even if China sought direct influence, it would face pronounced limits to its ability to do so. The Chinese government instead seems to have pulled back from extending substantial support to a government unable to convince Beijing it can seriously manage its crisis.

Such examples illustrate a wider theme, the relative strength of China's relations with African governing elites and political parties in different democratic and non-democratic polities, in contrast to a much more mixed status among civil society and other social groups that demonstrate wide support for democracy, human rights and genuinely sustainable development. As the US under the Trump administration made clear, the external context of democracy promotion in Africa and the world has changed markedly in recent years. The abolition of term limits during the 2017 19th CCP Party Congress and strong evidence of Xi Jinping's desire to remain in power for a third term in 2022 served as one example to African politicians. President Trump's approach to elections in 2020 served as another. Cases of extending presidential term limits in Africa included Togo, where a constitutional change in 2019 allowed President Faure Gnassingbé, in power since 2005 (following his father's seizure of power in 1967), to run for president two more times and saw him re-elected in February 2020. However, within African states there has been growing pressure for democratic politics. Afrobarometer survey evidence, for example, demonstrates consistent support for presidential term limits. Furthermore, on average, 75% of 'Africans interviewed in 2016/18 said they prefer to use regular, open and honest elections to choose their country's leaders'.[78] In contrast to Togo, in February 2020, Malawi's High Court annulled the results of its May 2019 presidential election, following months of mass protests against electoral fraud. The election was rerun in June 2020 and saw the opposition candidate win a historic victory.

CONCLUSION

China's New Era African relations has seen a new phase in the politics of the China model. Beijing now presents its approach to economic development and political organization as the optimal choice for Africa. Xi Jinping's CCP has been promoting its China model in pursuit of its continental and global ambitions, through direct means and helped indirectly by other factors, notably the Trump administration's America First policy and perceptions of US decline used to lionize perpetual single-party CCP rule. As a report on an international forum, 'The Significance of China's Social Governance to the

World' in November 2019, put it: 'China can provide wisdom to a world that is in need of new governance models.'[79] In keeping with how the China model has evolved over time, the COVID-19 pandemic brought into closer focus how issues concerning the politics of models will develop in the future amid intensified global politics.

Despite resonances with past relations, Xi Jinping's New Era China model is qualitatively more ambitious and promoted by more sophisticated means. One aspect of efforts to promote the China model is not so much transplanting or emulating this in economic development terms, although assisting economic relations with China is a supporting goal, but strengthening deeper, informal and personalized ties behind formal political party cooperation. In this way, on China's side, it may be not the formal content of training in Xi Jinping Thought or CCP doctrine that matters most, so much as demonstration effects, socialization and enabling connections. The CCP's political party training program is geared towards creating a community of politicians sympathetic to and supportive of the CCP. How successful this will prove to be remains to be seen but its more focused, determined, systematic, future-oriented and continental scope far exceeds comparable efforts by other, Western powers. New Era China is better able to promote such goals, given its economic stature in a geopolitical period when a more powerful China's role in shaping future world order is real. This makes China a compelling subject of political interest. As the Secretary General of Kenya's ruling Jubilee Party, Raphael Tuju, argued in June 2020: 'The Chinese Communist Party is the biggest political party in the whole world. Its grassroots organization is second to none. Jubilee Party can only aspire, and where possible learn some lessons ... what is wrong with learning from the most successful and the best run?'[80] The largest political party in the world is actually India's ruling BJP, with some 180m members in August 2019, and some argue India can provide a compelling model in the next few decades.[81]

The China model is also far more complex than any simple narrative about a Made in China political model being exported to and inter-nalized within African countries allows. One reason is the diversity of other external 'models' and accompanying relationships. For all the Chinese government's intensified efforts under Xi Jinping to promote China's model, China remains second to America as African's preferred development model according to Afrobarometer's 2019/20 surveys of eighteen African countries: 32% identified the US as their preferred model, and 23% preferred China. These also found younger Africans are more likely to favour the US model (36% of those aged 18–25 vs 25% of those over 65), with regard for China's model consistent across age groups.[82]

The hope and hype surrounding Xi's China model risked overshad-owing another, more significant reason, the need for approaches tailored to, embedded within and owned by African contexts. The argument that African countries should identify, own and pursue their own development paths – more Deng, less Xi, in other words – is neither new nor original. As one former Chinese ambassador Shu Zhan said in 2010: 'China is willing to share experiences in development with the Africans, yet it seems to me that Africa's development should be based on its own conditions and to follow its own path, that is, the [sic] African Models.'[83] This view is widely shared. The time when 'the West has the answers and African countries can only ask how high they should jump' has ended but because 'China is not the saviour either', African countries should direct their own development.[84]

5 | Chinese–African Relations _____

During his first trip to Africa as President in March 2013, Xi Jinping visited a memorial outside Dar es Salaam to Chinese workers who died in Tanzania. Like Hu Jintao at the same spot four years previously, he paid 'tribute to the Chinese martyrs who sacrificed their lives for the great cause of China–Tanzania and China–Africa friendship' building the TAZARA railway. The walled memorial features long lines of gravestones inscribed with the names of those buried. It has an air of official remembrance but reveals much more. Humanizing different generations of deceased individual Chinese workers, flowers and other offerings by gravestones show private remembrance, mourning and continuing human connections over distance. The memorial also provides a point of contrast between a time of limited, controlled Chinese engagement directed according to state-aid priorities and more recent trends. During construction of the TAZARA railway, after being trained, Chinese workers went to Tanzania and Zambia, completed their work under close supervision and returned to China.[1] While some Chinese corporations continue to wield significant control over their workforces, the expansion of independent Chinese migration to African countries in recent decades has been a significant and conse-quential departure.

Migration is uniquely emotive, as seen in some reactions to Chinese traders in African marketplaces, the size of China's population compared to a host of far smaller African states, or speculation that Chinese migration is connected to the Chinese government's higher future intent in Africa.[2] For some, Chinese migration is part of a grand plan connected to empire building, by design or default.[3] Others argue that Chinese migration is independent and, rather than cohering into a grand strategic design, is 'typified by a multitude of both public and private actors with independent motives'.[4]

The aim of this chapter is to change focus away from relations between China and African states, official state-backed People-to-People exchanges and the conflation of China with Chinese by redirecting attention towards relations between people, including Africans in China and Chinese in African countries. It seeks, in particular, to examine the ways in which migration has given rise to forms of politics involving Chinese or China. There are precedents to the politicization of Chinese and China in African countries, as seen with the example of Zambia, but concomitant with China's wider rise and internet-enabled social media age in which grievances are amplified, this has become more prominent in the New Era. Everyday dynamics of Chinese in African countries – and Africans in China – illustrate a complex diversity that simple narratives struggle to convey.

This chapter argues that the realities of Chinese migration are more complicated than Chinese government narratives of South–South cooperation or media-fuelled narratives about empire building.[5] Chinese migrants are 'not simply state agents' but 'have individual motivations, expectations and concerns, which are sometimes at odds with the state'.[6] At the same time, the presence and impact of African states and the CCP-state often affects migrant communities and has contributed to more prominent politics of Chinese migrants in which ideas about China and its relations with Africa can be and are mobilized in political ways. What follows is organized into three overlapping sections. The first concerns transnational trading networks involving African traders based in or moving between parts of China and Africa, and Chinese migrants in African countries. The second considers the ways in which the politics of Chinese – and China – have become more prominent in various African countries and how this can be affected by relations between China and African states. The third considers what this might mean going forward, and the chapter concludes by arguing that migration and the security of overseas Chinese has become much more significant for China's foreign policy.

MOBILITY AND MIGRATION

This section examines the theme of mobility in terms of Africans in China and Chinese in African countries, in the context of what have been dynamic transnational links often passing under the radar of formal coverage. Increasing Chinese exports to African countries from around 2000 was paralleled by growing numbers of African traders visiting China and Chinese migration to African countries, which contributed to enhanced informal trading networks.

Africans in China

Unprecedented numbers of Africans were visiting China in the first part of the twenty-first century until the 2020 COVID-19 pandemic halted mobility.[7] An important aspect of this involved African traders who were drawn to commercial hubs like Shenzhen or Yiwu by the easy, cheap supply of manufactured products and the business opportunities these offered. Many chose to migrate to China to operate trading businesses in Guangzhou, the capital of Guangdong Province and hub of the Pearl River Delta industrial heartland. Guangzhou has been called 'the central metropolis in the world where the goods of low-end globalization are bought and sold'.[8] Different to the globalization of large multinational corporations, low-end globalization involves mobile transnational traders moving between parts of China and African countries. It revolves around reputation and interpersonal trust, rather than legal contracts. Flexible low-end manufacturing enabled quick transitions from new product design to production and distribution in end markets in Africa.[9] Traders in Guangzhou moved goods to Africa via full containers, groupage, air cargo, formal courier services, or informal carrying of goods on planes as luggage and 'hand carry' services. Such trade is a small proportion of overall China–Africa trade but it has exercised disproportionate significance due to the political tensions it can generate. This is seen in persistent claims that 'China' is 'flooding Africa' with cheap products, a popular but misconceived idea because many Chinese-manufactured products get shipped to African countries through informal trade networks operated by African and Chinese traders. African traders are by no means the only ones active in such trade but are often overlooked.[10] In Mali's trade with China, for example, Malian importers were more successful in selling Chinese green tea than their Chinese counterparts due to their wider economic networks and knowledge of local tea.[11]

The African presence in China involves much more than just traders in Guangzhou but is multidimensional and more widely spread.[12] This presence is a small part of a small international migrant population (0.1% in 2019, according to the UN Population Division). Accurate statistics on the size of the African presence are not available, estimates varying from 20,000 to 130,000 African immigrants registered in Guangzhou in 2008. Nigerians constituted the most numerous group of African migrants in Guangzhou, forming three main categories: travellers on short business trips; people residing in China legally; and migrants staying in China without valid visas or residence permits.[13] The African community in Guangzhou has become organized with consulates, business associations and even underground churches.[14] There are also African communities in other parts of China, notably the business centre of Yiwu, Zhejiang Province, featuring more diverse occupations and business engagements.[15] As seen, while not new, the numbers of African students undertaking educational migration has been surging compared to the past.[16] This means that Africans in

China have involved a much more diverse business presence than just traders.[17]

Chinese migration to African countries

The Chinese presence in Africa reflects different layers of historical interactions and the influence of China's changing domestic economic and social context.[18] In the twentieth century, Chinese emigrants largely came from coastal regions like Zhejiang, Fujian or Guangdong. More recently, sending provinces have become more diverse.[19] Other divisions are based on class, occupation and geographical provenance. Perceptions of homogeneity can be generated by concentrations of Chinese businesses in African cities, but stereotypes like 'the Chinese stick together' are at odds with dispersed settlement patterns propelled by the pursuit of niche markets. Migrants make their own way to African countries or through informal chain migration.

No one knows how many Chinese there are in individual African countries or the continent. Nor is it possible to find out: many African countries are unable to compile accurate migration statistics, and Chinese embassies often seem to lack numbers. According to the Annual Report on Overseas Chinese Study, Africa was home to more than 1.1m Chinese immigrants in 2012.[20] In 2016, there were an estimated 1m Chinese across 54 African countries (meaning Chinese in Africa accounted for under 3% of Chinese outside China and under 0.1% of Africa's population). Of these, one third were affiliated to Chinese construction companies, independent migrants account for at least half, and the remainder are other professionals including diplomats, doctors and students.[21]

There are many categories of Chinese in Africa, from those in state employment, like diplomats, to professionals working on development schemes, contracted workers employed by SOEs on state-sponsored infrastructure projects and migrants. According to official Chinese sources, for example, there were 182,745 Chinese contract workers in Africa by the end of 2019, with Algeria, Angola, Nigeria, Zambia and Kenya accounting for 50% of all Chinese workers in the continent at the end of 2019 (Algeria alone accounting for 25%). In 2015, the number of Chinese workers in Africa peaked at 263,659.[22] The politics of Chinese companies' employment practices has been a major issue, with widespread perceptions of limited or non-existent opportunities for local African employment. Evidence from Ethiopia and Angola suggests that the employment of national workers by Chinese companies is substantially higher than assumed.[23] Outside of official employment, however, many more Chinese in countries across Africa are migrants operating family businesses in trade, small-scale manufacturing, farming or the service sector. Roughly between half and two-thirds of Chinese in Africa are migrants associated with small and medium businesses as owners, employees or family dependants. Private entrepreneurs engage in a highly diverse range of activities from health care, medicine, petty or wholesale trade, service sectors (such as restaurants, hotels, brothels), agriculture, small factories, mining or logging.

Chinese migration to Africa is driven by various factors that influence how numbers and patterns fluctuate, mostly in tandem with underlying economic conditions. Africa had been seen as an opportunity frontier where money could be made. In 2016, in the context of lower commodity prices and the slowest economic growth in two decades, however, the numbers of Chinese in many African countries declined. Between 2013 and 2017, for instance, an estimated 150,000 Chinese returned to China from Angola.[24] At the same time, countries like Ethiopia and Kenya saw rising numbers of Chinese immigrants. Chinese mobility to Africa is partly a barometer of socioeconomic shifts in China, even if this is only one aspect of the choices migrants make about which particular African countries to go to. In China, the migration frontier had been shifting from rural–urban to overseas migration. Overseas migration motivated by individual aspiration was an important path for upward social mobility for a generation of mainly male migrants, many of whom were former rural–urban migrants within China, who went to Ethiopia, for example, to earn a higher salary in order to craft a better life in China. The 'bitter reality' for many, however, was that the middle-class lifestyle gained through overseas employment could only be sustained by working abroad.[25] More recently, rising wages in China has meant the incentive for low-skilled workers to migrate to Africa has decreased. The BRI and new emphasis on industrial cooperation seemed to entail a shift from traders or contract labourers towards more business forms of migration.

Mobility was helped by more liberal African country visa regimes and improved transport connections. Visa changes boosted Chinese tourism before the disruption of the COVID-19 pandemic in 2020.[26] Such changes were also intended to assist business connections. In 2018, for example, South Africa announced it would grant Chinese business travellers a ten-year multiple-entry 'BRICS visa' without a requirement to apply in person (it did not relax restrictions to other African nationals). Other countries, including Angola, Botswana, Ethiopia, Rwanda and Zimbabwe, revised visa requirements to make it easier for Chinese nationals to travel. In 2019, around 28 African countries, from Morocco, Egypt, Tunisia to Equatorial Guinea, did not require visas or allowed visas on arrival for Chinese nationals. On top of such changes, travel has been aided by direct flights connecting Guangzhou and an increasing number of African airports. Prior to the disruptions of 2020, it was becoming much easier to travel between China and African countries, with air traffic increasing by over 600% between 2009 and 2019 for example.[27] This enhanced the circulation of people and goods.

Chinese migration is notable for its involvement in the informal sector across Africa. This involves everyday cooperation between Chinese entrepreneurs, African traders and businesses but can also produce grievances due to competition. A substantial part of cross-border trade in Africa is informal; informal trade accounted for the major part of trade in domestic products between Benin and Nigeria, for instance. Official statistics underestimate total trade by around 50% for imports and 85% for exports.[28] The intersection between Chinese migration and informal economies in many African countries can generate grievances, and grievances can have political effects. The presence of Chinese traders in street markets, for instance, can give rise to opposition, and such micro-encounters can, as in Nairobi's markets, escalate to become part of the national debate.[29] In April 2017 hundreds of Ugandans in Kampala protested about unfair competition from Chinese traders and called on them to leave. By contrast, Ethiopia's tougher approach to regulating retail and wholesale business by foreign nationals has meant such concerns have not been as present.

Box 2. Gold Mining in Ghana

The common idea that 'China' is doing something 'to Africa' simplifies and distorts myriad forms of Chinese and African collaboration, including the example of small-scale gold mining in Ghana. The Chinese engagement in Ghana is diverse, ranging from oil and gas to big projects like the Bui Dam. In 2019, Ghana established a consulate in Guangzhou, an indication of Ghanaian engagement in southern China.[30] The Chinese role in Ghana's mining sector is not limited to small-scale artisanal mining; since 2008, for example, the Chinese-owned Shaanxi Mining Company (Ghana Ltd) has operated in the mineral-rich northern district of Talensi and generated controversy over employment practices, mining accidents or expansion plans. Among other things, these have caused divisions between the paramount chief and traditional landowners in the areas affected. In another case, Ghanaian NGOs including A Rocha and Concerned Citizens of the Atewa Landscape filed a High Court complaint in July 2020 claiming that bauxite mining in Atewa, a globally significant biodiversity area in southeastern Ghana, infringed constitutional rights. The bauxite mining is intended to support a $2bn deal through which the Sinohydro Corporation will build infrastructure projects in Ghana.

Following a global gold price spike, between 2008 and 2013 approximately 50,000 Chinese migrants entered into Ghana's informal small-scale gold-mining sector. This became a major issue, illustrating the role and multifaceted impacts of Chinese migrants in this informal sector. The Chinese migrants working in Ghana's gold-mining sector mainly came from Shanglin County in Guangxi Province, and were 'marginal people travelling from one periphery to another in search of resources to make a livelihood, and hopefully strike it rich'.[31] In Ghana, they formed mutually beneficial relationships with local miners, both legal and illegal, and introduced machinery that substantially increased gold production. By law, small-scale mining is confined to registered Ghanaian citizens, meaning unregistered illicit Ghanaian and foreign miners are illegal, or 'galamsey'.

One study found that irregular migration into Ghana's informal gold-mining sector had long-lasting impacts. The economic significance of small-scale gold production increased, but such mining meant a loss of tax revenue for the state and played a significant role in the transformation of economic, political and physical landscapes. Arising from the mechanization of small-scale alluvial mining mainly due to new technologies introduced by Chinese miners, which were adopted by Ghanaian miners, the consequences have been 'significant and transformative' and have 'irreversibly changed the traditional way that alluvial mining was undertaken' in Ghana.[32] Such intensified mining has caused wide environmental destruction of land and waterbodies.

Where was Ghana's state during this gold rush? It was not absent. 'Foreign miners operated with impunity precisely because they were protected by those in authority, that is, public officials, politicians and chiefs, in return for private payments.'[33] Such mining thus cannot be reduced to Chinese vs Ghanaians. It has involved collaboration and collusion between Chinese miners, and local political and economic actors, such as in Awaso, Western Region.[34] The government was slow to respond. In 2013, media pressure pushed President John Mahama (2012–17) to establish a military taskforce against illegal mining. This resulted in the arrest and deportation of over 4,500 Chinese nationals and others from Togo, Niger and Russia. The number of Chinese miners in Ghana fell. Rather than ending, however, Chinese small-scale mining became more concealed. Another crackdown followed in 2017 together with a controversial ban by President Akufo-Addo's government on all small-scale mining.

The political impacts are also highly significant. As campaigning during Ghana's general election of December 2020 showed, the issue of what to do about galamsey in general and China's role in particular remains highly controversial. The role of Chinese miners has been a longstanding national political issue, even though miners from many other parts of the world are also involved. In 2020, as presidential candidate for the National Democratic Congress party, John Mahama attacked the incumbent President Akufo-Addo and his New Patriotic Party for allowing Chinese miners to operate in the small-scale mining sector. Mahama criticized the government for imprisoning 'our youth' but allowing 'a Chinese national and galamsey queen', Aisha Huang, to go free and return to China. He promised an amnesty to those convicted of galamsey if elected. The National Concerned Small-Scale Miners' Association of Ghana endorsed Mahama's campaign: 'Today, the so-called community mining is being operated by foreigners, especially the Chinese, under the endorsement of the current administration, while locals wallow in poverty in the various mining districts.'[35]

Rather than 'China' doing something 'to Ghana', the politics of such mining illustrates many fine-grained and wider themes in the political economy of resource extraction in Ghana. This despite a certain binary blame game conducted in public. Many in Ghana blame Chinese or use the issue as proxy in the pursuit of political gain. Chinese diplomatic officials in Accra, by contrast, have argued that 'Chinese illegal miners could not have come all the way from China to Ghana without the facilitation, support and shelter from local people, so Ghana is the root cause of the problem.'[36] Finally, the issue raises the question of what the official principles of China–Africa cooperation espoused by states, like 'win–win' or 'mutual benefit', mean in deeper socio-economic context beyond central state elites. Ghana exemplifies such trends but is not alone as small-scale mining in the DRC, Zimbabwe or Zambia, among others, also show in different ways.

CHINESE AND CHINA IN AFRICAN POLITICS

Chinese communities in African countries have in general become more established and organized over time. Chinese communities are often thought to self-segregate, but this is not always the case in practice.[37] The genesis and growth of Chinese associations in African countries was often propelled by adversity and crisis.[38] South Africa illustrates the growth of a more organized, active Chinese community. It is notable for historical reasons and because the Chinese population there accounts for as much as half of the total Chinese population in Africa in a country known as a 'gateway' for southern Africa and beyond. Despite the most recent wave of mainland Chinese immigrants becoming more established, together with a Chinese South African community bearing a long historical lineage, the Chinese community exists 'behind a curtain of incomprehension, largely unknown to other South Africans due to the nearly ubiquitous language barrier'.[39] The growth over the past two decades of Chinese associations in South Africa has contributed to more diverse, extensive and organized Chinese communities, characterized over time by different layers of organization and identity.

The spread of a social media era in African countries has meant an intensified, more immediate and compelling menu of instantly accessible gossip, conspiracy theories, memes, rumours or click-bait. An indirect result of the spread of smartphones and internet availability, in which Chinese companies are playing a leading role, has been to enhance the speed and circulation of rumours about China and Chinese immigrants.[40] Rumours about Chinese manufacturers producing substandard quality goods specifically for the African market, deliberately downgrading them in comparison with the same products produced for European or American markets, can exacerbate negative sentiments among local populations. The impact of social media should not be exaggerated but has amplified stories of Chinese misconduct and fed into the politics of what such incidents can be used for. In Kenya, for example, numerous publicized incidents have contributed to a popular backlash against Chinese, and China. Alongside bigger, more abstract questions like debt, personalized encounters resonate strongly, such as the arrest of a Chinese businessman in September

2019, after a video surfaced online of him calling 'every Kenyan ... like a monkey, even Uhuru Kenyatta. All of them'.[41]

Crime is a recurring challenge for Chinese communities in many African countries (although statistics are lacking) and responses to crime and everyday insecurity have varied. The Chinese government has mounted initiatives geared towards strengthening security cooperation, which extend to policing assistance. In June 2016, for example, a Chinese Committee of Joint Defence for Public Security in Angola was established to enhance protection for Chinese nationals. Attempts to incorporate Chinese nationals into Zambia's police force in 2017, and improve links with the Chinese community, were abandoned after public controversy and a social media backlash. In South Africa, high-profile crimes against Chinese prompted the Chinese Consulate-General to advocate a policy of keeping a low profile for Chinese people and tourists in South Africa.[42] The South African Chinese Community and Police Cooperation Centre, founded in 2004 on the initiative of two Chinese businessmen with the support of China's Embassy to deal with crime within the Chinese community as well as in wider South African society, plays a prominent role in responding to crime. With twelve offices throughout South Africa and one in Lesotho, it provides security, emergency response and other communal tasks.

The Chinese are not just victims but can be perpetrators of crime, seen in a range of criminal activity from kidnapping, robbery, to the ivory trade in Tanzania and East Africa, which illuminates the role of Chinese transnational organized crime in the illegal wildlife trade.[43] An investigation in Mozambique found a Chinese-led criminal syndicate trafficking ivory from Africa to Shuidong, its base in southern China.[44] This operated a sophisticated global operation, from local employment in Africa to using corruption and complex trade routes with numerous transit ports like Mombasa (Kenya), Singapore, Busan (Republic of Korea), and Hai Phong (Vietnam) to ship products from Africa to China.[45] With the profitability of East African tusks falling, the Shuidong syndicate moved to more lucrative forest elephant ivory and pangolin scales. Such a displacement effect was also seen when enhanced law enforcement efforts at Tanzanian ports resulted in ivory being shipped out of Pemba, Mozambique, and the emergence of Nigeria as 'a key source/transit country' for many ivory, rhino horn, pangolin and rosewood shipments.[46] The illegal ivory trade is one, albeit particularly important part of broader trade in illegal wildlife products. The conduct of Chinese in the ivory trade is unfortunately visible in other wildlife sectors. For example, in Ghana a pretence of legality overlays de facto Chinese ownership and running of 95% of the licensed fishing vessels.[47]

The role of some Chinese in African countries in illicit activities generates local blowback as well as regulatory challenges for the Chinese and African governments, seen in the example of donkey hides. Responses have included the targeting of Chinese gangs by local law enforcement sometimes cooperating with Chinese police. Since 2015, China has publicly committed to ending the ivory trade and in 2019, the China Customs Anti-Smuggling Bureau made convictions related to the Shuidong ivory smuggling. Less well known than ivory has been the impact of rising demand for *ejiao*, gelatin obtained from donkey hides and used in traditional Chinese medicine. The steep decline of China's donkey population meant *ejiao* producers sought to source elsewhere, including African countries. In Kenya, growing demand produced a sharp reduction in the donkey population (as much as half in the past ten years), and four licensed abattoirs created to meet demand were closed in 2020. High demand and declining donkey numbers have meant higher prices, theft and thriving cross border trade. In 2019, six African governments banned donkey skin exports in response.

The politicization of China and Chinese in domestic African politics has become a more visible trend. As the example of Zambia showed, this pre-dated Xi Jinping's leadership but has evolved significantly since 2012. As President of Zambia from 2011–14, Michael Sata toned down his anti-China rhetoric, but his example became widely known and joined by others. It illustrated a trend in which criticism of or campaigns against China can be partly genuine but also rooted in domestic political factors, and can mean Chinese are targeted. As such, these become hybrid grievances in which China can be readily invoked as a high-profile justification for political mobilization, which has greater actual or potential political impact now that China is a major power. In this way, the issue of China, Chinese workers and migrant entrepreneurs can channel discontent, for example, with 'land, Jobs [sic], debt, corruption, immigration and rule of law' and complaints about the 'slow colonization of Zambia'.[48] In September 2018, China was accused of using loans to create openings in government-run bodies, such as the national electricity supplier Zesco and the state broadcaster. These claims were exaggerated but did reflect the terms of build-operate-transfer models that involve Chinese management for several years.[49] Zambian government denials didn't stop protesters taking to the streets of Lusaka in September 2018. In November 2018, there were xenophobic protests in the Copperbelt town of Kitwe after a rumour circulated that the government had sold the Zambia Forestry and Forest Industries Corporation to a Chinese company to service its debt. Opposition leader Haikande Hichilema of the United Party for National Development was detained after being accused of making anti-China statements, and inciting the Kitwe protests.[50] Online campaigns like '#saynotoChina' channelled criticism of Zambia's ruling government.

Many Chinese in African countries are necessarily attuned to politics and political cycles, as these can mobilize anti-Chinese sentiment and action. During Gabon's 2016 presidential elections, for instance, politics was seen to produce security problems; one Chinese resident in the capital, Libreville, noted, for example, that 'Police are robbers and the military gendarmes are arrogant predators.'[51] Violence flared after President Ali Bongo Ondimba was narrowly re-elected. In 2015, political demonstrations in Kinshasa, DRC against a proposed change in the electoral law to allow President Joseph Kabila to remain in office after 2016 saw attacks on many Chinese-owned shops in Ngaba and Kalamu neighbourhoods.[52] Although specific grievances were aired against Chinese business, one motivation appears to have been President Kabila's close relations with China and such violence was part of a broader pattern; some protesters burned and looted police stations, one courthouse, surveillance cameras and 'buildings associated with majority party officials, and other places seen as being close to or representative of Kabila and his government.'[53]

In South Africa, there have been three main responses to rising anti-Chinese sentiment. Some Chinese South Africans and Chinese nationals have left the country, a phenomenon linked to the state of South Africa's economy but also the high rate of crimes against Chinese.[54] Some choose to continue in South Africa. A third response is to 'fight back via legal channels and a media campaign.'[55] In December 2019 South Africa saw a seminal legal case brought by The Chinese Association in the Equality Court against anti-Chinese social media 'genocidal hate speech', in which four people admitted guilt. In a context of xenophobia against foreigners, the case arose after a viral video showed donkeys being slaughtered, allegedly for their skins to be exported to China. The 'social media mob' that followed featured what The Chinese Association's chairman Erwin Pon termed 'a barrage of hateful, hurtful insults' and racial slurs.[56]

CHANGING STATE RELATIONS

Although Chinese migrants in African countries are not agents despatched by the Chinese state, and have their own agendas, private migration remains unavoidably 'entangled with Chinese state policies and processes' and ties with African states.[57] One idea that captures this is the existence of an 'overseas Chinese state' among migrant communities in Africa, which refers to local institutions of the Chinese state in African countries, like embassies, aid missions or SOEs.[58] The Chinese government has been actively engaging overseas Chinese for over three decades but in recent years its political outreach has been growing and links with Chinese associations in African countries increasing. The CCP's New Era has exposed Chinese migrants in African countries to more political winds that reach further and can impact more, due to the internet.

China's New Era nationalism has been evolving in the context of the CCP's rejuvenation narrative and project. State visits by Xi Jinping to African capital cities provide opportunities not just to showcase relations but also to unify Chinese communities around his CCP New Era flag. Under Xi Jinping, such nationalist ripple effects are to be expected, since these are connected to how China has become more powerful, and perceived as such around the world. The context has changed by virtue of China's economic development and global role under Xi Jinping, but both the Chinese state and CCP has a deeper history of seeking to invoke and mobilize Chinese identity in order to bolster their legitimacy.[59] Nor should this upstage the different, sometimes contested understandings of 'Chineseness' and the ways in which 'Chinese and African actors possess agency to reimagine meanings of "Chineseness" that exist alongside the Chinese government's construction of Chinese national identity.'[60]

In the context of China's ascendancy as a great power, one recent trend has been for 'Chinese new migrants to internalize the "national interests" of the remote motherland.'[61] Migration can make some migrants more susceptible to the discourses of Chinese cultural, ethnic and state nationalism.[62] Many Chinese communities seek to support and show support for causes closer to China, like demonstrating in favour of the One-China principle. The China Council for the

Promotion of National Reunification, for example, a branch of the CCP's United Front Work Department, has chapters in around 27 African countries, including five in South Africa, and has mobilized to support Beijing's One China principle. In January 2017, for example, the independent South African Chinese news agency and newspaper *African Times* published a notice by the All-Africa Association for Peaceful Reunification of China, strongly condemning the business trip by Solly Msimanga, an opposition Democratic Alliance party member and Tshwane mayor, to Taiwan in December 2016. And 106 Chinese organizations in South Africa published a joint letter to leaders of the Democratic Alliance requesting an apology for Msimanga's visit.[63]

The case of Zambia also illustrates how the mostly urban associational life of new Chinese migrants can be 'highly politicized and connected to the bigger picture of China–Africa relations' to the extent that 'many contemporary Chinese associations serve as a vital extension of Beijing's diplomacy in Africa'.[64] One study found that contemporary Chinese associations in Zambia, mostly founded after 2014, serve as bridges 'connecting individual Chinese, the Chinese embassy, and local society' and are 'active actors' in relations with China, categorizing these into three types: Chinese associations founded by new migrants, including civic and self-governing groups; semi-official commercial groups (like the Association of Chinese Corporations) subject to Chinese embassy supervision; and more politicized groups, such as those that focus on other semi-official issues (women, Taiwan, or cultural promotion), and act 'as the extended arm of the Chinese state apparatus'.[65] In Zambia, a 'pyramid of power' exists within Chinese associations from the Chinese embassy at the top, to associations and individual Chinese and companies; some associations 'may even take orders directly from homeland governments (provincial or municipal) and promote subnational and party policies within the Chinese community in Zambia'.[66] The participation of these different types of Chinese associations in local Zambian and Chinese politics means these are 'potential players in the China–Africa arena, as inter-mediaries, defenders of China's image, or implementers of China's foreign policy'.[67] Zambia is a particular case but shares similarities with other, contrasting examples, such as Nigeria, in terms of the limits on the Chinese embassy's ability to manage demanding consular protection work. The limits of official protection in Zambia mean necessary self-help by well-connected Chinese associations, including those which function to respond to security challenges.

That such examples can't be generalized is demonstrated well through 'the indifferent Chinese state' in Nigeria.[68] Small-scale Chinese entrepreneurs fall under the regime of both Nigeria, as the host country, and China as their country of origin. Chinese migrants face the actual and potential unwillingness or inability of China's embassy or consulate to assist them, such as by helping to protect against extortion by Nigerian officials. This can mean that 'small-scale Chinese entrepreneurs are likely to be ignored by the Chinese state', despite depending on good relations between Nigeria and China for their businesses to continue.[69] As a result, the consulate is not 'received favourably by small-scale Chinese entrepreneurs and does nothing about their vulnerable situation'.[70]

Nigeria also illustrates the impact of changing inter-state relations on Africans in China and Chinese in Africa. Variations in state relations can 'give rise to a chain reaction' of what appear to be tit-for-tat actions; Chinese policy towards Africans in China has been linked, for example, to 'Nigerian policy towards Chinese in Nigeria'.[71] Previous campaigns against illegal foreign migrants in China had repercussions in Nigeria: a 100-day crackdown was launched on 15 May 2012 in Beijing after which, in a move widely seen as retaliation, Nigerian immigration arrested nearly 100 Chinese immigrants in Kano and Lagos. Both states tightened visa regulations. Nigeria played a leading role in responses to the April 2020 'Guangzhou incident', continuing a pattern seen in previous tensions involving mutual backlash. Abuja saw protests in September 2019, for example, after a Nigerian pastor was allegedly killed in a police visa raid in Guangdong. The Nigeria–China Diaspora Group called on Nigeria's federal government to ensure 'China stop maltreating and killing Nigerians in China' and demanded that the Chinese government 'accord Nigerians the same freedom Chinese enjoy in Nigeria'.[72] In the aftermath of what happened in April 2020 in Guangzhou, Chinese migrant businesses came under the scrutiny of the Nigerian authorities and other events not directly connected, like the arrest of two Chinese men alleged to have attempted to bribe a member of Nigeria's anti-corruption agency, seemed to chime with citizen support.

UNCERTAIN FUTURES

Three contrasting themes stand out as windows onto general trends going forward for Africans in China and Chinese in African countries. The first concerns changing circumstances of Africans in China after 2020, which reached a visible turning point when many of the issues that had been present under the surface came to a head. In 2020, the COVID-19 pandemic saw a rapid halt to the dynamic circulation of people and products between African countries and Guangzhou, Yiwu and other places in China. However, the boom had been slowing for a number of years before the pandemic, meaning that 2020 may have been a visible turning point but many of these issues had been in motion for some time. To begin with, in the context of greater competition and the rising costs of made-in-China goods, before 2020 some Africans had already been leaving Guangzhou and moving to Vietnam, Laos, Cambodia or Sri Lanka, for example. Second, visa regulations had been tightened at various points before 2020. In 2014, trying to assuage fears of a potential spread of Ebola, Guangzhou's government reported that some 16,000 Africans were legally residing in the city.[73] In May 2020, local authorities reported that the whole legally resident African population, some 4,500 individuals, had been tested, suggesting a sharp decline over six years. Trading connections continued but, disrupted by the COVID-19 pandemic, faced new, more uncertain circumstances. Some argued that the prospect of a new, more restrictive post-pandemic regime within China meant that 'migration between Africa and China may never be the same'.[74]

The second theme concerns the indeterminate, in-between and contingent status of many Chinese migrants in Africa. This can be seen in Ghana, for instance, where Chinese communities remain in a state of flux and 'Chinese migrants experience an in-betweenness and struggle with notions of belonging'.[75] Chinese migrants in other countries like Kenya grapple with the challenges of localization (*bentu hua*). Some parts of the Chinese presence remain in an indeterminate state. 'Many Chinese in Africa are convinced they are adapting to host societies, but have not integrated into them'.[76] Many Chinese migrants do not seek to become permanent settlers or citizens of their host African countries; their presence is both indefinite and contingent upon a range of personal, socio-economic, and political factors. One result can be continuing mobility characterized by diverse patterns of movement, with some Chinese leaving Africa to go elsewhere, or leaving one African country for another while sending their children to school in Europe or the US.[77]

Box 3. Chinese in Namibia: Becoming a Single Social Field?

To date, China's influence in African countries has been regarded as external and Chinese and Africans (of various kinds) seen as separate groups. Beyond the headlines about backlash are signs suggestive of underlying changes in some African countries, involving ongoing processes of long-term change pointing towards new social formations.

A revealing example is Namibia.[78] With a small population of around 2.5m, and income inequality among the highest in the world, Namibia depended for decades on resource extraction creating political rents for ruling elites. This meant that over the past two decades, the Chinese presence fed into, but did not create prevailing conditions. In Namibia, the commodities boom of the early 2000s, largely caused by China's market entry and its economic growth, led to the creation of new mines at a pace unprecedented since early colonial times. This generated income and created political rents, producing plentiful opportunities for politically connected middlemen and women. It spilled over into other sectors: construction, in which Chinese companies play an important role, or imported manufactured goods often produced in China. The interlinkages between Namibian elites and Chinese investors that resulted contributed towards increased inequality in Namibia, while embedding Chinese investors into Namibia's political economy in ways that makes effective regulation much more difficult, since regulation can only be effective if 'regulator and regulated remain separate entities'.

The links between Namibian elites and Chinese investors are the most crucial factor for the consequences "the rise of China" is having for Namibia – not any inherent differences between Western and Namibian ways of doing business.' A rift was identified 'between a sceptical majority progressively disillusioned with the Chinese involvement, and a well-connected elite convinced of the benefits closer cooperation with China can have'. The presence of Chinese actors does much more than change Namibia's external relations. 'By adding resources and providing new avenues of external integration, it influences the distribution of economic, social and cultural capital within Namibia and engenders shifts in the internal balance of power.' Alliances between Namibian elites and Chinese investors emerged that 'reaffirm the social and economic exclusion of large parts of the population'. Such alliances demonstrated that 'Chinese' investments in Namibia could not be regarded as just an external factor any more. The upshot is that 'Chinese and African actors have become part of a single social field in which the focus on nationality is more often misleading than helpful.'[79] Namibia may be a particular case but does offer potentially transferable insights into the changing political economy in other African countries.

The final theme presents a contrast by involving processes of longer-term social change. The deepening Chinese role in some African countries has been taking on a longer-term quality of emerging African–Chinese or Chinese–African communities, outside countries like South Africa that have a longer history. There are wide variations in terms of how long Chinese communities have been present, or the degree of rootedness in African countries. In contrast to dispersed patterns of Chinese migrants seeking new spaces with no or less competition, the appearance and development of Chinese community clusters and Chinatowns are part of ongoing urban change bearing the imprint of Chinese construction and takes on different forms in African towns and cities. Such a perspective, illustrated by the example of Namibia, shows change across time, including inter-generational change involving Chinese born in African countries. It also helps take analysis beyond any focus on the entry of Chinese migrants into African spaces, or visible episodes of friction, and instead considers the nature and implications of change over time. In Namibia, this has involved the emergence and development of Chinese–African communities and associated identities that bring into question the common idea that China's influence is a force that is somehow external to African societies.

CONCLUSION

This chapter examined different aspects of Chinese–African relations that have advanced in significant and consequential ways since the days of the construction of the TAZARA railway, when Chinese workers went to Africa, completed their work and returned to China. The official memorial to these and other Chinese aid workers outside Dar es Salaam illustrates how much has changed following decades of Chinese migration to African countries and flows of African traders to and from parts of China. Controversy over a proposed Chinese memorial cemetery in Lusaka, Zambia, in 2018 also demonstrated how much has changed in terms of politics. Chinese migration to African countries is diverse, evolving and much more multifaceted than reductionist treatments or narratives suggest.

There is now a diverse range of examples of how Chinese, willingly or not, are caught up in the domestic politics of different African states, and are subject to the vagaries of developments in official state relations with China. Each example reflects the particular circumstances of the given contexts, even if these are now more interconnected due to social media and information sharing. A widespread theme remains the unique salience of Chinese and China as an actual or potential issue in domestic politics. A common denominator in concerns about Chinese migration and the role of migrants in Africa was how these reflected 'broader concerns about the role of Beijing in African politics and African futures, including South African affairs'.[80] Whether these represented ongoing adjustments or were a sign of things to come remained to be seen. Beyond transient flows of entrepreneurial migrants, the deepening Chinese role in some African countries like

Namibia is taking on a longer-term quality organized around emerging African–Chinese communities.

One response of many Chinese communities to such problems as crime, as seen in South Africa or Angola for instance, has been self-help. Threats to Chinese in African countries, however, introduced new security challenges for China's foreign policy, illustrating the connections between everyday life of ordinary Chinese and higher foreign-policy concerns. In the New Era, there was heightened sensitivity to the treatment of Chinese and, ultimately, CCP legitimacy. Migration and the security of Chinese citizens became a key driver of Chinese government efforts to enhance its force projection capability in Africa, showing how bottom-up pressures facing Chinese in Africa influenced China's expanding peace and security engagement in Africa.

6 Security: A New 'Pillar' ——————

The opening of Beijing's first ever overseas naval base in Djibouti in 2017 was a defining event in China's New Era and represented a historic departure in China's foreign policy as well as Africa relations. The idea of opening overseas military bases had been debated before, with influential scholar Shen Dingli of Fudan University making waves in 2010 by criticizing the Chinese government's dogmatic adherence to the claim it had never nor would it ever establish an overseas military base. Insisting that establishing overseas military bases was 'our right', he argued that China needed to be able to safeguard overseas interests, protect Chinese and economic interests, and defend China against 'foreign invasion'.[1] For long, however, the Chinese government had insisted that its global economic expansion would not be joined by a global expansion of its military. It criticized overseas military bases as instruments of American hegemony and neo-colonialism. The idea of a naval base in Djibouti was long denied or downplayed as merely a 'logistics support base' to support economic interests and safeguard regional peace. The opening ceremony of the base, on 1 August 2017 or the ninetieth anniversary of the founding of the PLA, inaugurated a new phase in China's global military expansion, and relations with Africa. This, however, was one especially prominent and strategically significant part of a process that had seen China's security engagement expand and become more multifaceted, in which the evacuation of Chinese in distress was one high-profile example.

Xi Jinping declared that security was a 'major pillar' of China–Africa relations in 2015, having only been formalized at the 2012 FOCAC. Xi Jinping thus inherited a policy theme but under his leadership this has been expanding. Chinese military connections with Africa are by no means new. In becoming prominent, and the focus of US geostrategic concern, however, these have been at the foreground of a more diverse security engagement. Security encompassed much more than traditional military forms. Indeed, while such high-profile and important events as the opening of the Djibouti base have attracted wide attention, less has been paid to various forms of non-traditional security cooperation. In 2014, China's 'big security concept' set out a comprehensive range of meanings, from economic, social, information and ecological to 'political security', underscoring the imperative of protecting the CCP's socialist system. In a context where domestic and overseas security have blurred, reforms to party-state structures have sought to enhance China's ability to manage overseas security challenges. In this process, Africa has been a prominent frontier of foreign-policy innovation.

This chapter examines why and how security has become a defining theme in China's New Era relations with Africa. Security exemplifies how much more established China's engagement in the continent has become, and the challenges China's party-state-military has faced in responding, but also the importance of cooperation in 'non-traditional' realms, in which law forms an emerging foundation of more advanced and integrated ties. The following sections begin by setting out the main drivers of China's security engagement, before examining the different ways in which security has become part of China's Africa relations in bilateral, multilateral and other, more localized domains. Finally, it discusses key themes and ongoing debates, suggesting that security demonstrates notable departures for the Chinese government's policy engagement if judged from Beijing's perspective, but in the African security context represent more familiar trends. Exploring a different aspect of China's evolving power in Africa, security reveals much about China's actual changing role and longer-term prospects in light of deepening interests and the multifaceted dilemmas these entail.

CHINA'S EXPANDING SECURITY ENGAGEMENT

China's permanent membership of the UNSC ensures that its Africa security role proceeds from more than its own partnership.[2] This is one dimension of China's many security engagements that are continuing to evolve at different levels, involving different drivers, actors and contexts. At the same time, the CCP-state is guided by overall strategic objectives. The following section sets out some of the main drivers for China's expanding security engagement.

China's more established role in Africa has involved a shift in its exposure to risk and security threats. The transition from China's market entry strategy of the mid 1990s onwards, to playing a more involved role 25 years later on the back of established interests, has been marked. The pace of China's expansion outstripped the Chinese government's ability to respond, meaning an 'eyes falling behind the feet' effect.[3] The practical reality of China's greater involvement in politics and exposure to conflict, insecurity, terrorism and risks of political instability in the continent has also raised the importance of investment protection for SOEs, private corporations or entrepreneurs. The 2019–21 FOCAC Action Plan confirms this transition, stating that the security of 'major domestic economic projects' and 'safety of Chinese nationals, Chinese companies, and major projects' will be prioritized in intelligence, military and police cooperation. Some two decades ago, however, the role of Chinese companies during Sudan's civil war, in post-war Sierra Leone or Liberia contributed to a popular narrative that Chinese investment was immune from conventional risk. Chinese companies did venture into such risky conflict-affected environments but proved to be as vulnerable as other external investors, as CNPC's experience in Sudan from 1995 showed. The Chinese government and national oil companies were regarded as best friends of the government of Sudan, which was the enemy of Southern Sudan's main rebel movement, and this meant Chinese interests, notably oil, were militarily targeted by rebel groups in attempts to exert pressure on the Sudanese government. Furthermore, it also showed how China could be dragged into the politics of armed conflict. Many wondered what leverage Beijing might have over the government of Sudan, but in important respects China was being leveraged by Southern rebels to advance their political ambitions of secession. Sudan also showed how China's rise in Africa was accompanied by increasing expectations and pressure on Beijing to contribute more to security, thereby balancing its perceived emphasis on business.

Conflict and insecurity have posed mounting threats to Chinese investment and economic interests in Africa, as seen from Nigeria to Somalia and Mali in the Sahel region. Threats to proposed infrastructure projects, such as the state-owned China Railway Construction Corporation Ltd company's planned rehabilitation of a railway in Mali, raised concerns about the safety of Chinese workers but also threats to future economic opportunities. Security concerns and future interests were notable reasons behind the Chinese government's decision to participate in the UN peacekeeping force in Mali, the UN Multidimensional Integrated Stabilization Mission in Mali (MINUSMA) from 2013. As this and the BRI now shows, China's security engagement is evolving in a different context of its foreign policy. However, China's exposure to risk is not unusual, and applies to other projects, like the French multinational company Total's $20bn gas export project in northern Mozambique, which was threatened by Islamic State-affiliated insurgents.

The security of Chinese in Africa is one reason behind China's expanding security engagement, which involves the legitimacy of the CCP-state through the party's ability to protect Chinese citizens abroad. The presence of Chinese in many of the continent's most unstable regions, like northern Nigeria, Mali, northeastern DRC or Somalia, as well as Chinese sailors off the Gulf of Guinea for instance, has resulted in numerous kidnappings, attacks or acts of piracy. Citizen security became more pressing under Xi Jinping due to a more systematic, determined push by the CCP-state to connect with and involve the Chinese diaspora, and the interconnections between China's domestic politics and foreign policy arising from the issue of Chinese in danger abroad. Some four months after a car bomb attack against the hotel in Mogadishu housing China's Somalia embassy, for example, in late November 2015 came an assault on the Radisson Blu hotel in Bamako, Mali, which killed nineteen people, including three senior Chinese employees of the China Railway Construction Corporation. Xi Jinping condemned the attack. The issue of Chinese citizen security was popularized through China's highest grossing film of all time, *Wolf Warrior II* (2017), which featured a maverick former special forces officer heroically protecting Chinese in danger (and defeating an American mercenary) in Africa. It also depicted militarized nationalism, proudly flying China's flag and declaring that 'whoever offends China will be hunted down wherever they are'. In this vein, and showing how the sensitivities of Chinese abroad at risk has become a more political issue, Wang Yi declared in December 2018: 'We will never sit idle when our citizens' rights and interests are infringed upon and subjected to bullying.'[4]

Reputational factors also inform China's expanding security engagement. First, the Chinese government sought to demonstrate support for the UN through UN peacekeeping, and thereby gain credit for its contribution to multilateralism and global security. Second, UN peacekeeping – and support for the AU – allows China to demonstrate its credentials as a 'responsible stakeholder'. Beijing can use its now formalized security engagement in Africa to promote China's self-ascribed status as a responsible power committed to global peace and security in word and deed. The Chinese government cites its

UN peacekeeping role as proof that China is a 'responsible stakeholder in global peace and security'[5] Finally, from 2020 the COVID-19 pandemic underscored how prominent and inter-connected biosecurity and China's reputation had become.

Gaining experience through an applied approach of learning by doing has been a further driver, and one that dovetails with China's reputational enhancement objectives. The PLA has sought to gain valuable operational experience by participating in overseas UN peacekeeping deployments in conflict zones. Such experience is otherwise hard to come by or to simulate within China or in its neighbourhood. The very risks and threats to economic interests and Chinese citizens were not just opportunities for the PLA to learn about overseas security operations through multilateral means but also to gain credit for UN peacekeeping. As China's 2015 Military Strategy white paper noted, by participating in UN peacekeeping or undertaking international disaster rescue or humanitarian assistance, China's armed forces can fulfil 'international responsibilities and obligations' but 'also enhance their own capabilities and expertise'[6] This shows how China has been using participation in UN peacekeeping operations as one part of wider efforts to modernize the PLA and transform it into a global force. UN peacekeeping has thus been playing a notable role in the PLA's own equivalent 'going global' process.

New Era foreign policy
Since 2012, the Chinese government's more ambitious major power foreign policy has been underpinned by military modernization and expansion, and featured a prominent position of the BRI as a global initiative involving but going far beyond Africa. More than anything, China's first overseas naval base in Djibouti signified that Xi's New Era was departing from China's previous relations with Africa and its foreign policy. Prior to Xi Jinping's leadership there were vigorous debates in China about how best to respond to the changing nature

and extent of global Chinese economic interests. Many defended 'traditional' approaches based on restraint, non-interference, and 'keeping a low profile'; others advocated bolder measures and argued that China's expanding global economic interests required a new playbook. For example, one view was that China should learn from the US and 'carry a sword whilst doing business' (*chijian jingshang*) and could simultaneously pursue national and international interests, for instance by conducting anti-piracy patrols off the Somali coast.[7] While bolder initiatives in China's Africa security were set in motion before 2012, the shift since then has been tangible. Furthermore, an important part of the enabling context for this shift has proceeded from within China. As well as reforms to enhance the PLA's operational capability, China's legal framework has been revised to establish and strengthen the legal basis for overseas intervention. China's 2015 counterterrorism law, for example, states (Article 71) that the PLA and the People's Armed Police 'may assign people to leave the country on counterterrorism missions as approved by the Central Military Commission'. In late 2020, proposed revisions to the National Defence Law stated that China's armed forces could be deployed when 'development interests' – such as overseas Chinese, investments and interests – were threatened.

The BRI has been a further driver of China's expanding global security engagement in which Africa is one prominent part. One public face of the BRI is developmental and benevolent, but it is also underpinned by harder-edged security concerns. While the BRI, in keeping with the CCP's directive amplified by Xi Jinping to 'tell stories about China well and spread China's voice well', is formally presented with the language of peace, it has also been seen as an opportunity to expand China's global military footprint, via peaceful posturing.[8] Indeed, some argue a more engaged role of the PLA and other security organs – from the Chinese state and private companies – is required if the BRI is to succeed. In this light, the BRI is much more than a 'national development strategy': it is also a 'national security strategy and an external leadership strategy.[9] The BRI is seen in this sense as a long-term, comprehensive global strategy to promote China's rejuvenation, and move from being 'rule followers' to global rule makers as part of a Chinese version of globalization in which the Chinese government would imprint itself on global governance reform.

The evolving place and role of Africa in China's global security strategy can be seen in how some Chinese analysts regard the continent as being a 'fulcrum for *fuqiang*', or China's rise to global wealth/power. This means Africa being identified as increasingly significant for China at a global level when competition between the US and China for global hegemony is intensifying. China's relations with the US have added a geopolitical driver to its security engagement. As seen (Chapter 2), China and US strategic competition means that rivalry is being transferred onto Africa, mainly in political ways to date but including security dimensions.

A final factor concerns the role of African states and other organizations led by the AU in enhancing security cooperation with China, paralleled by various less official, non-state dynamics. Since the early 2000s, the AU has prioritized its African Peace and Security Architecture (APSA), grounded in the firm belief that Africa should take ownership of finding solutions to the continent's security problems. More importantly, the AU views APSA as an amalgamation of governance, security, and development. As a result, relaxing the boundaries between security and development, and viewing these as necessarily interdependent, is compatible with the Chinese state's views on security.[10] For this reason, one influential driving factor is the role of African states, regional organizations and the AU in seeking to forge relations with China in the field of security. Beyond this state level of interaction, sub-state dynamics have also contributed towards a more diverse Chinese security engagement at the corporate and citizens levels. In Angola, for instance, crime was one factor behind efforts to create a protection force. In Sudan, an attack by a rebel militia against

CNPC that killed five oil workers in October 2008 led to a series of reforms within the company (see below, page 190).

MAINSTREAMING SECURITY INTO CHINA–AFRICA RELATIONS

The processes by which security has been mainstreamed into China–Africa relations have involved a wide range of actors and expanding, connected CCP-state-military, corporate and citizen levels, which are not always harmonized or well-coordinated. Most obviously, security has become prominent in the FOCAC process and in China's relations with the AU. The 2012 FOCAC declared that a China–Africa Cooperative Partnership for Peace and Security would be established. With turmoil in north Africa, this came at the end of Hu Jintao's administration. In 2013, the head of the MFA's Department of African Affairs suggested that China's inadequate involvement in African peace and security was a weakness in China's Africa policy and urged greater engagement. Security was duly elaborated further in China's second Africa policy and at the 2015 FOCAC, when Xi Jinping elevated it to one of five foundational 'pillars' of the China–Africa 'comprehensive strategic partnership'. Xi's speech to the 2018 FOCAC talked about building 'a China–Africa community with a shared future that enjoys common security' and declared that China was 'ready to play a constructive role in promoting peace and stability in Africa and will support African countries to strengthen their independent capacity for safeguarding stability and peace'. FOCAC 2018 also aligned China–Africa security cooperation with the BRI.

Djibouti naval base
China's naval base in Djibouti greatly enhances the PLA's ability to conduct military operations in Africa, including potentially securing BRI projects.[11] Soon after the base opened, Chinese forces, including

tank destroyers, engaged in live fire exercises in the heavily fortified base, which can accommodate up to 10,000 troops, a dozen helipads, and a pier to dock a naval flotilla. China's Ministry of National Defence cited three official roles for the base: deploying peacekeeping troops, providing logistical support for antipiracy naval patrols, and supporting humanitarian assistance and disaster relief operations. In reality, it has other functions, such as providing medical services, refuelling and servicing naval task groups, and is capable of supporting a range of activities from China's counter-piracy operations, to intelligence collection, non-combat evacuation, and counterterrorism. The base will act as a hub for joint Chinese military operations and assist the growing role of Chinese special forces in the region. There are thus three additional reasons why the base is significant. First, though touted as supporting peace, it enables China's military capability and has operational significance, even if exactly how remains unclear. Second, it provides the basis for a new chapter in the PLA's operational military learning on the ground – and sea – in a location where there are also American, Japanese and other foreign bases. Third, the strategic value of the base extends beyond its stated role in other ways, being important to Xi Jinping's declared goal of transforming China into a 'strong maritime country'.

The Djibouti base will also assist China's expanding 'maritime cooperation' with Africa, which encompasses naval visits and exchanges, and a broader range of activities, including under the BRI. Following its anti-piracy deployment off Somalia's coast, for example, the PLA Navy's 28th escort task force visited Ghana, Cameroon, and Gabon in June 2018 before concluding its African tour in South Africa. China's Vision for Maritime Cooperation under the BRI (2017) identifies further areas of cooperation, such as combating 'non-traditional security issues such as crimes on the sea'; search and rescue and marine disaster prevention and mitigation, and the BeiDou Navigation Satellite System, which was completed in June

2020. Additionally, it sets out areas for 'strengthening cooperation in maritime law enforcement', from enforcing fishing law to 'anti-terrorism and anti-violence on the sea'.[12]

The new base illustrated the different faces China's military now has in Africa: benign, cooperative and 'responsible' (fulfilling international responsibility on UN peacekeeping or anti-piracy, supporting the APSA); concerned and responsive (undertaking humanitarian missions, protecting Chinese in Africa, demonstrating capability and willingness to use force if necessary); and a more militaristic face demonstrating power and signalling that a logic of further military expansion is underway. These are codified in official policy. China's 2019 White Paper on defence asserts that the 'fundamental goal of China's national defense in the new era' is 'resolutely safeguarding China's sovereignty, security and development interests'. China's national defence aims include 'safeguard China's overseas interests' and supporting 'the sustainable development of the country'. Declaring overseas interests to be 'a crucial part of China's national interests', it states: 'One of the missions of China's armed forces is to effectively protect the security and legitimate rights and interests of overseas Chinese people, organizations and institutions.'[13]

Arms merchant and defence partner

Chinese arms sales to Africa have increased in recent years. China accounted for a 5.5% share of global major arms exports between 2015 and 2019 and ranked as the fifth top exporter, behind the US (36%), Russia (21%), France (7.9%) and Germany (5.8%). Between 2015 and 2019, North Africa was responsible for 74% of African arms imports, with Algeria alone accounting for 79% of all North African arms imports of which 67% came from Russia, 13% from China and 11% from Germany. China accounted for 19% of arms imports in sub-Saharan Africa between 2015 and 2019, when the subregion took up 26% of all African arms imports (Russia accounting for 36%

Table 7. Top Arms-Supplying Countries to African Countries, 2014–2019

Country	Total Arms Imports (TIV US$ mn*)	Top Supplying Countries			Chinese Imports as % of Total
Egypt	8,816	Russia (2,980)	France (2,971)	US (1,434)	China (430)	0.48
Algeria	6,766	Russia (4,444)	China (864)	Germany (707)	Italy (306)	12.7
Morocco	1,792	US (1,126)	France (643)	Italy (10)	-	0
Angola	736	Russia (501)	Lithuania (60)	Belarus (40)	China (37)	5
Nigeria	573	Russia (216)	China (115)	US (82)	-	20
Sudan	396	China (163)	Russia (125)	Belarus (87)	-	41
Tunisia	364	US (192)	Netherlands (134)	Turkey (29)	-	0
Cameroon	176	China (85)	Russia (38)	France (11)	-	48
Senegal	153	France (70)	China (36)	Slovakia (10)	-	23.5
Zambia	138	China (65)	Italy (35)	Russia (14)	-	47
Ethiopia	130	Russia (69)	Ukraine (26)	Israel (10)	-	0
Tanzania	87	China (35)	France (32)	Netherlands (20)	-	40

Source: Elijah N. Munyi, "The Growing Preference for Chinese Arms in Africa: A Case Study of Uganda and Kenya,' CARI Policy Brief 49, 2020: 2, using SIPRI Arms Transfer Database.

*Trend Indicator Value (military capability price of military equipment, combining financial value and capability of the procured equipment) and France 7.6%), with Angola, Nigeria, Sudan, Senegal and Zambia accounting for 63% of all arms imports by states to the subregion.[14]

China has been more willing to proliferate than competitors like the US, as the example of armed drones in Nigeria shows. In 2018, the Nigerian Air Force confirmed that unmanned aerial vehicle pilots had been trained to operate the attack drone CH-3A, manufactured by China Aerospace Science and Technology Corporation, which have been deployed in Nigeria's northeast, against Boko Haram. The previous importance after the Cold War of cheap Soviet-era surplus material from former Warsaw Pact states in African defence markets is being displaced by Chinese defence exports, now characterized by Chinese-designed equipment (rather than Soviet-era copies).

Commercial motivations for arms sales are a driving force for Chinese companies like the state-owned defence corporation NORINCO, but 'China's growing position in the African defence market reflects the broader growth of Beijing's influence and investment on the continent.'[15] Beyond state transfers, Chinese manufactured small arms and light weapons are a significant feature in conflict contexts across the continent, including in central Africa and the Horn. After revelations that NORINCO had shipped arms, ammunition and related materiel to South Sudan's government in July 2014, the Chinese government's complicated exposure became evident on top of the fact that such transfers came during a particularly destructive civil war and followed the indirect effects of the government of Sudan's secondary retransfer of Chinese arms to allied armed groups in South Sudan.[16] The incident risked not just a damaging political backlash but also armed blowback on Chinese oil interests and UN peacekeepers; China subsequently declared a moratorium on arms sales to South Sudan. One trend has thus seen attempts by the Chinese government to control arms transfers, and a slow evolution of policies on proliferation. This is partly due to reputational concerns but also awareness of blowback risks. At the same time, arms are one part of a widened array of defence ties.

Military partner

China has a long track record as a military partner to African states. In this way, military cooperation and training represent another area of continuing, enhanced cooperation involving several hundred military officers from African countries studying in China each year, going to the China Military Academy, the Dalian Naval Academy, the Air Force Aviation Academy, or the PLA's National Defence University. At the same time, 'China–Africa military relations in a new era', an official new phase in a longer history of bilateral military ties between China and African countries, has seen the advent of forums for military cooperation geared towards supporting 'New Era' relations, and efforts to institutionalize these. This has involved an upgrade in military connections, attempts to forge a more continental level of engagement, enhance bilateral military ties, and educate African militaries in New Era political doctrine. In June–July 2018, for example, China's Ministry of National Defence held the first China–Africa Defence and Security Forum featuring the participation of military representatives from fifty African countries and the AU over two weeks. In July 2019, the first China–Africa Peace and Security Forum was held in Beijing.

UN peacekeeping

UN peacekeeping is a cornerstone of China's security-related activities in Africa and is prominent in China's evolving global foreign security policy. Over 80% of Chinese peacekeepers are stationed, and 75% of its peacekeeping financial contributions are used, in Africa.[17] China has participated in UN peacekeeping in the continent since 1989, but the nature of its participation evolved notably in September 2014 when Beijing announced it would deploy a 700-strong infantry battalion to the UN Mission in South Sudan (UNMISS). China had deployed its first security forces to MINUSMA in Mali the year before, but this new UNMISS deployment was the PLA's first infantry battalion to participate in a peacekeeping mission and had a broader UN mandate than the protection unit sent to Mali. The new frontline combat role illustrated the PLA's attempts to gain operational experience through UN peacekeeping and how challenging this was in practice (see Box 4 opposite).

Addressing the UNGA in September 2015, Xi Jinping made the dramatic announcement that China would join the UN's new

Table 8. China's Contribution to UN Peacekeeping by Mission in Africa, 2020

UN Peacekeeping Mission	Total Contingent	Total Police	Total Experts	Total Staff
MINURSO (UN Mission for the Referendum in Western Sahara)	-	-	15	-
MINUSCA (UN Multidimensional Integrated Stabilization Mission in the Central African Republic)	-	-	-	7
MINUSMA (UN Multidimensional Integrated Stabilization Mission in Mali	413	-	-	9
MONUSCO (UN Organization Stabilization Mission in the Democratic Republic of the Congo)	218	18	7	5
UNAMID (AU–UN Hybrid Operation in Darfur) [completed its mandate on 31 December 2020]	364	9	-	-
UNMISS (UN Mission in South Sudan)	1031	2	5	23

Source: UN Department of Peacekeeping, 'Summary of Contribution to UN Peacekeeping by Mission, Country and Post: Police, UN Military Experts on Mission, Staff Officers and Troops', 31 December 2020

Peacekeeping Capability Readiness System and create 'a permanent peacekeeping police squad and build a peacekeeping standby force' of 8,000 troops. In November 2018 a spokesman for China's Ministry of National Defence stated that the UN had deemed all thirteen units of the force deployable.[18] UN peacekeeping is used to exemplify China's support for the UN, and its newfound interest in 'big power' diplomacy. It is also used to promote China's status as a 'responsible stakeholder in global peace and security'.[19] In this way, a 2015 white paper on military strategy affirmed that China's armed forces would 'do their utmost to shoulder more international responsibilities and obligations, provide more public security goods, and contribute more to world peace and common development'.[20]

Box 4. South Sudan: Gaining Experience Under Fire
China's aim of gaining military experience via UN peacekeeping is clear in theory but is much harder in practice. This was illustrated in South Sudan's capital Juba, following the outbreak of fighting between forces of the president and opposition leader on 7 July 2016. The day after, fighting moved closer to UN House, the headquarters of UNMISS, and intensified around two adjacent Protection of Civilian (POC) camps, POC1 and POC3, housing some 37,000 internally displaced persons (IDPs). UNMISS found itself in the middle of full-blown hostilities between two fighting forces.

Chinese peacekeepers were responsible for protecting the POC1 camp. During the attack, Chinese peacekeepers manning POC1 guard towers, which were not adequately protected from gunfire, withdrew to ditches and vehicles below. At around 6:30 p.m. on 10 July, a rocket-propelled grenade exploded near a Chinese-manned UN armoured personnel carrier inside POC1.

One soldier died that evening, and another died the next day after bleeding out without receiving adequate medical care. The exact circumstances of the incident, including whether the Chinese troops were accidentally caught in the crossfire or targeted because government troops thought the UN was shielding rebels, are hard to determine accurately. However, the incident caused POC1 to be vulnerable, with peacekeepers withdrawing to UN House and about five thousand IDPs fleeing POC1 to also seek refuge in the headquarters' compound. Many peacekeepers abandoned their posts. Making the deaths of the Chinese peacekeepers even worse was the possibility that Chinese-supplied arms were involved.

The next day, 11 July, a nearby hotel, the Terrain Hotel compound was attacked by government soldiers, who raped at least five international aid workers, physically or sexually assaulted at least a dozen others, and executed a South Sudanese Nuer journalist. Several departments within UNMISS received information about the attack shortly after it began. Orders were given directing a Quick Reaction Force to respond. None did – with Chinese and Ethiopian battalions refusing to go.

In response, China's MFA and embassy in Juba activated its emergency response mechanism. Two seriously wounded peacekeepers were flown to Beijing on a military medical rescue plane. Over 330 Chinese workers were evacuated to Nairobi, and Chinese embassy staff, members of a medical team and twenty employees of Chinese companies were evacuated to Kampala. In China, the deaths of Chinese peacekeepers shocked the public. Footage of Chinese troops under fire and attempting to administer emergency first aid to bleeding colleagues was broadcast on television. The dead soldiers were mourned with public funerals.

It was a rude awakening at a time when the realities of dangerous overseas deployments were upstaged by Chinese government narratives about China's growing power, and subsequent glorified portrayal of armed intervention in Africa in popular culture, not just the film *Wolf Warrior II* (2017), but also films like *Chinese Peacekeeping Forces* (2018), loosely based on China's experience in South Sudan.

The UN's official investigation attributed the 'chaotic and ineffective response to the violence' to 'a lack of leadership' from key senior UNMISS personnel. The actions – or in some cases non-actions – of UNMISS forces during this episode did not constitute an effective implementation of UNMISS's Chapter VII mandate, which authorizes it to 'use all necessary means' to protect civilians. The mandate of UNMISS is ambitious – to protect a vulnerable population of more than twelve million in the midst of a harrowing political, economic, security and humanitarian crisis. But the role of the Chinese peacekeepers during the violence in Juba – to guard a fixed site and respond to hostile fire – was not. Nor were such tasks unusual in military or peacekeeping terms. The shortcomings of the Chinese peace-keepers in July 2016 thus cannot be simply ascribed to the challenges inherent in UNMISS's mandate.

For UNMISS, the fighting demonstrated systemic short-comings, of which two are particularly relevant to the deaths of the Chinese peacekeepers. One was the lack of appropriate medical trauma facilities and blood banks, and medical and casualty evacuation capability, which went against previous recommen-dations about enhancing UN peace operations. Second, there was a breakdown of mission command and control. During the disruption caused by the fighting, the Chinese Battalion

Commander at UN House was appointed by the UNMISS Force Commander as the acting commander in charge of operations there, giving him authority to lead other UN contingents. Yet reports suggest that, in addition to communication difficulties caused by language barriers, the fact that the Chinese Battalion Commander had the same military rank as the leaders of the other UN contingents impeded his ability to get them to obey orders.

As China's commitment to and role in robust peacekeeping missions has grown, Chinese personnel have been increasingly put in harm's way. Just how much the PLA has learned from the Juba incident remains to be seen; learning lessons on paper is one thing, converting them into operational practice quite another. On the one hand, the incident in Juba represented exactly the kind of frontline experience China's leadership had sought for the PLA: an opportunity to test itself in dangerous conditions and to learn from its conduct. On the other hand, despite the government's carefully crafted media images aimed at domestic Chinese and international audiences, the tragic incident demonstrated just how far the PLA had to go before it was fully capable of effectively undertaking a robust Chapter VII mandate.

Aspiring peacemaker and peacebuilder
China has become more involved in peace diplomacy and, in limited often unofficial ways, conflict mediation. This is readily seen in terms of China's more involved UN role in conflict. Despite US opposition, for instance, UN Secretary-General António Guterres appointed Ambassador Xia Huang, whose career included serving as China's ambassador in Niger, Senegal and the Republic of Congo, as his Special Envoy for the Great Lakes region from January 2019.

Previously, and in part reflecting its peripheral, outsider role, China was not active in conflict resolution or mediation processes, deferring to other powers, preferring to play a secondary support role or concentrating political energy on its own bilateral relations. It had an experimental approach, as seen in the aftermath of the eruption of conflict in South Sudan in December 2013 for example, when much was made of China's mediation role. It even convened a meeting of belligerents in Khartoum in January 2015, formally to support the regional peace process. China's engagement had mediation-like aspects but did not conform to a strict definition of the term. Instead, it represented a diplomatic–political intervention to try to promote a negotiated settlement, protect China's interests, assist the formal mediation process and gain credit for doing so. China's diplomatic engagement on South Sudan was mostly confined to a supporting role positioned carefully behind the lead regional body, the Intergovernmental Authority on Development, and the AU. Beijing has sought to present itself as active in conflict mediation in Africa, but it is not immediately obvious how. In February 2019, for instance, China's then Assistant Foreign Minister Chen Xiaodong said: 'China is actively involved in mediating hotspot issues in Africa, and supports African people in resolving African issues in the African way.'[21] In reality, this was case specific and encompassed a range of different types of mediation-like brokering roles, including discrete shuttle diplomacy between Eritrea and Ethiopia when these were in conflict.

China's role in post-conflict reconstruction and peacebuilding has been more engaged in a variety of ways, from supporting the UN Peacebuilding Fund, to the AU and country-specific engagements. In this, China emphasizes economic development as the means by which conflict can be overcome and peace, understood as more than the absence of fighting, can be realized. This emphasis is prominent in the overall rationale behind China's engagement.

Corporate and citizen security

Chinese corporations pioneered security in their operations, to the point of being ahead of the Chinese state. CNPC's '10.18' incident in Sudan on 18 October 2008, when five Chinese oil workers were killed, was instrumental in pushing the corporation to improve its security and risk-management practices, in Sudan and elsewhere. This process took time but helped CNPC's operations during conflict in South Sudan after December 2013.[22] The company's efforts to enhance protection of its operations included a strategy of attempting to cultivate better ties with communities, political opposition groups and religious leaders. Realizing the limitation of only engaging the official government, CNPC's International Department 'called for the company to go beyond its government-focused approach by establishing ties with local communities, major political opposition groups and religious leaders.'[23]

Chinese enterprises have been driven by more pressing and localized security concerns and one recent departure has involved turning to private security firms for assistance. Private security contractors have a range of benefits, from providing a hands-on approach to protecting overseas interests (especially where local security forces can't be relied on), to creating employment for veterans and being an effective tool that can be mobilized under the banner of overseas investment protection without direct PLA involvement.[24] Former PLA military personnel have established private security companies; DeWe Security Service Group, for example, has provided protection to Chinese companies in South Sudan and other African countries. Other companies involve joint ventures, like HW Raid Security Pty Ltd, created by Shandong Huawei Security Group and Raid Private Security from South Africa in December 2014.[25]

Citizen security has been promoted in numerous ways, producing a contrast between the efforts by China's party-state and a profusion of non-state self-help initiatives. The plethora of more localized forms of citizen security initiatives have been often driven by concern at crime and are linked to, but often occurring outside of, connections to China's party state. In terms of further measures at the Beijing level, the Chinese party state has attempted to respond more effectively to citizens in danger, not merely through military means but also improved consular response and protection. In September 2018, the MFA launched Foreign Ministry (*waijiaobu*) 12308, a smartphone app enabling Chinese nationals to call an MFA hotline any time for free, as well as via Wechat and Weibo, and providing alerts, advice and information. The hotline was created in 2014 by the MFA's Global Consular Protection and Service Emergency Call Centre, but this app enabled internet access.

Non-traditional security
Non-traditional security has not just emerged as a more established, high-profile and politicized theme; it has also been the subject of myriad forms of engagement involving a range of subjects, from anti-terrorism, anti-corruption and climate change to legal cooperation. Health cooperation was one established example. China mobilized to respond to the outbreak of Ebola in Guinea, Liberia and Sierra Leone in 2014, after which the Chinese government contributed $2m to support the creation of the Africa Centres for Disease Control and Prevention (Africa CDC). In December 2020, the ground-breaking ceremony for construction of the Africa CDC headquarters building, mainly financed by the Chinese government and built by Chinese contractors, was held in Addis Ababa and, with the backdrop of the COVID-19 pandemic and praise from AU officials, represented a timely public diplomacy achievement for China.

Legal cooperation became a more discernibly significant New Era theme. 'Judicial cooperation' had featured in inter-state China–Africa relations before; there were two short paragraphs about it in the 2006 FOCAC Action Plan, for instance. The 2018 FOCAC Action Plan offered a more detailed set of action areas, grouping stated priorities into 'Military, Police and Anti-Terrorism', and 'Anti-Corruption, Consular Affairs, Immigration, Judiciary and Law Enforcement'. Using a language of 'harmonizing' laws, or enhancing law enforcement capacity (from border controls, customs, military policy, taxation and cooperation with Afripol, the African Police Cooperation Organization), this also includes BRI-focused security cooperation measures. In part, such processes involved necessary updates, such as to old investment treaties for example; additionally, it represented the progressive integration of African legal systems with China (at times framed as supporting UN agreements, like on anti-corruption). Such an agenda seemed to be pushed by the Chinese government but represents areas where African states have reciprocal interests in better managing and regulating relations, including over Chinese corporate or citizen conduct. It was testament to how important this has evolved to become and will continue to be, as part of the recalibration of longer-term, thickening ties. It had not just expanded but done so in context of Xi Jinping's New Era, meaning more politically attuned motivations, processes and objectives.

NEW ERA SECURITY

Given how far security has advanced in a relatively short period of time, this multifaceted theme now intersects with many aspects of China–Africa relations, especially when approached as a full spectrum of concerns extending much beyond traditional, or military security. A number of themes have become particularly notable since 2012, in which the following stand out: peace through development, investment protection, non-interference, China's approach to and role in intervention in African countries, and African activism and adaptation.

First, China champions the notion that economic development can resolve armed conflict and produce peace – indeed, that development is the highest form of security – in a manner that reinforces

China's economic strengths. President Xi told the 2015 FOCAC that 'Development holds the key to solving all problems'. China's Foreign Minister, Wang Yi, repeated this message at the September 2019 UNGA, promising that Beijing would 'actively explore and apply a Chinese approach to addressing hotspot issues, and play a constructive role in upholding international peace and security'. For China's government, economic development has an almost magical status. China's domestic and global development are connected: China needs a peaceful international environment to develop, and China's growth in turn will help drive development and stability at global level. In this way, development is part of China's foreign policy.

Of course, this way of thinking about development, peace and security is not unique to China. But it is ubiquitous in China's peace and security engagement, and used in different ways: as a commonsense mantra (investment can overcome conflict); political discourse (in public relations); causal claim (economics determines politics) and in particular policy areas (like UN peacekeeping or peace-building). Efforts to develop Chinese approaches to development as an alternative to liberal approaches informed by democracy, rights and market economics generated debate about China's normative role in African peace and security.[26] However, an underlying shift away from transformative prescriptions and towards a broad consensus on stabilization meant this was superseded by broad consensus around political stability. Additionally, there were indications of a changing approach to UN peacekeeping operations beyond large complex missions, or involving operations sanctioned by the UNSC and the AU's Peace and Security Council like the G5 Sahel, together with questions about how African Standby Force could operate.

China's official emphasis on security through development tended to marginalize or displace the politics of armed conflict, including regional and global dimensions. Despite this, there has been recognition in Chinese quarters that economic development can't be divorced from politics and governance. By stressing economic development as the means to overcome conflict in Africa, Beijing seeks to advance a distinctive approach with Chinese characteristics allied to its practical capability to rapidly mobilize finance and corporate deployment in order to assist with building infrastructure. In political terms, under Xi Jinping there have been more ambitious claims about China's ability to address hotspot issues, and the efficacy of economic development, as the example of China's engagement in Mali shows.[27] For all China's claims to an alternative approach to intervention in Africa, this represented a quiet form of convergence around a counter-terrorism and stabilization agenda to support market-driven economic activities. In countries like the DRC, however, this approach does not offer any clear route to peace and development; instead, China's and Western involvement there 'provide possibilities for continued insecurity, rather than any fundamental break from previous patterns and structures of politics.'[28]

The second area concerns investment protection in the New Era, which has evolved over the past two decades and in much more conspicuous ways since 2012. Protecting overseas interests is now an explicit part of China's foreign policy. At the Tiananmen Square military parade in Beijing on 1 October 2019, which commemorated the 70th anniversary of the founding of the PRC, Xi Jinping spoke about how 'China's strong military aims to safeguard its overseas interests', contributing to peace and security but 'protecting China's overseas interests', citing the development of 'overseas logistical facilities' and maritime evacuation as areas of PLA activity. Efforts to undertake investment protection now take many direct and indirect forms, such as UNSC resolutions.[29] Indicative of a wider range of threats to economic interests, these go far beyond simple military measures. As noted, the 2019–21 FOCAC Action Plan states that the security of 'major domestic economic projects' and 'safety of Chinese nationals, Chinese companies, and major projects' will be prioritized in intelligence, military and police cooperation. Investment protection now assumes a more prominent political aspect based on the need for a more vocal role in advocating China's position. Increasingly, much investment protection involves legal processes or politics. Under Xi, the most difficult question is not whether but how to protect overseas interests.

Third, China's principle of non-interference is unavoidable in debates about its security role, and for good reasons. Non-interference in the internal affairs of African countries remains China's dominant thinking and declared policy at a strategic level, but China's policy-makers have been gradually adopting a more flexible view of the principle in tactical terms. Non-interference was far more coherent and easier to plausibly sustain when China lacked significant economic interests in Africa. Now that it has developed these, it has become far harder to reconcile the principle with actual practices as attempts to do so, such as 'influence without interference', show.[30] Nonetheless, non-interference still matters. It is perhaps the most popular principle in formal China–Africa inter-state political relations, being China's signature brand, but also because it is one side of the state sovereignty coin and therefore reinforces the central place of state sovereignty in Africa (even allowing for AU reforms). For China, it matters in large part as it externalizes Beijing's preferred way of being treated itself: by preaching non-interference to others, the Chinese government asks for the same in return.

There is a wide range of potential forms of 'interference' in internal affairs of African states, which extend into political territory. This raises questions about the nature of economic influence and forms of interference by other means, which can be formally separated from official non-interference (Sierra Leone's elections in 2018 provided one example). The notion that there is a red line of interference that China can cross is a misnomer in the face of the now wide reper-toire of economic, political and other means (such as education) by which China in functional terms seeks to or can exert influence. Based substantially on an elite political compact, rhetoric and performances, the Chinese government's insistence that it practises, more than preaches, non-interference, has struggled to convincingly counter perceptions about China's exploitative role or 'real' aims. Overall, non-interference is better able to express declared intent than the effects of China's role today.

In contrast to public presentation, non-interference is in practice a double-edged sword for the Chinese government: it generates wide political capital among African ruling elites but formally constrains China's ability to fully respond to an increasing range of challenges. One reason why private security is attractive to Chinese companies in African countries is in order to negotiate the difficult balance between the public, state principle of non-interference and ensuring the security of Chinese investments. The Djibouti naval base and expanding military role are presented as both conforming to non-interference and enhancing, among other things, China's ability to undertake UN or AU authorized military interventions. This distinction may sound semantic but reflects important differences between two principles that are often wrongly conflated: for the Chinese government, 'interference' against the wishes of any given African state is formally opposed, but 'intervention' when legally sanctioned by a (preferably) UN or AU mandate and host state consent can be acceptable.

A fourth theme thus concerns the evolution of China's approach to and role in military intervention in African countries, alongside the continuity of and efforts to strengthen its non-interference rhetoric under Xi Jinping's leadership. A key claim to China's difference from Western powers derives from its approach to intervention. China has objected to outside intervention in African conflicts on normative and practical grounds. Military intervention was seen as deeply questionable in normative terms and because it did not work in practice. One change in Beijing's approach, however, has involved maintaining opposition to foreign intervention in principle but accommodating this more pragmatically in practice. Mali, for instance, saw a remarkable turnaround in China's approach to armed intervention in the continent: after initial blanket condemnation of France's neo-colonial military Operation Serval in January 2013, which aimed at ending jihadist control over northern Mali, China went on to actively support and participate in MINUSMA. In debates about intervention, those advocating restraint and adherence to traditional principles have mostly seemed to prevail, at least in formal terms, but vigorous debates reflect different institutional interests and agendas in China's party-state and military.

Fifth, although debates around China and intervention are often framed in terms of how China is adjusting to new realities in Africa, an important set of influences shaping China's engagement – like those of other powers – comes from African initiatives of various kinds. Most obviously, as conflict in Sudan's Darfur region showed from 2005, part of China's learning on intervention in Africa concerned the need to balance non-interference with the doctrine of 'non-indifference' enshrined in the AU Constitutive Act (which mandates non-interference but recognizes 'the right of the Union to intervene in a Member State ... in respect of grave circumstances, namely: war crimes, genocide and crimes against humanity').[31] But beyond such legal and normative issues, African elites have found ways of harnessing intervention for their own purposes, including by reframing intervention as a way of restoring order.[32]

Beijing insists that it follows the guiding principle of 'Africa-proposed, Africa-agreed and Africa-led' in security cooperation, but its engagement has also been guided by necessity and strategic direction. At the same time, this has been Africa-influenced in unintended and unforeseen ways. Despite continuing to formally support the principle of non-interference, the evolution of intervention with Chinese characteristics in Africa continues. This has been partly pushed and shaped by activist African states, and various non-state factors, which have been at the forefront of redefining intervention in the continent. The adversarial shift in China's relations with the US introduced new pressures. Overall, the best means of comprehending China's engagement was not by starting with the hallowed principles of non-interference and sovereignty, but by actual ground practices in African political domains, including conflict-affected states.

Finally, a related further dynamic involved African roles across a range of security questions, including particular ways of involving China to helping protect investments and deployment of African state security forces to protect Chinese interests. Examples included Nigeria's efforts to secure counter-terrorism assistance from China over Boko Harem, Uganda's announcement in November 2018 that it would deploy its military to protect Chinese companies in response to attacks and robberies on Chinese nationals, and the training by China's security services of a special police unit to protect the Mombasa–Nairobi railway in Kenya. Another method has involved African militaries providing assistance to Chinese corporations, such as in the DRC's mining sector. Such trends pointed to evolving hybrid collaborations and efforts to share responses.

CONCLUSION

Approached from the perspective of African security, China represents a comparatively new, well-resourced and increasingly influential external power. Approached in terms of past African peace and security experience, the trajectory of China's security engagement in light of its economic role had familiar historical resonances. Just how and how far China continues to be incorporated into the APSA and whether this can manage China in its own terms, remains to be seen across a range of important areas. The January 2020 AU summit 'Silencing the Guns: Creating Conducive Conditions for Africa's Development' sought to renew an ambition set out in 2013 to end war and prevent genocide in Africa by 2020. It also showed how slow progress has been.

One relatively rapid change, however, has been the expansion of a multi-stranded Chinese security engagement. In less than a decade, security has gone from being largely absent to a pillar of China–Africa relations and in the process, initiatives that used to be ad hoc or managed within bilateral relations have become more organized and institutionalized, from FOCAC, relations with the AU and African regional organizations to coordination at the UNSC. With China's first naval base becoming part of the strategic landscape in the Horn of Africa as an established, less controversial fact, Beijing's role looked set to become more involved. In 2020, the Chinese government's defence budget increased by 6.6%. China's expanding security engagement in Africa has contrasted with America's engagement. To date, the US has had a far more militarized presence in Africa, but the Trump administration furthered the prospect of a military drawdown in Africa from current troop levels of around 9,000 military personnel (of which 7,000 are special forces). US military engagement continued, however, as seen for instance with the 8th African Land Forces Summit in Addis Ababa in February 2020. This was co-hosted by the Ethiopian National Defence Force and the US Army Africa, whose promotion of the event as 'the largest gathering of military leaders on the African continent ever' implied a certain competition with China but also provided a reminder that China is one of many external military partners that the AU, African countries and militaries work with.

China's naval base in Djibouti has established itself as a hub for regional military operations serving UN and Chinese government's policy purposes and extending the global possibilities for naval and other expeditionary actions. It represents a step towards the original China Dream; that is, developing military power commensurate with China's economic status,[33] such as by providing necessary facilities for future ocean-going aircraft carriers. The base broke a taboo on creating overseas military facilities, paving the way for new bases in Africa and elsewhere. Given China's evolving engagement in Africa, protecting bilateral interests and promoting China's leadership credentials via multilateral contribution looks set to continue to be complementary goals in an expansion strategy. In January 2019, a senior PLA officer stated that whether China establishes new overseas military bases will depend 'primarily on whether a new base is needed to help China better fulfil missions given by the United Nations and host country approval'.[34] The question is now when and where, not whether, China will develop new military facilities in Africa.

China's 'traditional security' engagement in Africa, exemplified by its Djibouti naval base, is set to become more important but should not divert attention from the mounting importance of a range of connected areas of 'non-traditional security' cooperation. With security having many meanings within China's domestic context and as an applied theme in China's Africa relations, the basic challenge of governance has become a more central, if not always visible, policy theme. In order to attempt to create conditions conducive to African development, and at the same time promote China's interests, part of China's 'new thinking' involves support for a raft of legal issues. The less visible, quotidian and cumulative impact of legal cooperation running concurrently with hard security cooperation centred on what Xi Jinping termed 'foreign-related rule of law work' pointed to a significant underlying shift, further binding relations together.

Conclusion

'We try to separate politics from business', Chinese government officials used to argue.[1] Under Xi Jinping, politics has been central to China's New Era Africa relations and inseparable from business and economic relations. This has been evident in public debate about China in African countries and when normally tightly controlled and choreographed official relations veer off script to reveal tensions concerning China's power in Africa. Before the 2018 FOCAC summit, for example, China's ambassador to Namibia Zhang Yiming told the country's President Hage Geingob that he should 'speak highly of China–Africa economic relations … and affirm Africa's political support for China and that of Namibia'. President Geingob replied: 'You should not tell us what we should do. We are not puppets.'[2] This episode showed discord and pushback by an African leader concerning Beijing's efforts to control every aspect of relations, pointing to deeper debates about China's role in Namibia and a greater complexity, which Beijing's official foreign-policy vocabulary and vision does not reflect.

Against the conventional wisdom that China's relations with Africa are based primarily on economics, this book has argued that while economics remain central, these are bound up in diverse types of politics indicative of China's more established role in African countries and continental affairs. Politics always mattered in China's post-colonial relations with Africa but, from 1978, China's leaders prioritized economic development and, from around the mid 1990s until 2014–2015, economic drivers dominated relations. Since coming to power, Xi Jinping has prioritized politics, through CCP renewal within China, major power diplomacy and the goal of national rejuvenation. The reasons why politics has become the defining feature of China–Africa relations are thus rooted in but go far beyond Xi's leadership of China.

China's ascendancy under General Secretary Xi Jinping as a self-proclaimed major power with global leadership ambitions and a leading power in Africa represents a major change. At the 2017 CCP Congress, Xi Jinping set the goal of China's becoming 'a global leader in terms of composite national strength and international influence'. The CCP's goal is to make China a global leader in economic, political and military strength. China's rise as a global economic power holding the world's largest financial reserves ($3.154trn in August 2020) forms the basis for China's economic statecraft. This entails using financial and other economic instruments to promote relations with other countries and provide them with incentives to support China's foreign policy.[3] Xi Jinping's New Era has seen different types of Chinese power become more manifest and consequential in its Africa relations. China's security and military engagement form one face of Chinese power in Africa, but this follows and is bound up in China's more advanced and involved political-economic role in the continent.

This conclusion examines three connected themes that draw together and expand on the contents of this book. The first concerns China as an established power in the continent, a key theme underpinning the politics of China's New Era relations with Africa. Second, the New Era has rendered the mismatch between the traditional language the Chinese government uses to frame its Africa relations – and actually existing relations – more pronounced. Third, the conclusion considers emerging directions in China's New Era African relations in a phase where previous certainties have eroded and the contours of revised relations have been taking shape. The previous teleology about the inevitability of future convergence and ties has been replaced by uncertainty.

CHINA: AN ESTABLISHED POWER IN AFRICA

China has gone from being a traditional, marginal and distant partner of Africa to attaining a leading position in continental affairs in just over two decades. It is now a major economic and political partner for individual African countries and the continent, sharing a clear agenda for developing long-term future ties. It is also a self-styled champion of Africa in international affairs, with Foreign Minister Wang Yi noting in late 2020: 'The African people must be involved as equal participants and important contributors to global governance.'[4] China once challenged established powers such as the UK, France or the US in Africa. Now it is an established, if still expanding, power, as seen in three overlapping areas: military, economic and political.

One face of China's power in Africa is military, part of an accelerated, far-reaching shift in the Chinese security engagement. This defining characteristic of China's New Era Africa relations is also indicative of the more established economic interests China has on the continent, the presence of Chinese citizens and opportunities for reputational enhancement and experiential learning. Security is often associated with China's expanding military engagement, symbolized by UN peacekeeping and now its naval base in Djibouti, which raises the issue of whether China's future role will be peaceful. However, China's security engagement is wide ranging. Non-traditional security issues have become prominent, exemplified by thickening legal cooperation, or China's efforts to promote its COVID-19 vaccines. China's military engagement should not be overstated, remaining small in comparison to America's militarized role; but achieving military power and capability commensurate with economic status remains a core part of the Chinese government's strategic aims.

Another central aspect of China's power concerns economic development. In the recent past, a spirit of Afro-optimism propelled by China's economic momentum and, conveyed by generic 'Africa Rising' narratives, inspired hopes of a new age of transformative development. China still gains by addressing economic development priorities held by African states. The basic aims of the AU's Agenda 2063 are widely supported. However, any faith that China could succeed where others failed – within and outside Africa – is now tempered by greater realism brought about by over two decades of experience. China is the major supporter and champion of structural transformation in Africa. This is advanced for good reasons but represents wishful thinking. It is presented officially in a continental framework but in practice only a handful of African countries demonstrate progress. Of these, Ethiopia has received outsized attention from Chinese, international media, African and many Western researchers. As a comparatively successful but particular case, Ethiopia is not Africa and, furthermore, faced new military conflict and political instability from late 2020. African resource-rich economies continue to export raw commodities, not higher value processed goods. From 2014, the downturn in commodity prices and the onset of the first Africa-wide recession for 25 years in 2020 affected relations and took these into a different phase. There is little evidence that ruling African political elites, assuming they have the will, have the power to change the structural basis of their economies.[5] This suggests that, going forward, the Chinese government would continue to revise its approach.

A number of African states experienced economic distress before the 2020 COVID-19 pandemic but this brought key underlying challenges into focus. For Angola, Mozambique, Zambia or Zimbabwe, this was partly because of the unsustainable debt burdens owed to China.[6] Much is at stake in how China manages its African debt issue and how far the structural transformation agenda advances, since otherwise the dominance of resource trade characterizing China–Africa economic relations is unlikely to change meaningfully. This would mean a continuation of Africa's historic subordination in the global economy. Debt has also sharpened and channelled concerns about deeper challenges concerning China and new forms of actual or potential dependency. That China is the largest bilateral holder of African debt represents a highly significant change. Debt became a key lightning rod for diverse grievances, but the larger issue is how far African countries are becoming dependent on China.

A historical conundrum for Tanzania was how to maintain a special relationship with but 'not become economically and politically dependent on China'.[7] Today this conundrum is more acute and widespread. Outwardly committed to both the 'self-development' of African countries and 'co-development' with China, Beijing denounces dependency as a historic phenomenon of African economic and political relations with neo-colonial Western states. For nearly six decades, the Chinese government has affirmed that the purpose of its development aid 'is not to make the recipient countries dependent on China but to help them embark step by step on the road of self-reliance and independent economic development'.[8] It appears less able to acknowledge and respond to concerns about emerging forms of dependency deriving from the nature of its own economic relations. In this sense, even if China's actual economic status is prone to exaggeration, perceptions of its economic power influence political reactions within African countries.

In terms of China's political power in Africa, different dimensions of China's actual and potential political influence within African countries have come to the fore. This remains hard to fathom. Much remains unknown about deeper impacts the Chinese engagements have been having within different African polities, and what these will mean going forward. Beyond the obvious material signifiers of China's concrete role, such as infrastructure projects, there are dynamics concerning how China's engagement may enable leverage to certain political elites, influence policy and affect relations between African states and civil societies. How 'this may be transforming the African state is not yet well understood'.[9]

The New Era has seen an important shift from downplaying to promoting the Xi Jinping incarnation of the China model, which more or less officially now exists. What is new is not the attempt to promote China's model but the China that is promoting it: Xi Jinping's China based on his form of authoritarian single-party state capitalism. The cross-generational efforts China has been making to invest in current ties with African political parties and future political relations, to influence ideas about governance and enhance links, are concerted, systematic and far reaching. Previous experience, whether China's or that of other external powers, suggests that the actual effects of such ideological education should not be overstated. What matters most is not what the Chinese government may try to promote by way of its ideas about politics, but how these are understood, selectively incorporated and used by African political elites, ruling political parties and others. Governing elites in African states will continue to pursue their own agendas, picking and choosing among external powers and exercising their own forms of extraverted political agency in the process. Nonetheless, 'the mechanisms and operations of China's influence remain underexplored'.[10] And the question of how the thickening of investment in education, trainings and governance exchanges, including between the CCP and African political parties, may translate in future power terms remains to be answered.

The multiplying challenges China faces in Africa test the ability of its party-state-military to respond effectively. China is attempting to respond to its more established role in Africa, as seen for example in institutional terms with the creation of the China International Development Cooperation Agency. China maintains a formal continental Africa policy but in practice has developed many African country and regional engagements. This also shows the various ways in which China's African state partners exercise influence and themselves have sought to make comparable institutional adjustments to better manage relations with China. The limits of China's traditional principles in the face of new realities, however, have become more tangible.

TRADITIONAL PRINCIPLES, NEW REALITIES

In the New Era, the mismatch between the traditional language China uses to frame its Africa relations and actually existing relations has become more pronounced. This can be seen in four areas: solidarity, equality and mutual respect, win–win development, and most importantly, sovereignty and non-interference.

The historic language of solidarity continues to be used and, on an inter-state basis, does convey aspects of current relations. While still suited to relations between different kinds of African states, from democracies to military dictatorships, and imbued with a powerful post-colonial symbolism, this is less well suited to a time when China's relationship with African countries has become more diverse and has gone much beyond state and political elite ties. Indeed, as controversy about African debt in 2020 showed, the notion can be a liability exposing the absence, perceived or otherwise, of actual solidarity. The political will and practical content behind the Chinese government's proclamations of solidarity in terms of global action for Africa remain questionable. Nonetheless, the very fact that China – and other powers like India – is attuned to Africa's predicament, positions itself as a leading part in addressing this, and does so via such tangible recent initiatives as COVID-19 vaccine support, is significantly more advantageous than the engagements of other Western powers.

The core principles of equality and mutual respect remain very present and integral but in the context of stark asymmetrical relations. While exercised via the notable personal investment by China's leadership in cultivating relations with African counterparts, for example, in practice these principles fail to mask already profound and deepening economic and political asymmetries. Xi Jinping prefers the language of China as 'the largest developing country and the largest developing continent', not that of a major power, in his African interactions. Yet, the power hierarchy is clear: China's relations with African states are now conspicuously unequal in unprecedented ways. The Chinese government talks equality but operates according to a hierarchy of relations in which some African states, including South Africa, Nigeria, Egypt or Kenya, are more important than others. Normally, this would not be surprising, especially given the sheer number of African states with which China maintains diplomatic relations, but China maintains firm public protestations of equality. Mutual respect, a principle often tied to equality, has also been under strain. In 2018, for example, after President Kenyatta called for a halt to imported Chinese tilapia to protect local fishing, China's acting ambassador to Kenya called the move a 'trade war', threatening sanctions and to withdraw SGR funding in response.[11] Hardly a model of 'mutual respect', this heavy-handed response was strikingly discordant, a vivid departure from the normal script, but provided a possible glimpse onto future relations.

'Win–win development' is an attractive slogan, predicated as it is on shared interest and mutual gains, but in practice is more complicated in the face of the wide variations in African country circumstance. This is seen, in simple terms, in just how difficult it has been for Namibian beef, Ugandan flowers or Kenyan avocados to be exported to China and for the wider agenda of African trade diversification to advance.[12] Official efforts within China–Africa relations to qualify the win–win premise by using 'sustainable', for instance, are contradicted by blatantly unsustainable intensive industrial fishing in west Africa, illegal forestry or other forms of environmentally harmful resource extraction. There are many such examples apart from China.[13] However, the Chinese government sets the bar high, including through its 'green development' rhetoric. In development cooperation, China presents itself as a partner different from Western and multilateral donors and development funders. This includes providing grants and loans for development purposes supposedly without political conditions, on more beneficial and 'equal' terms since China is also a developing country. At the same time, China continues not to be transparent about development finance and aid. Further, as seen in Zambia, for example, accusations about corruption are rife.[14] Outside such problems, however, China continues to be an inspiration for economic development on the basis of demonstrable Chinese domestic achievements. These continue to confer a basic credibility, which is often lost on Western decision-makers and publics.

The principles of sovereignty and non-interference have taken on new applied meanings at a time when China is no longer an outsider in African affairs. China's sovereignty doctrine has formed the bedrock for its relations with African states. Sovereignty has also become a banner around which African politicians and various civil society groups now mobilize vis-à-vis China. One factor behind the potency of mobilizing sovereignty is the very fact that this is a cornerstone of China's domestic and foreign policy, as well as the Chinese government's formal organizing principle for a world based on the rights of sovereign states, not rights-bearing individuals. The politicization of African state sovereignty has been seen in fierce controversy in Kenya or Nigeria, for example, about debt terms and clauses in contracts with China that have been interpreted, rightly or wrongly, as ceding sovereignty and paving the way for China to take future control. This is a powerful, emotive basis for political critique and mobilization, and means that China can and has become a useful proxy for various forms of domestic political opposition to incumbent African governments. As seen in the context of Zambia, the DRC or Nigeria, for example, Chinese migrants can be caught up in the fallout of deteriorations in inter-state relations.

The language of sovereignty and non-interference also obscures a more far-reaching and ongoing shift in China's engagement with

African politics. China generally refrained from publicly criticizing its African partners, except on exceptionally sensitive issues like Taiwan. Recently, Chinese officials have pointed to the political constraints on African development, sometimes in unusually forthright terms. The former Chinese ambassador to South Africa, for example, described President Cyril Ramaphosa as 'the last hope' of South Africa and argued that Chinese investors needed reassurance about the institutional integrity of managing such entities as Eskom, which he described with the loaded phrase 'debt trap', in order to explain that China was wary of providing further financial support to it.[15] The bigger point this raised was the centrality of politics to future development in Africa. It implied what had been apparent elsewhere but not publicly vocalized by Chinese officials – in South Sudan, to cite one example – which was that technical cooperation was necessary but insufficient for advancing economic development, and functioning political institutions were vital to any meaningful such process.

Given the unavoidable importance of politics, it is unsurprising that China's role in the governance of African countries has been deepening in ways that bring received wisdom about non-interference into question. The Chinese governance engagement and attendant legal aspects, which is linked to but goes beyond political training around the China model, has been quieter but important, slowly shifting the nature of relations and taking these into new territory. The Chinese government's former 'hands off' approach to African governance has in some cases much evolved in the face of day-to-day challenges. Placing Chinese officials directly in Zimbabwean government ministries and parastatal offices in 2015, to promote reform and provide oversight, evoke classic IMF methods and conditionalities in ways that are not lost on African civil society and governments. Whether or not this is 'interference' can be debated; in general China goes with, not against, the grain of a multitude of different political systems in Africa. Nonetheless, it represents a functional form of interference that indicates Chinese government practice is converging with aspects of what has hitherto been deemed 'Northern' practice.

The practical tensions between ground realities and abstract high political principle are more evident in China's path towards a more interventionist role in African security. The issues of Chinese citizens at risk in the continent, the exposure of significant economic interests operated by SOEs, the future of the BRI and China's relations with some African states may necessitate a more interventionist approach, whether bilaterally or through UN missions, as in Mali. This has been happening in all but name. China's Djibouti naval base represented a remarkable departure in China's foreign policy but has already become a normal part of China's engagement. Beijing plays up the role of the base helping China fulfil UN responsibilities, or assisting the AU in promoting continental security, but this also serves to project hard power and further China's global ambitions. The Chinese government has become 'able to intervene directly overseas'.[16] Going forward, and in light of CCP efforts to build a 'world-class military' by 2050, as Xi Jinping stated in his 2017 19th Party Congress report, future military bases in Africa will only assist this, and China's wider global goals.

Solidarity, equality and mutual respect, win–win development, sovereignty and non-interference: addressing criticism within African countries and without, the Chinese government's efforts to double-down on traditional principles by framing its Africa relations through slightly revised but essentially more robust versions of traditional principles – such as Xi Jinping's 'five no' statement in 2018 – sought to reaffirm and even renew its credentials as both a peer developing country and a Southern power engaging in major power diplomacy. The principles of 'sincerity, real results, amity and good faith and of pursing [sic] the greater good and shared interests' articulated at the 2018 FOCAC indicate awareness of deeper challenges and realistic purpose. However, these complement, rather than supersede, the higher-order principles of official inter-state cooperation and, overall, render 'power relations less visible/confrontational and therefore more successful'.[17]

Despite maintaining inflexible principles in public rhetoric, China's approach as actually applied has been adaptive, innovative and often responsive to African demands, even if contentious issues like market access to China remained unresolved. In keeping with China's historic blending of high principle and pragmatism, this meant that the essential starting point for any attempt to grapple with China's Africa engagement in the New Era is arguably not Beijing but seeking truth from the distant and grounded granular facts of myriad African contexts. China's Africa engagement appears to be more coherent from the outside than it is in practice: the CCP leads on everything but can't control everything, including SOEs.

China's advancing role in Africa has been generating more conspicuous gaps between the traditional language the Chinese government uses to frame its Africa relations and actually existing, far more complex relations. Principle and pragmatism have characterized China's Africa relations for decades. The New Era has continued to involve a combination of a heavily principled approach with greater flexibility in practice. The continued use of China's general foreign-policy principles dating back to 1954/55 is striking. It matters because such principles define China's claimed difference from other external powers in Africa, not just in declared intention but outcomes. These thus serve to set expectations and as a means to measure conduct. China's relations with Africa in Xi Jinping's New Era have rendered the gaps between rhetoric and real relations more apparent. The actual politics of China–Africa relations, in other words, has outpaced the official state-based vocabulary with which these are formally directed and represented, and the hallowed historic principles of South–South cooperation have become more evidently abstract post-colonial categories removed from the new realities of relations.

Such trends are unlikely to meaningfully affect the continued use of a vocabulary that serves political relations well. For all the myriad counter-reactions in African countries, this vocabulary remains popular – not just in terms of governing elites – when taken literally as signifying China's declared intent, as with non-interference, as opposed to the effects of Chinese engagement, which are invariably part of more diverse African political relations. China's official language of its Africa relations remains too important to change, or change significantly. It will endure. The basic framing of official relations continues to matter in terms of image projection, and an attractive, compelling shared language governing elites can use to represent official relations in public. China's attempts to update, reinforce and reaffirm this language signal indirect recognition of the distance between the vocabulary and narratives of official China–Africa relations and actual relations. Nonetheless, the Chinese government insists its Africa relations are to be understood on the basis of formal principles, codifying what these are supposed to be but revealing little about real relations.

Beyond official rhetoric, the practical consequences of the expansionary success of China's engagement in Africa have been generating seeds of change, in institutional, regulatory or even personnel terms. These mean that adjustment has been inevitable and necessary, as part of ongoing processes of change.[18] All manner of the practices of different Chinese actors have been changing, but its official language remains constant. Instead of morally charged rhetorical South–South claims, outcomes and results now matter more in a context of greater demand on the part of Africans, not just for accountability in African countries but also ensuring that China together with African governments contributes to broader, longer-term, and lasting development in the continent. The deepened interaction that China's more established engagement with African countries has entailed has produced complications, tensions and political differences in a range of areas, from interpersonal relations to trade, development projects or geopolitics.[19]

China's engagement is thus symptomatic of broader challenges in twenty-first-century South–South cooperation, which continues to revolve around mid twentieth-century post-colonial principles but in conditions of more advanced economic attainment and power hierarchies within and between Southern states. In this, China stands out for the systemic importance of its role, not just in Africa but its wider engagement in the global South. No longer the 'poor helping the poor', as Premier Zhou Enlai described Mao-era China–Africa relations, China is now at the forefront of emerging relations between and within the global South involving a separation between the 'Power South' and the 'Poor South'.[20] The more visibly exposed position China has in Africa, and the far more consequential impact of its role, ensures greater and wider scrutiny. This does not sit well with Beijing's default preference for not being open about the terms of major deals or relationships.

Where once, even before China's 'going global' strategy made this more evident from 1999, Africa held a distinctive, pioneering position in China's strategy of overseas expansion, the continent now is far less distinctive in global terms as China's engagement with the global South has broadened, deepened and evolved. The issue of how the New Era will evolve is not just about China's Africa relations but its wider global role.

THE FUTURE OF THE NEW ERA

The New Era now encompasses highly diverse engagements, in which the place, role and future of Chinese migrant communities in African countries is notable in not just political respects but also for deeper social changes evident in some countries. African migration to and business in China was evolving in the context of the political and regulatory changes caused or accelerated by the COVID-19 pandemic from 2020. The deepening Chinese role in some African countries like Namibia is taking on a longer-term quality organized around emerging

African–Chinese communities. This brings into question the common idea that China's influence is a force that is somehow external to African societies, since this involves evolving hybrid combinations that cut across and complicate any such simple divisions. In terms of key trends going forward, however, interconnected economic and political issues stood out.

The economic importance of Africa for China is often overstated. As noted, Africa is significant in the Chinese government's global foreign aid (officially receiving 45% between 2013 and 2018). Total combined Africa trade, however, itself dominated by a small number of resource-rich African exporters, counts for a fraction of China's overall global trade. China matters far more to African trade than African trade, including resource exports, matters to China. Unlike two decades ago, when Chinese oil imports from Angola or Sudan mattered (China imported around one third of its oil from Africa in 2008), China has diversified its existing or potential supplies of raw materials beyond African producers, diminishing their importance. In addition, China is not currently the top investor in Africa, although that is likely to change, nor does the continent represent a sizeable proportion of global Chinese FDI. Even before 2020, when this was confirmed, it was evident that the Chinese government's appetite for large-scale financing had waned, meaning that the familiar pattern of substantially increasing or matching FOCAC funding pledges every three years is unlikely to continue. This did not preclude future investment, even though China's New Era has repositioned the economic importance of Africa to China in global terms. China has been advancing ties with other strategically important regions, including the Middle East, revising the seemingly special treatment extended to Africa. The BRI shifted Beijing's focus to a global scale in which African countries were one part of a more far-reaching project.

Despite this, China's economic importance for African countries and the continent looks set to remain and grow, albeit in changing circumstances. That Africa is less important in narrow economic terms to China than often assumed is indicative of the continent's structural marginalization in the global economy. The dominant feature of many African economies continues to be extremely high sensitivity to global economic conditions, meaning that the story of economic development in the continent has been one of cyclical patterns of boom and bust.[21] Putting recent economic relations into context is not to minimize these, nor preclude future expansion, but it is to attempt to shift analysis of China–Africa relations beyond simple, reductionist accounts based on resource extraction and, above all, recognize the greater complexity of relations now bound together by politics at various local, national, regional or global levels.

China's economic engagement with Africa is continuing to evolve, as its own domestic economy evolves in a changing global context. The 'express train of China's development' that Xi Jinping invited African countries to board in 2018 is proceeding at a slower, more uncertain pace and faces numerous barriers. China's approach to economic development was moving towards 'domestic circulation'. Amid a reassessment of China's overseas lending, and tightening of lending criteria, banks and SOEs were shifting attention to domestic projects. The COVID-19 pandemic seemed to generate greater interest and demand for domestic health investment within China, meaning an additional constraint on overseas lending.[22] For Africa, the prospects seemed to entail lower lending, higher scrutiny and interest in sustainability. Debt and attention to China's lending has generated more interest in Africa in what Chinese money has been used for, and how far this has contributed to wider development as opposed to elite enrichment. A further trend involves African states looking beyond China to other partners as part of efforts to diversify economic relations, such as South Africa and ASEAN. A final trend, more significant within Africa, concerned the efforts of African countries to develop economic relations between themselves. The launch of the

AfCFTA in January 2021 had symbolic value, and provided a future vision, but the more difficult work of building the legal and practical foundations to make the project work was only just beginning.

Post-colonial historical connections between China and African countries remain present in China's statecraft, used to promote its own engagement and delegitimize others, but as a factor influencing current ties, China's recent history exerts more tangible and varied influences. For all Beijing's investment in 'telling China's story well' and its attempts to use its version of the past as proof of future benign conduct, many of the most contentious political challenges between China and African countries derive from the recent past and experience. Beijing can mostly control official African governing elite discourse but struggles to exert the same control over its version of history within heterogeneous African countries, especially those characterized by open debate and keen historical awareness like Nigeria, South Africa or Kenya. One example that speaks volumes is the politics of China's past money in Angola, where President João Lourenço has sought to recover what he estimated as at least $24bn in stolen money, stolen under his predecessor, José Eduardo dos Santos. In his October 2020 state of the nation address, President Lourenço noted that this amount was larger than the approximately $20bn debt Angola owes to China, its main creditor.[23] The crackdown has targeted key allies of the former president as prime suspects in a corruption scandal concerning the China International Fund, a venture of a secretive 88 Queensway Group based in Hong Kong. President Lourenço's campaign against corruption, which has had selective political motivations, was proceeding at the same time as the Angolan government was trying to renegotiate debt with China. This example demonstrated the importance of large resource-backed Chinese financing through elite political appropriation and use in a country that may have been Africa's third largest economy for much of the last two decades but where poverty and inequality remain entrenched.[24] Simply put, this politics of Chinese financing shows how bound together politics and economics are in practice and also the very different stage of Angola's relations with China in the face of these challenges. A major question in Angola and in Africa more generally is how relations with China will develop without the exponential increases in funding witnessed thus far and how this would change views on China's political appeal.

Namibian President Hage Geingob's 'We are not puppets' comment also drew attention to a number of potential opportunities that African countries could attempt to better manage and balance ties. The actual continental aspects of Africa's relations with China are not as developed as the bilateral relations between 53 African countries and China. One priority is the need for more strategic, better managed and coordinated African strategies on China, such as around debt. This theme, which is not unique to African countries since it now applies around the world, has been much discussed but little acted on. In 2006, for instance, the then AU Commission Chairman and former president of Mali, Alpha Konaré, spoke about Africa's need to develop strong relationships with 'partners of the future', including China, and affirmed: 'The terms and the conditions should be set by us.'[25] With examples of best practice by African governments in negotiating with China, including allowing technical ministries to direct negotiations, or hiring external expertise, there are 'plenty of stratagems and tactics on the African side. What is required is a more coordinated and coherent approach.'[26] Another priority concerned the ability of African governments to better manage disclosure of the terms of financing deals and undertake open due diligence concerning the sustainability of borrowing. African governments can do more to address the glaring lack of public information about key aspects of financial dealings with China, for example, through legislation to require loan terms to be made public. Such measures are meaningless, however, when there is a shared interest in opaque financial dealings. This raised another issue concerning the broadening and deepening of participation in China relations not only by civil society groups but by citizens of African states as well. Finally, one notable trend is organized around reciprocity and involves greater interest in matching China's declared language of its Africa partnership with meaningful reform. Taken up by incumbent and opposition African politicians alike, as well as civil society groups, this takes various forms that, revolving around efforts to balance relations and add substance to slogans, commonly rest on the intent to achieve genuine reciprocity with China. In economic relations, this means addressing trade deficits, the barriers African producers face to accessing China's market or calls by African leaders and ministers on China to open its markets further. As Kenya's President Kenyatta asserted in 2017, 'just as Africa opens up to China, China must also open up to Africa.'[27] In more political ways, demands for the equal treatment of Nigerians in China and Chinese in Nigeria, to cite one prominent example, echo widely held sentiment in other African countries. Such African-authored initiatives represent signs of good health if these can meaningfully address common complaints about a China-dominated one-way street. How far such initiatives can advance remains in question, especially given that a key asymmetry in relations concerns 'the negotiating capacities of African and Chinese governments.'[28]

The political importance of Africa for China's global role continues. This is clearly seen in African state support for the Chinese government's foreign policy and the political importance of 53 African states and potential votes in multilateral settings. Nonetheless, Beijing cannot take the support of African states for granted, since these remain necessarily pragmatic. Despite closer relations and common interests, questions about the actual extent to which China will act to advance African interests remain. Until recent US–China geopolitical competition opened up the prospect of global divergence, China's new leadership of globalization had been a reality experienced in African countries and had shaped African understandings of China–Africa relations.[29] This is likely to continue but in the context of prospective divergent trends revolving around US–China relations, which, in the future, seem likely to affect topics such as global internet governance, and contending visions of world order.

For China's leadership, at a time when the balance of global power is changing and 'the East is rising, the West is declining', China is in 'an important period of strategic opportunities'.[30] The COVID-19 pandemic has catalysed such opportunities. Despite risks, there are major opportunities for China that the pandemic has accelerated.[31] Amid questions about the BRI's future, the global economic context is undergoing uncertain transition defined by the US–China techno-trade war. This will have implications for African countries. Global economic uncertainty offers a sharp reminder of the imperative of continued intra-African economic reform and African-authored development paths now that the relatively benign era of cooperative coexistence between emerging Southern powers led by China and established OECD donors has reached an uncertain juncture.

Changing geopolitical winds look certain to affect the course of future relations. Despite wide calls by African leaders and others for Africa not to choose between Washington and Beijing, there is growing concern about the direction and implications of US–China global strategic rivalry. There are sound reasons behind calls for Africa to 'chart a new course' but this will be far harder to convert into practice.[32] Nonetheless, the emerging geopolitics is not just about China, the US and Africa but extended to other powers, from Japan, India, Turkey or Russia as well as the EU.

On issues from Xinjiang, Hong Kong, Huawei to development, African states were more supportive of China, including on the Chinese government's interest in promoting Made in China technology standards like a digital currency or 'human rights with Chinese characteristics'. As became more apparent in 2020 with pushback against China in many parts of the world, which the COVID-19 pandemic exacerbated, Africa stood out as being still open to China, at least at the level of governing elites, on such issues. European policy-makers, by contrast, were taking steps to end a 'long period of asymmetric openness to China.'[33]

As seen in the militarization of the South China Sea or boycotts to damage Taiwan, 'China is unafraid to wield its power in profoundly nonliberal, noncooperative ways.'[34] Africa thus far has not seen such equivalents (apart from over Taiwan), but the example of China's confrontation with Australia is not lost on African politicians and decision-makers, civil society groups and wider publics. In order to diversify external partnerships, a growing number of African countries like Angola are re-evaluating ties with China and, in large part due to the question of debt, reconsidering future options. Furthermore, popular reactions and civil society engagement means pressure from within on African states such as Zimbabwe, Ghana, Guinea or Kenya about the terms of their China relations. There has been no major divergence of interests between China and an African state thus far. It remains uncertain as to how China might respond, given domestic nationalism and social media connections, to a significant test of the system for protecting overseas investments, starting with political but now backed up by greater logistical capability and a stronger legal basis.

POLITICS AND THE END OF TELEOLOGY

Debates in African media, among African elites and beyond, as well as external observers, often use terms such as 'neo-colonialism' as proxy for all sorts of growing Chinese ascendancy in different sectors of daily life. This book's larger point is not that twenty-first-century China as a leading global power is the architect of a new colonialism, with Africa as a primary target. In an era where the locus of global power appears to be shifting to China, instead it is that African states and their governing elites will be confronted by the challenges of explaining and responding to Chinese economic and political dominance.[35] That power produces resistance was well understood by Deng Xiaoping, who called on people to 'expose', 'oppose', and 'together with Chinese people, overthrow' any future China that became an imperialist superpower.[36] Where China once was seen to represent a potential source of emancipation, it now more evidently represents a potentially hegemonic power.

The big question, then, is whether China will become a (or the) hegemon in Africa, or be a leading part of more multipolar power structures and orientations on the continent shaped by African agency in conjunction with other external powers. In a turbulent geopolitical context of transition, a number of scenarios were present. First, there were good reasons why China appeared set to become more dominant. These included the nature of its engagement and questions about the extent to which other powers, notably a US preoccupied with domestic priorities and reforging a global role after the Trump administration, would seriously engage.[37] Second, China could end up being the hegemon by default, not necessarily design, though much will depend on the actions and engagement of other powers. Third, China's more established position is changing how many African countries have and will engage with it and other external powers. China has transitioned from being an empowering anti-hegemonic alternative to being a proto or actual growing hegemonic power, in perception if not consistent or uniform fact. Where some African states sought to employ China to balance other external powers, now some seek to use other external powers to balance against China as part of a developed strategy of managing competition to attempt to avoid dependency and pursue relative autonomy. After over two decades of 'Looking East', primarily but not only to China, and following a deeper history of such behaviour, African states are now looking to use diversified external partners to maximize their own interests.[38] Finally, then, and shaped by forms of African agency, China could become a leading part of more multipolar power structures and orientations on the continent.

Years before the 2020 COVID-19 pandemic, debt crisis and economic challenges, a longer-term vision for China–Africa relations stood out. This can be dated to China's Africa relations under President Jiang Zemin in the 1990s and was predicated on future economic integration and global political partnership. More recent versions of this vision identify Africa as crucial to China's national fate in the twenty-first century based on future demographic growth.[39] With a current median age of twenty, the population of Africa is projected to double by 2050 and reach 2.5bn.[40] Looking forward, Chinese analysts identify demand from expanded future African markets, based partly on projections that the economic growth China experienced after 1978 can also happen in African countries, which are destined to be the growth story of the future.[41]

China and Chinese relations with Africa and its peoples will continue long beyond Xi Jinping's New Era. The roads there, however, and whether Africa can become the growth story of the future, are far less certain, much as are the prospects for China's future global role. Whether the Chinese government will have the political will to continue to expand relations with Africa, for instance, cannot be taken for granted. In a global context, whether China is ready and able to become a global leader remains questionable.[42] Much remains in flux, including the fallout of the US Trump administration and implications for human rights and democracy as well as the future of the CCP's China model. China–Africa relations in the New Era ultimately stand out because of the ways in which the previous teleology that characterized relations as inevitably marching towards closer future partnership was ending, in effect, even if this was maintained in rhetoric. Beijing's Africa relations have been ever more defined and determined by politics, meaning that the future of China–Africa relations has become much more uncertain.

Notes

Introduction

1 'Wang Yi, South-South Cooperation was Elevated to a New Level', 11 December 2018 (https://www.fmprc.gov.cn/ce/ceus/eng/zgyw/t1621540. htm).

2 See Chris Alden, *China in Africa* (London: Zed Books, 2007); Li Anshan, 'China and Africa: Policy and challenges', *China Security* 3 (3) 2007: 69–93; Kweku Ampiah and Sanusha Naidu, eds, *Crouching Tiger, Hidden Dragon? Africa and China* (Scottsville: University of KwaZulu-Natal Press, 2008); Deborah Bräutigam, *The Dragon's Gift: The Real Story of China in Africa* (Oxford University Press, 2009); Ian Taylor, *China's New Role in Africa* (Boulder, CO: Lynne Rienner, 2009); David Shinn and Joshua Eisenman, *China and Africa: A Century of Engagement* (Philadelphia: University of Pennsylvania Press, 2012).

3 Minxin Pei, 'China's expensive bet on Africa has failed', *Nikkei Asian Review*, 1 May 2020.

4 Lauren Johnson, 'China–Africa economic transitions survey: Charting the return of a fleeting old normal', Proceedings of the 38th African Studies Association of Australasia and the Pacific Conference (February 2016), 10, citing Chris Alden, *China in Africa*.

5 See Chris Alden, Daniel Large and Ricardo Soares de Oliveira, eds, *China Returns to Africa: A Continent and a Rising Power Embrace* (London: Hurst Publishers, 2008).

6 Elizabeth Economy, *The Third Revolution: Xi Jinping and the New Chinese State* (Oxford University Press, 2018).

7 Xi Jinping, 'Secure a decisive victory in building a moderately prosperous society in all respects and strive for the great success of socialism with Chinese characteristics for a new era', Speech delivered at the 19th National Congress of the CCP, 18 October 2017: 9.

8 'China's exports to its three major trading partners all increased by

more than 10%', *Hellenic Shipping News*, 24 August 2020 (https://www. hellenicshippingnews.com/chinas-exports-to-its-three-major-trading-partners-all-increased-by-more-than-10/).

9 UNCTAD, 'Key statistics and trends in regional trade in Africa, 2019', p. 1.

10 Irene Yuan Sun, *The Next Factory of the World: How Chinese Investment is Reshaping Africa* (Harvard: Harvard Business Review Press, 2017).

11 See, for example, Tatiana Carayannis and Lucas Niewenhuis, 'China–Africa: State of the literature 2012–2017' (New York: Social Science Research Council, December 2017).

12 Cobus Van Staden and Yu-Shan Wu, 'Media as a site of contestation in China–Africa relations', in Chris Alden and Daniel Large, eds, *New Directions in Africa–China Studies* (Abingdon: Routledge, 2019), pp. 88–103. See chinaafricaproject.com for up-to-date news and analysis.

13 See Derek Sheridan, 'Chinese peanuts and Chinese *machinga*: The use and abuse of a rumour in Dar es Salaam (and ethnographic writing)', in Alden and Large, eds, *New Directions in Africa–China Studies*, pp. 145–57.

14 See Alden and Large, eds, *New Directions in Africa–China Studies*. For broader Africa–Asia scholarship, see Ross Anthony and Uta Ruppert, eds, *Reconfiguring Transregionalisation in the Global South: African–Asian Encounters* (Palgrave Macmillan, 2019).

15 See, for example, Bräutigam, *The Dragon's Gift*.

16 Marcus Power, Giles Mohan and May Tan-Mullins, *China's Resource Diplomacy in Africa: Powering Development?* (Houndmills: Palgrave Macmillan, 2012); Alison J. Ayers, 'Beyond myths, lies and stereotypes: The political economy of a "new scramble for Africa"', *New Political Economy* 18 (2) 2013: 227–57.

17 Ching Kuan Lee, *The Specter of Global China: Politics, Labor, and Foreign Investment in Africa* (Chicago: University of Chicago Press, 2017).

18 Li Xing and Abdulkadir Osman Farah, eds, *China–Africa Relations in an Era of Great Transformations* (Farnham: Ashgate, 2013).

19 Algeria, Angola, Benin, Botswana, Burkina Faso, Burundi, Cameroon, Cabo Verde, Central African Republic, Chad, Comoros, Republic of Congo, Côte d'Ivoire, Democratic Republic of Congo, Djibouti, Egypt, Equatorial Guinea, Eritrea, Eswatini, Ethiopia, Gabon, Gambia, Ghana, Guinea, Guinea-Bissau, Kenya, Lesotho, Liberia, Libya, Madagascar, Malawi, Mali, Mauritania, Mauritius, Morocco, Mozambique, Namibia, Niger, Nigeria, Rwanda, Saharawi Republic, Sao Tome and Principe, Senegal, Seychelles, Sierra Leone, Somalia, South Africa, South Sudan, Sudan, Tanzania, Togo, Tunisia, Uganda, Zambia and Zimbabwe.

20 Nic Cheeseman, *Democracy in Africa: Successes, Failures, and the Struggle for Political Reform* (Cambridge University Press, 2015).

21 John Ryle, 'The many voices of Africa', *Granta* 92 (2005).

22 Pang Zhongying, 'China's non-intervention question', *Global Responsibility to Protect* 1 (2) 2009: 237–51.

23 Rebecca Lo, 'Why 'Chunwan', China's Lunar New Year gala, is the world's most-watched TV show', *South China Morning Post*, 1 February 2019.

24 Roberto Castillo, 'What "blackface" tells us about China's patronising attitude towards Africa', *The Conversation* (online), 6 March 2018.

25 Hannah Getachew and Runako Celina Bernard-Stevenson, 'Racism – with Chinese characteristics: How Blackface darkened the tone of China's Spring Festival celebrations', Black Livity China, 6 April 2018 (published on https://blacklivitychina.com/).

26 John K. Cooley, *East Wind over Africa: Red China's African Offensive* (New York: Walker and Company, 1965), p. 7.

1 The New Era in Context

1 See Martin Bailey, 'Tanzania and China', *African Affairs* 74 (294) 1975: 39–50.

2 See Philip Snow, *The Star Raft: China's Encounter with Africa* (London: Weidenfeld and Nicolson, 1988).

3 See Jamie Monson, *Africa's Freedom Railway* (Bloomington: Indiana University Press, 2009).

4 See Linda Jakobson and Dean Knox, *New Foreign Policy Actors in China* (Stockholm: SIPRI, 2010).

5 See Niall Duggan, *Competition and Compromise Among Chinese Actors in Africa: A Bureaucratic Politics Study of Chinese Foreign Policy Actors* (Palgrave Macmillan, 2020).

6 See Alexandra Budabin, 'Genocide Olympics: How activists linked China, Darfur and Beijing 2008', in Daniel Large and Luke Patey, eds, *Sudan Looks East: China, India and the Politics of Asian Alternatives* (Oxford: James Currey, 2011), pp. 139–56.

7 Richard McGregor, *The Party: The Secret World of China's Communist Rulers* (Penguin, 2010), p. 1.

8 Signifying the CCP's new importance in the MFA, the former CCP Organization Department deputy head, Qi Yu, was appointed MFA party secretary in 2019.

9 Yang Jiechi, '*Zai Xi Jinping waijiao sixiang zhiyin xia fenli tuijin zhongguo tese*

daguo waijia (Strive to promote diplomacy of big countries with Chinese characteristics under the guidance of Xi Jinping's diplomatic thought); *Qiushi (Seeking Truth)*, 1 September 2019 (http://www.qstheory.cn/dukan/qs/2019-09/01/c_1124940423.htm).

10 Weifeng Zhou and Mario Esteban, 'Beyond balancing: China's approach towards the Belt and Road Initiative', *Journal of Contemporary China* 27 (112) 2018: 487–501.

11 Liza Tobin, 'Xi's vision for transforming global governance: A strategic challenge for Washington and its allies', *Texas National Security Review* 2 (1) 2018: 154–66.

12 This is not a new trend. For example, China has had three Special Envoys for Africa since 2006. The first, Ambassador Liu Guijin, was appointed to deal with China's crisis over Darfur. More recent reforms have, however, been more significant and far reaching.

13 Marina Rudyak, 'The ins and outs of China's International Development Agency', Carnegie, 2 September 2019 (https://carnegieendowment.org/2019/09/02/ins-and-outs-of-china-s-international-development-agency-pub-79739).

14 For example, FOCAC established a China–Africa Environmental Cooperation Center with the UN Environment Program in Nairobi, and the UN in China established a 'China in the World Theme Group'.

15 Ian Taylor, 'The institutional framework of Sino-African relations', in Arkebe Oqubay and Justin Yifu Lin, eds, *China–Africa and an Economic Transformation* (Oxford University Press Scholarship Online, 2019), p. 119.

16 The China Gezhouba Group Co., Ltd, for example, which describes itself as 'the top infrastructure constructor' in Africa, cultivates and uses extensive and high-level connections with African leaders; for example, President Museveni of Uganda.

17 Denghua Zhang and Graeme Smith, 'China's foreign aid system: Structure, agencies, and identities', *Third World Quarterly* 38 (10) 2017: 2330–46.

18 Steve Tsang, 'Party-state realism: A framework for understanding China's approach to foreign policy', *Journal of Contemporary China* 29 (122) 2019: 304–18.

19 Giles Mohan and Ben Lampert, 'Negotiating China: Reinserting African agency into China–Africa relations', *African Affairs* 112 (446) 2012: 92–110.

20 Cobus Van Staden, Chris Alden and Yu-Shan Wu, 'In the driver's seat? African agency and Chinese power at FOCAC, the AU and the BRI', SAIIA Occasional Paper 286, 2018.

21 Ian Taylor, *Africa Rising? BRICS – Diversifying Dependency* (Oxford: James Currey, 2014).

22 Van Staden, Alden and Wu, 'In the driver's seat?'.

23 See Chris Alden, Alvaro Mendez and Daniel Large, 'The Western way of development: A critical review', in Yijia Jing, Alvaro Mendez and Yu Zheng, eds, *New Development Assistance* (Singapore: Palgrave Macmillan, 2020), pp. 19–38.

24 Jon Phillips, 'Who's in charge of Sino-African resource politics? Situating African state agency in Ghana', *African Affairs* 118 (470) 2019: 101–24.

25 Christopher Clapham, *Africa and the International System: The Politics of State Survival* (Cambridge University Press, 1996).

26 Barnaby Dye and Mathias Alencastro, 'Debunking Brazilian exceptionalism in its Africa relations: Evidence from Angola and Tanzania', *Global Society* 34 (4) 2020: 125–46.

27 Jean-François Bayart, 'Africa in the world: A history of extraversion', *African Affairs* 99 (395) 2000: 217–67.

28 Jonathan Fisher and David M. Anderson, 'Authoritarianism and the securitization of development in Africa', *International Affairs* 91 (1) 2015: 131–51.

29 'Sierra Leone scraps project for Chinese-built airport', *AFP*, 11 October 2018.

30 Johanna Malm, '"China-powered" African agency and its limits: The case of the DRC 2007–2019', SAIIA Policy Insights 96, November 2020.

31 See Rirhandu Mageza-Barthel, 'Beyond the state in Sino-African relations?', in Arndt Graf and Azirah Hashim, eds, *African–Asian Encounters: New Cooperations and New Dependencies* (Amsterdam University Press, 2017), pp. 103–31.

32 Barney Walsh, 'China's pervasive yet forgotten regional security role in Africa', *Journal of Contemporary China* 28 (120) 2019: 965–83.

33 Development Reimagined, 'Who does China prioritise?', 30 January 2018 (https://developmentreimagined.com/2018/01/30/who-does-china-prioritise-our-first-investigation/).

34 Chinese aid appears to disproportionately benefit politically privileged regions in years when incumbents face upcoming elections and when electoral competitiveness is high. Axel Dreher, Andreas Fuchs, Roland Hodler, Bradley C. Parks, Paul A. Raschky and Michael J. Tierney, 'African leaders and the geography of China's foreign assistance', *Journal of Development Economics* 140, 2019: 44–71.

35 Folashadé Soulé-Kohndou, 'Bureaucratic agency and power asymmetry in Benin–China relations', in Alden and Large, *New Directions in Africa–China Studies*, pp. 189–204.

36 AU Commission, 'Agenda 2063: The Africa we want' (2015): 1.

37 The French newspaper, *Le Monde*, alleged that China had bugged the AU headquarters but this was rejected by African leaders and China.

38 Bob Wekesa, 'A call for an African policy framework towards China', in Philani Mthembu and Faith Mabera, eds, *Africa–China Cooperation: Towards an African Policy on China?* (Palgrave Macmillan 2021), p. 12.

39 Paul Kagame, The Imperative to Strengthen our Union: Report on the proposed recommendations for the institutional reform of the African Union, 29 January 2017.

40 Francis A. Kornegay, Jr and Chris Landsberg, 'Engaging emerging powers: Africa's search for a "common position"', *Politikon* 36 (1) 2009: 171–91.

41 For instance, see 'Taming the dragon? Defining Africa's interests at the Forum on China–Africa Co-operation' (Centre for Conflict Resolution and the Institute for Global Dialogue, 2009).

42 Francis A. Kornegay Jr, 'Regionalizing Sino-African diplomatic engagement: Kagame and overcoming the "one and the many" paradigm', in Mthembu and Mabera, eds, *Africa–China Cooperation*, p. 33.

43 Julia C. Strauss, 'The past in the present: Historical and rhetorical lineages in China's relations with Africa', *The China Quarterly* 199, 2009: 777–95.

44 Yoon Park, 'One million Chinese in Africa', 12 May 2016, at ⟨http://www.saisperspectives.com/2016issue/2016/5/12/n947s9csa0ik6kmkm0b zb0hy584sfo⟩.

45 Nis Grunberg and Katja Drinhausen, 'The party leads on everything', *MERICs China Monitor*, 24 September 2019: 5.

46 Lucy Corkin, *Uncovering African Agency: Angola's Management of China's Credit Lines* (Farnham: Ashgate: 2013), p. 5.

47 Pádraig Carmody and Francis Owusu, 'Competing hegemons? Chinese vs American geoeconomic strategies in Africa', *Political Geography* 26 (5) 2007: 504–24.

2 China and Africa in Global Politics

1 Yang Jiechi, 'Zai Xi Jinping waijiao sixiang zhiyin xia fenli tuijin zhongguo tese daguo waijia'.

2 Dikarabo Ramadubu, 'Khama blasts China', *Botswana Guardian*, 17 August 2017.

3 *Xinhua*, 'China appreciates 37 foreign ambassadors' joint letter supporting Xinjiang policy', 15 July 2019 (http://www.xinhuanet.com/english/2019-07/15/c_138229200.htm).

4 Jane Perlez, 'China wants the world to stay silent on Muslim camps. It's succeeding', *New York Times*, 25 September 2019.

5 Kevin Pinner, 'China on the offensive about Xinjiang', *SupChina.com*, 25

September 2019 (https://supchina.com/2019/09/25/exclusive-china-on-the-offensive-about-xinjiang-raises-issue-at-u-n/).

6 *Vanguard Newspaper*, 'Using vocational education to tackle extremism: the Xinjiang Experience', 23 August 2019: 30.

7 *Xinhua*, 'UN envoys from 8 countries visit Xinjiang', 2 September 2019.

8 Song Shengxia, Bai Yunyi and Liu Xin, 'Geneva-based envoys get clearer picture of China's policy in Xinjiang during visit', *Global Times*, 3 September 2019 (http://www.globaltimes.cn/content/1163560.shtml).

9 Ibid.

10 The South African poet Dennis Brutus visited China in 1973 and quoted Zhou Enlai as saying: 'We support you in your struggle for freedom in South Africa'. Dennis Brutus, *China Poems* (Austin: University of Texas, 1975).

11 Zheng Zhuqiang, 'Five questions, answers on what is happening in Hong Kong', *New Vision*, 25 August 2019.

12 Rosemary Foot, '"Doing some things" in the Xi Jinping era: The United Nations as China's venue of choice', *International Affairs* 90 (5) 2014: 1085–100.

13 'Speech by H. E. Li Keqiang Premier of the State Council of the People's Republic of China at the AU Conference Center', AU Commission, 5 May 2014.

14 'Chinese FM calls for solidarity of China, Africa', *Xinhua*, 27 September 2019.

15 'Keynote Speech by Wang Yi State Councillor and Foreign Minister of the People's Republic of China at the Opening Ceremony of the Coordinators' Meeting on the implementation of the follow-up actions of the Beijing Summit of the Forum on China–Africa Cooperation', 25 June 2019 (https://www.fmprc.gov.cn/mfa_eng/wjdt_665385/zyjh_665391/t1675596.shtml).

16 See Katrin Kinzelbach, 'Resisting the power of human rights: The People's Republic of China', in Thomas Risse, Stephen C. Ropp and Kathryn Sikkink, eds, *The Persistent Power of Human Rights: From Commitment to Compliance* (Cambridge University Press, 2013), pp. 164–81.

17 'China and the world in the New Era' (Beijing: The State Council Information Office of the People's Republic of China, September 2019).

18 Ibid.

19 Including the 2nd Ministerial Meeting of the Forum of China and Community of Latin American and Caribbean States in Santiago, Chile; and the 8th Ministerial Meeting of the China–Arab States Cooperation Forum in Beijing.

20 China–Latin America trade increased from $17bn to almost $315bn between 2002 and 2019.

21 See Timothy R. Heath, 'China prepares for an international order after US leadership', Lawfareblog.com, 1 August 2018 (https://www.lawfareblog.com/china-prepares-international-order-after-us-leadership).

22 '*Canyu quanqiu jingji zhili tixi biange* (Participate in the transformation of the global economic governance system)', *People's Daily*, 27 February 2019: 1.

23 Congress Report, English version, p. 54.

24 Pádraig Carmody, Niheer Dasandi and Slava Jankin Mikhaylov, 'Power plays and balancing acts: The paradoxical effects of Chinese trade on African foreign policy positions', *Political Studies* 68 (1) 2020: 224–46.

25 See Pádraig Carmody and Peter Kragelund, 'Who is in charge? State power and agency in Sino-African relations', *Cornell International Law Journal* 49, 2016: 1–23.

26 See Large and Patey, eds, *Sudan Looks East*.

27 Foreign Ministry spokesperson Zhao Lijian, Press Conference, 17 November 2020 (https://www.fmprc.gov.cn/mfa_eng/xwfw_665399/s2510_665401/2511_665403/t1833054.shtml).

28 Stephen N. Smith, 'Harmonizing the periphery: China's neighborhood strategy under Xi Jinping', *The Pacific Review* 34 (1) 2021: 58–9.

29 For instance, the 2018 FOCAC Beijing Declaration (para. 18) affirms support for reforming the UNSC. In 2005, the AU's Ezulwini consensus had called for a reformed UNSC featuring African representation.

30 Xi Jinping, 'A new starting point for China's development: A new blueprint for global growth', B20 Summit, Hangzhou, 3 September 2016.

31 See Adriana Erthal Abdenur, 'Brazil–Africa relations: From boom to bust?', in Dawn Nagar and Charles Mutasa, eds, *Africa and the World* (Palgrave Macmillan, 2018), pp. 189–208.

32 For context, see Ajay Kumar Dubey and Aparajita Biswas, eds, *India and Africa's Partnership* (Springer, 2016).

33 *IANS*, 'India marks presence on world stage with Africa summit', 29 October 2015 (http://www.newindianexpress.com/nation/India-Marks-Presence-on-World-Stage-With-Africa-Summit/2015/10/29/article3103713.ece).

34 See Ruchita Beri, 'Towards India–Japan development cooperation in Africa', in Sachin Chaturvedi, Anita Prakash and Priyadarshi Dash, eds, *Asia–Africa Growth Corridor* (Springer, 2020), pp. 227–34.

35 Keynote address by Shinzo Abe, opening session of TICAD 7, 28 August 2019.

36 DFID, 'Economic development strategy: Prosperity, poverty and meeting global challenges' (London: DFID, 2017).

37 Boris Johnson, 'Africa is a mess, but we can't blame colonialism', *The Spectator*, 2 February 2002.

38 See Tom Bayes, 'China in francophone West Africa: A challenge to Paris', MERICS, 28 May 2020.

39 See Anna Katharina Stahl, *EU–China–Africa Trilateral Relations in a Multipolar World: Hic Sunt Dracones* (Palgrave Macmillan 2018), p. 156.

40 European Commission, 'EU–China – a strategic outlook', 12 March 2019.

41 European Commission and High Representative of the Union for Foreign Affairs and Security Policy, 'Joint communication to the European Parliament and the Council: Towards a comprehensive strategy with Africa', Brussels, 9 March 2020.

42 Brenthurst Foundation, 'Summary of Africa–China–US Trilateral Dialogue Council on Foreign Relations', 13 September 2007.

43 Thomas Christensen, Deputy Assistant Secretary of State for East Asian and Pacific Affairs, and James Swan, Deputy Assistant Secretary of State for African Affairs, testimony to Senate Foreign Relations Subcommittee on African Affairs, 4 June 2008.

44 Hillary Rodham Clinton, 'Remarks on building sustainable partnerships in Africa', Secretary of State, University of Cheikh Anta Diop, Dakar, Senegal, 1 August 2012.

45 'Remarks by National Security Advisor Ambassador John R. Bolton on the Trump Administration's New Africa Strategy', Washington, DC, Heritage Foundation, 13 December 2018.

46 Arwa Damon and Brent Swails, 'China and the United States face off in Djibouti as the world powers fight for influence in Africa', CNN, 27 May 2019.

47 Speaking during the US House of Representatives Committee on Foreign Relations, 'Hearing on democracy, development, and defense: Rebalancing US–Africa policy', 16 May 2019.

48 Tibor P. Nagy, speaking at the 'Hearing on democracy, development, and defense'.

49 'Remarks by National Security Advisor Ambassador John R. Bolton.'

50 Peter Fabricius, 'Chinese ambassador to South Africa blasts Donald Trump', *Daily Maverick*, 23 August 2018 (https://www.dailymaverick.co.za/article/2018-08-23-chinese-ambassador-to-south-africa-blasts-donald-trump/).

51 See, for example, Lin Songtian, 'The US willful and bullying acts threatens to plunge the world economy into a severe recession', *The Star* (South Africa), 10 September 2019.

52 Lina Benabdallah, *Shaping the Future of Power: Knowledge Production and Network-Building in China–Africa Relations* (University of Michigan Press, 2020).

3 New Era Economics

1 Felicia Omari Ochelle, 'Why African countries should emulate China's development model', 15 December 2017 (http://venturesafrica.com/africa-needs-to-seize-the-golden-opportunity-to-promote-economic-trans formation-helen-hai/).
2 Taylor, *Africa Rising?*
3 FDI is used here but is termed 'Overseas FDI' in official Chinese usage.
4 Willemien Viljoen, 'The China–Africa trade relationship', TRALAC, 18 November 2019 (https://www.tralac.org/publications/article/14319-the-china-africa-trade-relationship.html).
5 WTO, 'World Trade Statistical Review 2019', p. 53.
6 African Export–Import Bank, *African Trade Report 2018: Boosting Intra-African Trade*: 58.
7 Deborah Brautigam, Xinshen Diao, Margaret McMillan and Jed Silver, 'Chinese investment in Africa: How much do we know?', PEDL Policy Insight Series No. 3, 1 December 2018.
8 *Hellenic Shipping News*, 'China's exports to its three major trading partners'.
9 Lawrence Edwards and Rhys Jenkins, 'The impact of Chinese import penetration on the South African manufacturing sector', *Journal of Development Studies* 51 (4) 2015: 447–63.
10 Girum Abebe, Margaret S. McMillan and Michel Serafinelli, 'Foreign direct investment and knowledge diffusion in poor locations: Evidence from Ethiopia', *NBER Working Paper* No. 24461 (2018).
11 Raphael Kaplinsky, 'What does the rise of China do for industrialization in sub-Saharan Africa?' *Review of African Political Economy* 35 (1) 2008: 7–22.
12 Nelson Oppong, Luke Patey and Ricardo Soares de Oliveira, 'Governing African oil and gas: Boom-era political and institutional innovation', *The Extractive Industries and Society* 7 (4) 2020: 1165.
13 IMF, 'Regional economic outlook: Sub-Saharan Africa recovery amid elevated uncertainty', April 2019: 9.
14 Janet Eom, Jyhjong Hwang, Lucas Atkins, Yunnan Chen and Siqi Zhou, 'The United States and China in Africa: What does the data say?', CARI Policy Brief 18, 2017: 1.
15 See Jeremy Stevens, 'Manufacturing for Intra-Africa trade: A focused response to China's dominant position in Africa for South Africa', in Chris Alden and Yu-Shan Wu, eds, *South Africa–China Relations: A Partnership of Paradoxes* (Palgrave Macmillan, 2021), pp. 107–35.
16 Viljoen, 'The China–Africa trade relationship'.

17 See 'China's Foreign Aid' (Beijing: Information Office of the State Council of the PRC: April 2011).

18 'China's international development cooperation in the New Era', State Council, January 2021.

19 For background, see Raphael Kaplinsky and Mike Morris, 'Chinese FDI in sub-Saharan Africa: Engaging with large dragons', *European Journal of Development Research* 21 (4) 2009: 551–69.

20 UNCTAD, World Investment Report 2020: 13.

21 CARI data. The largest single Chinese investment in Africa was the 2007 Industrial and Commercial Bank of China acquisition of a 20% stake ($5.5bn) in Standard Group, South Africa's largest bank.

22 Thierry Pairault, 'Investment in Africa: China vs "traditional partners"', China in Africa: The Real Story blog, 31 July 2020 (http://www.chinaafricareal-story.com/2020/07/guest-post-investment-in-africa-china.html).

23 UNCTAD's ranking of top investor economies by FDI stock in Africa in 2018 was: the Netherlands ($79bn), France ($53bn), UK ($49bn), US ($48bn), China ($46bn), South Africa ($35bn), Italy ($29bn), Hong Kong ($21bn), Singapore ($26bn) and Germany ($14bn). UNCTAD, World Investment Report 2020: 28.

24 Lucas Atkins, Deborah Brautigam, Yunnan Chen and Jyhjong Hwang, 'Challenges of and opportunities from the commodity price slump', CARI Economic Bulletin 1, 2017: 4; Eom et al., 'The United States and China in Africa': 4.

25 Thierry Pairault, 'China in Africa: Goods supplier, service provider rather than investor', *Bridges Africa* 7 (5) 2018: 17.

26 See CARI, Chinese Investment in Africa, 2003–19 (http://www.sais-cari.org/chinese-investment-in-africa).

27 Chris Alden and Martyn Davies, 'A profile of the operations of Chinese multinationals in Africa', *South African Journal of International Affairs* 13 (1) 2006: 83–96; Kartik Javaram, Omid Kassiri and Irene Yuan Sun, *Dance of the Lions and Dragons: How are Africa and China Engaging, and How Will the Partnership Evolve?* (McKinsey, June 2017).

28 Brautigam et al., 'Chinese investment in Africa', p. 3.

29 Christina Wolf and Sam-Kee Cheng, 'Chinese overseas contracted projects and economic diversification in Angola and Ethiopia 2000–2015', IDCEA Working Paper No. 2, SOAS, University of London, 2018.

30 See CARI, Data: Chinese Contracts in Africa, citing National Bureau of Statistics of China (http://www.sais-cari.org/data-chinese-contracts-in-africa).

31 These were ranked 5th, 17th and 26th by *African Business* magazine's

2018/2019 Top 100 most admired brands in Africa (Nike ranked 1st, Apple 7th).

32 Carlos Lopes, 'Defining structural transformation in Africa', *CODESRIA Bulletin* 1&2, 2016: 3.

33 Deborah Brautigam, Tang Xiaoyang and Ying Xia, 'What kinds of Chinese "geese" are flying to Africa? Evidence from Chinese manufacturing firms', *Journal of African Economies* 27, AERC Supplement 1, 2018: i29–i51.

34 Justin Yifu Lin and Wang Yan, *Going Beyond Aid: Development Cooperation for Structural Transformation* (Cambridge University Press, 2016).

35 Chris Alden and Lu Jiang, 'Brave new world: Debt, industrialization and security in China–Africa relations', *International Affairs*, 95 (3) 2019: 641–57.

36 Lin Songtian, 'The new thinking and new measures of China's policy to Africa: Helping boost transformation and development of African Economy', speech at Policy Dialogue between China and IDA, 7 June 2016 (https://www.fmprc.gov.cn/ce/ceke/eng/zfgx/t1372756.htm).

37 Paul Nugent, 'Africa's re-enchantment with big infrastructure: White elephants dancing in virtuous circles?', in Jon Schubert, Ulf Engel and Elisio Macamo, eds, *Extractive Industries and Changing State Dynamics in Africa* (Routledge, 2018), p. 22.

38 Javaram, Kassiri and Sun, *Dance of the Lions and Dragons*, p. 23.

39 See The Infrastructure Consortium for Africa, 'Infrastructure financing trends in Africa – 2018' (Abidjan: ICA, 2018) (https://www.icafrica.org/fileadmin/documents/IFT_2018/ICA_Infrastructure_Financing_in_Africa_Report_2018_En.pdf).

40 See Brautigam, *The Dragon's Gift*, p. 47. Commodity-secured financing in Africa had a longer history as well.

41 Ana Cristina Alves, 'China's "win–win" cooperation: Unpacking the impact of infrastructure-for-resources deals in Africa', *South African Journal of International Affairs* 20 (2) 2013: 207–26.

42 Scott Wingo, 'The rise and fall of the resource backed loan', CACR, 18 February 2020 (Parts 1&2).

43 Javaram, Kassiri and Sun, *Dance of the Lions and Dragons*.

44 'Chinese phone maker celebrates 100-mln-USD export milestone in Ethiopia', *Xinhua*, 21 November 2018.

45 Sun, *The Next Factory of the World*, 53–4.

46 Ying Xia, 'Assessing Chinese manufacturing investments in East Africa: Drivers, challenges, and opportunities', CARI Briefing Paper 2, 2019.

47 Alden and Jiang, 'Brave new world', p. 652.

48 Hunan Provincial Government, 'Ethiopian–Hunan industrial park under

construction', 7 September 2018 (http://www.enghunan.gov.cn/SP/SP201 8/4thInvesting/4thInvesting_news/201809/t20180917_5096277.html).

49 Justin Yifu Lin, 'Industry transfer to Africa good for all', *China Daily USA*, 20 January 2015 (http://usa.chinadaily.com.cn/opinion/2015-01/20/ content_19353085.htm).

50 Yuen Yuen Ang, 'Demystifying Belt and Road', *Foreign Policy* 22 (2019).

51 Wang Weixing, '*Quanqiu shiye xia de yidai yilu fengxian yu tiaozhan* (Risks and challenges to the Belt and Road from a global perspective)', 5 June 2015 (http://www.cssn.cn/zzx/gjzzx_zzx/201506/t20150605_2024182. shtml?COLLCC=3527704886&).

52 David Dollar, 'Understanding China's Belt and Road infrastructure projects in Africa' (Brookings: September 2019).

53 According to one study, the 2019 figures represented a 71% drop in global energy finance from 2018. See Xinyue Ma, Kevin P. Gallagher and Yanan Guo, 'China's global energy finance 2019', GCI Brief 004 (02/2020).

54 The RMB's addition to the IMF's Special Drawing Rights basket of currencies in October 2016, and approval as an official reserve currency, was another notable shift.

55 'BRI promotes yuan internationalization despite trade war', *Global Times*, 4 June 2019.

56 Deborah Brautigam, 'A critical look at Chinese "debt-trap diplomacy": The rise of a meme', *Area Development and Policy* 5 (1) 2019: 1–14.

57 As Eric Olander noted, 'African leaders push back on Western-led debt narrative, US, European officials should take note', 9 December 2019 (https:// chinaafricaproject.com/analysis/african-leaders-push-back-on-western-led-debt-narrative-u-s-european-officials-should-take-note/).

58 Anzetse Were, 'Debt trap? Chinese loans and Africa's development options', *SAIIA Policy Insights*, 11 September 2019.

59 Deborah Bräutigam and Kevin Gallagher, 'Bartering globalization: China's commodity-backed finance in Africa and Latin America', *Global Policy* 5 (3) 2014: 348.

60 Kevin Acker, Deborah Brautigam and Yufan Huang, 'Debt relief with Chinese characteristics', CARI Working Paper 39, June 2020.

61 Another figure was China made up 20% of external debt in 2018; Jubilee Debt Campaign, 'Africa's growing debt crisis: Who is the debt owed to?' (October 2018).

62 Acker, Brautigam and Huang, 'Debt relief with Chinese characteristics'.

63 According to CARI data, 2020.

64 Matthew Hill and Eric Martin, 'Angola may see biggest win in $12 billion G-20 debt-relief plan', *Bloomberg*, 19 June 2020 (https://www.

bloomberg.com/news/articles/2020-06-19/angola-may-see-biggest-win-in-12-billion-g-20-debt-relief-plan).

65　Liu Qinghai, 'Feizhou jingji weilai zouxiang ji Zhongguo duice (The future of African economy and China's countermeasures)', Zheshida Feizhou guancha 2 (Zhejiang Normal University Africa Watch 2), 10 September 2019 (https://www.thepaper.cn/newsDetail_forward_4387906).

66　Mail & Guardian, 'China puts screws on Zim', 23 January 2015 (www.mg.co.za/article/2015-01-23-china-puts-screws-on-zim.htm).

67　Alves, 'China's "win–win" cooperation', p. 219.

68　Alden and Jiang, 'Brave new world'.

69　Yinka Adegoke, 'Africa's rising "unsustainable" debt driving a wedge between the World Bank and other lenders', Quartz Africa, 16 February 2020 (https://qz.com/africa/1803280/world-bank-imf-worry-on-africa-rising-debt-to-china-afdb/).

70　One review of Chinese loan contracts found that most include language about a waiver of sovereign immunity regarding arbitration and enforcement, if disputes can't be resolved by 'friendly consultation'. The venue for arbitration is not always specified, although Kenya's SGR loan, for example, specifies Beijing, but contracts are generally governed by Chinese law. A general lack of public information and opaque negotiating processes means that politics can easily mobilize in response. See Deborah Brautigam and Won Kidane, 'China, Africa, and debt distress: Face and fiction about asset seizures', CARI Policy Brief 47, 2020.

71　Rodney Muhumuza, 'As China builds up Africa, some in Uganda warn of trouble', AP, 24 October 2019.

72　Obiageli Ezekwesili, 'China must pay reparations to Africa for its coronavirus failures', The Washington Post, 16 April 2020; Sun Saixiong, 'Stop dancing to other's tune', Guardian (Nigeria), 3 May 2020.

73　In relation to bilateral debt service payments owed by the 76 International Development Association-eligible countries and Angola, including 40 African countries.

74　Acker, Brautigam and Huang, 'Debt relief with Chinese characteristics'.

75　Ma Tianjie, 'How will China handle multiple debt repayment crises?', Panda Paw Dragon Club, 21 June 2020.

76　Yun Sun, 'China's debt relief for Africa: emerging deliberations', 9 June 2020 (https://www.brookings.edu/blog/africa-in-focus/2020/06/09/chinas-debt-relief-for-africa-emerging-deliberations/).

77　Edward Friedman, 'How economic superpower China could transform Africa', Journal of Chinese Political Science 14 (1) 2009: 14, 18.

78　Taylor, Africa Rising?

79 AU Development Agency and NEPAD, 'First Continental Report on the Implementation of Agenda 2063', February 2020.

80 Allianz SE, 'Heading for a China-less recovery', 10 November 2020 (https://www.allianz.com/en/economic_research/publications/specials_fmo/2020_11_10_EmergingMarketsChina.html).

81 Calestous Juma, 'Globalization as we know it has failed. Africa has an alternative', World Economic Forum, 6 July 2016 (https://www.weforum.org/agenda/2016/07/globalization-as-we-know-it-has-failed-africa-has-an-alternative/).

82 Heiwai Tang, Douglas Zhihua Zeng and Albert Zeufack, 'Assessing Asia – sub-Saharan Africa global value chain linkages', Kiel Working Paper 2159, June 2020.

83 See UNCTAD, Economic Development in Africa Report 2019 (UNCTAD: Geneva 2019).

84 Lopes, 'Defining structural transformation', pp. 3–5.

85 For context, see Maddalena Procopio, 'Kenyan agency in Kenya–China relations: contestation, cooperation and passivity', in Alden and Large, eds, New Directions in Africa–China Studies, pp. 173–88.

86 A 2013 agreement by Kenya, Uganda and Rwanda to fast-track construction of rail connections between Nairobi, Kampala and Kigali was in question.

87 Ian Taylor, 'Kenya's new lunatic express: The standard gauge railway', African Studies Quarterly 19 (3–4) 2020: 43.

88 Lin Songtian, 'The new thinking and new measures of China's policy to Africa'.

89 Carmody and Kragelund, 'Who is in charge?', p. 1.

90 Alden and Jiang, 'Brave new world', p. 657.

4 Xi's China Model, African Politics

1 MFA, 'Wang Yi talks about the essence of major country diplomacy with Chinese characteristics', 19 October 2017 (www.fmprc.gov.cn/mfa_eng/zxxx_662805/t1503756.shtml).

2 See Benabdallah, Shaping the Future of Power.

3 Christopher Clapham, 'Fitting China in', in Chris Alden et al., eds, China Returns to Africa: A Continent and a Rising Power Embrace (London: Hurst, 2008), pp. 361–9.

4 See Daniel Bell, The China Model: Political Meritocracy and the Limits of Democracy (Princeton University Press, 2015).

5 Emmanuel John Hevi, *An African Student in China* (London: Pall Mall Press, 1963), p. 100.

6 Yuen Yuen Ang, *How China Escaped the Poverty Trap* (Cornell University Press, 2016).

7 Wei Wei Zhang, 'The allure of the Chinese model', *International Herald Tribune*, 1 November 2006.

8 See Joshua Ramo-Cooper, *The Beijing Consensus* (London: The Foreign Policy Centre, 2004).

9 Matt Ferchen, 'Whose China Model is it anyway? The contentious search for consensus', *Review of International Political Economy* 20 (2) 2013: 390–420.

10 These included the Suzhou model (a government-led economic development model), the Wenzhou model (economic development model guided by market), the Dongguan model (using foreign investment to develop manufacturing industry) and 'new left' approaches (reasserting state control).

11 Yuen Yuen Ang, 'Autocracy with Chinese characteristics', *Foreign Affairs* 97 (3) 2018: 39–46.

12 Tai Ming Cheung, 'The Chinese national security state emerges from the shadows to center stage', *China Leadership Monitor*, 1 September 2020.

13 *China Daily*, 'Full text of Xi Jinping's report at 19th CPC National Congress', 4 November 2017, (https://www.chinadaily.com.cn/china/19thcpcnationalcongress/2017-11/04/content_34115212.htm).

14 Speech by Xi Jinping, 'Work together to build the Silk Road Economic Belt and the 21st-century Maritime Silk Road', 14 May 2017 (http://www.xinhuanet.com//english/2017-05/14/c_136282982.htm).

15 'Xi Jinping: Working together to build a better world', 1 February 2018 (http://ca.china-embassy.org/eng/sgxw/t1531148.htm).

16 'China and the world in the new era' (Beijing: State Council Information Office, September 2019).

17 As Renmin University's Wang Yiwei remarked in relation to the 2017 CPC in dialogue with World Political Parties High-level Meeting. See Ting Shi, 'China gets 300 parties to endorse Xi as peacemaker', *Bloomberg*, 4 December 2017.

18 'Celebrating the 40th anniversary of reform and opening up', *Xinhua*, 18 December 2018 (http://www.xinhuanet.com/politics/zbggkf40/wzsl.htm).

19 See 'China and the world in the New Era'.

20 Nectar Gan, 'Economist Zhang Weiying slams "China model" that "inevitably leads to confrontation with the West"', *South China Morning Post*, 26 October 2018; Gabriel Wildau, 'Chinese economists blame "China model" for US trade war', *Financial Times*, 30 October 2018.

21 Song Wei, 'China–Africa governance exchange nothing like the export of Western institutions', *Global Times*, 29 September 2019 (http://www.globaltimes.cn/content/1165870.shtml).

22 Luke Patey, *How China Loses: The Pushback against Chinese Global Ambitions* (Oxford University Press, 2021).

23 Zhou and Esteban, 'Beyond balancing'.

24 Lina Benabdallah, 'Contesting the international order by integrating it: The case of China's Belt and Road Initiative', *Third World Quarterly* 40 (1) 2019: 102.

25 Zheng Zhuqiang, 'Five questions, answers on what is happening in Hong Kong', *New Vision*, 25 August 2019 (https://www.newvision.co.ug/new_vision/news/1506172/questions-answers-happening-hong-kong).

26 'Secretary of State Rex Tillerson on US–Africa relations: A new framework', George Mason University Fairfax, Virginia, 6 March 2018 (https://translations.state.gov/2018/03/06/remarks-secretary-of-state-rex-tillerson-on-u-s-africa-relations-a-new-framework/).

27 By contrast, in the 2017/2018 academic year, there were 39,479 African higher education students in US universities (https://www.iie.org/Research-and-Insights/Open-Doors/Data/International-Students/Places-of-Origin).

28 Yun Sun, 'The political significance of China's latest commitments to Africa', 12 September 2018 (https://www.brookings.edu/blog/africa-in-focus/2018/09/12/the-political-significance-of-chinas-latest-commitments-to-africa/).

29 'Vice Foreign Minister Zhang Ming makes new requests to Chinese research institutes for enhancing original research on Africa', 14 September 2017 (http://www.fmprc.gov.cn/mfa_eng/wjbxw/t1493456.shtml).

30 Wang Yi, 'Build on 20 years of proud achievements and open up a new chapter in China–Africa relations', 14 November 2020 (https://www.iol.co.za/business-report/belt-and-road/build-on-20-years-of-proud-achievements-and-open-up-a-new-chapter-in-china-africa-relations-6de2f883-e1d3-41ee-abf8-d63b2f7fa729).

31 Development Reimagined, 'Who's helping young African people become global citizens?', 9 September 2018.

32 Benabdallah, *Shaping the Future of Power*, p. 134.

33 Forum on China–Africa Cooperation Action Plan 2018, at 5.5.2 (http://www.focac.org/eng/zywx_1/zywj/t1594297.htm).

34 Yun Sun, 'The political significance of China's latest commitments'.

35 Jing Gu and Richard Carey, 'China's development finance and African

infrastructure development', in Oqubay and Lin, eds, *China–Africa and an Economic Transformation*, pp. 147–72.

36 Eric Olander, 'China appears to be using African mass media to try and sway public opinion on Xinjiang', 20 November 2019 (https://chinaafricaproject. com/analysis/china-appears-to-be-using-african-mass-media-to-try-and-sway-public-opinion-on-xinjiang/).

37 Dani Madrid-Morales, 'Chinese media in the Global South: A historical overview of an enduring asymmetric relationship', 27 May 2019, presentation at ICA 2019.

38 Herman Wasserman and Dani Madrid-Morales, 'How influential are Chinese media in Africa? An audience analysis in Kenya and South Africa', *International Journal of Communication* 12, 2018: 20.

39 'More Batswana are turning to social media – for better and for worse', Afrobarometer, 22 May 2020 (http://afrobarometer.org/press/more-batswana-are-turning-social-media-better-and-worse).

40 Internet users in Africa as of December 2020 were estimated at 590,296,163 (https://www.internetworldstats.com/stats.htm). Out of a total continental population of 1.356bn, 62% were using the internet in southern Africa in 2020, 56% in northern Africa, 42% in west Africa, 26% in central Africa and 24% in eastern Africa. At the same time, the number of unconnected people remains high in some regions (with 238 million unconnected people in western Africa, and 341 million in eastern Africa), and countries (85% of Liberia's population are not using the internet, the largest percentage in the world). See We Are Social, *Global Digital Report 2021* (https://wearesocial. com/digital-2021).

41 David Bandurski, 'PSC converges for media convergence', 29 January 2019 (https://chinamediaproject.org/2019/01/29/psc-converges-for-media-convergence/).

42 Benabdallah, *Shaping the Future of Power*.

43 For instance, Guo Yezhou, Vice-minister of the ID-CCP, met with a cadre study group of Kenya's Jubilee Party in July 2019, a senior MPLA cadre study group in September 2019, and François Xavier Ngarambe, Secretary General of the Rwandan Patriotic Front in October 2019.

44 Christine Hackenesch and Julia Bader, 'The struggle for minds and influence: The Chinese communist party's global outreach', *International Studies Quarterly* 64 (3) 2020: 723–33.

45 See Lu Jiang and Zhan Shu, '"There was no real information about China in South Africa": Revisiting the history of the establishment of diplomatic relations between South Africa and China (1950s–1990s)', *South African Journal of International Affairs* 26 (3) 2019: 455–79.

46 Hackenesch and Bader, 'The struggle for minds and influence', p. 727.

47 Susan Booysen, 'Hues of the ANC's Chinese homecoming', *Daily Maverick*, 1 August 2018 (https://www.dailymaverick.co.za/opinionista/2018-08-01-hues-of-the-ancs-chinese-homecoming/).

48 African National Congress, National General Council 2015 Discussion Document, 'International Relations', p. 161, para. 32.

49 Gertrude Makhafola, 'Tshwane mayor's Taiwan visit an act of treason: ANC', 28 December 2016 (https://www.iol.co.za/news/politics/tshwane-mayors-taiwan-visit-an-act-of-treason-anc-7286678).

50 Caiphus Kgosana, 'ANC looks to China for election strategy and tactics', *The Times Live*, 28 June 2018 (https://www.timeslive.co.za/news/2018-07-28-anc-looks-to-china-for-election-strategy-and-tactics/).

51 See Chris Alden and Yu-Shan Wu, 'Leadership, global agendas and domestic determinants of South Africa's foreign policy towards China: The Zuma and Ramaphosa years', in Alden and Wu, eds, *South Africa–China Relations*: 37-63.

52 Lina Benabdallah, 'Power or influence? Making sense of China's evolving party-to-party diplomacy in Africa', *African Studies Quarterly* 19 (3–4) 2020: 102.

53 Ibid., p. 103.

54 Such adaptation to politics in African countries also applies to Chinese migrants and SOEs, among others. As Chapter 6 noted (p. 190), CNPC's efforts to develop better community relations in Sudan can be said to have been ahead of the curve when it came to more sophisticated attempts to understand and engage politics.

55 See Benabdallah, *Shaping the Future of Power*.

56 *AFP*, 'Tanzanian President Magufuli says his party will rule "forever"', 17 July 2018 (https://www.theeastafrican.co.ke/news/ea/Tanzania-John-Magufuli-ccm-in-power-forever/4552908-4667434-oosawgz/index.html).

57 Benabdallah, *Shaping the Future of Power*, p. 147.

58 For example, Cooley, *East Wind over Africa*.

59 For example, David E. Kiwuwa, 'Why China's removal of term limits is a gift to African despots', *The Conversation*, 8 March 2018 (https://theconversation.com/why-chinas-removal-of-term-limits-is-a-gift-to-african-despots-92746).

60 Bayart, 'Africa in the world'.

61 See Chris Alden, 'A Chinese model for Africa', in Alden and Large, eds., p. 280.

62 William Gumede, 'China [*sic*] impact on African democracy', *The Namibian*, 28 August 2018.

63 Giovanni Marco Carbone, Vincenzo Memoli and Lia Quartapelle, 'Are lions democrats? The impact of democratization on economic growth in Africa, 1980–2010', *Democratization* 23 (1) 2016: 27–48; Robin Harding, *Rural Democracy: Elections and Development in Africa* (Oxford University Press, 2020).

64 Abimbola Adelakun, 'Nigerian politicians and the China Fallacy', 5 December 2019 (https://punchng.com/nigerian-politicians-and-the-china-fallacy/).

65 Nimot Sulaimon, '"China closed its borders for 40 years and they're better now" –NCS', *Nigeria News* 4 November 2019 (https://www.pmnewsnigeria. com/2019/11/04/china-closed-its-borders-for-40-years-and-theyre-better-now-ncs/).

66 Elsje Fourie, 'China's example for Meles' Ethiopia: When development "models" land', *Journal of Modern African Studies* 53 (3) 2015: 289–316, p. 295.

67 Alex de Waal, 'The theory and practice of Meles Zenawi', *African Affairs* 112 (446) 2013: 153.

68 See Berhan Taye, 'Targeted, cut off and left in the dark', *Access Now*, 2019.

69 Eniola Akinkuotu, 'Social media bill: China also hangs corrupt politicians, Nigerians reply Aisha', 30 November 2019 (https://punchng.com/social-media-bill-china-also-hangs-corrupt-politicians-nigerians-reply-aisha/).

70 This matters particularly where print media are government controlled, and the internet is the main source of trustworthy information. In June 2019, for example, following the role of social media in the overthrow of former president Bashir, the Sudanese government switched off the internet as paramilitary soldiers killed protesters in Khartoum, stopping protesters documenting violence on social media.

71 Iginio Gagliardone, *China, Africa, and the Future of the Internet* (London: Zed Books, 2019).

72 Gumede, 'China impact on African democracy.'

73 Yuan Wang and Uwe Wissenbach, 'Clientelism at work? A case study of Kenyan Standard Gauge Railway project', *Economic History of Developing Regions* 34 (3) 2019: 280–99.

74 See Damaris Parsitau, 'Wajinga nation: The rising popularity of protest music in Kenya', *The Elephant*, 25 January 2020 (https://www. theelephant.info/features/2020/01/25/wajinga-nation-the-rising-popularity-of-protest-music-in-kenya/).

75 'Figures of China's bilateral support to Zimbabwe in the budget statement

shall be revisited', 19 November 2019 (http://zw.china-embassy.org/eng/xwdt/t1717059.htm).

76 Stephen Chan, 'China/Africa: New departures', *The Africa Report*, 18 April 2018 (https://www.theafricareport.com/670/china-africa-new-departures -3/).

77 Such as claims that China sought to have Mnangagwa promoted to become vice-president in 2014, and recent displeasure at Mnangagwa and preference for Chiwenga, who became co-vice president in 2017, as a future leader.

78 Michael Bratton and Sadhiska Bhoojedhur, 'PP58: Africans want open elections – especially if they bring change', Afrobarometer Policy Papers 58, 2019: 2.

79 'China shares wisdom of social governance with world', *Xinhua*, 19 November 2019 (http://www.xinhuanet.com/english/2019-11/19/c_138567460.htm).

80 'Tuju admits Jubilee Party has its challenges', *Sunday Nation*, 7 June 2020.

81 Samir Saran and Akhil Deo, *Pax Sinica: Implications for the Indian Dawn* (Rupa Publications India, 2019).

82 See Naunihal Singh, Josephine Appiah-Nyamekye Sanny and E. Gyimah-Boadi, 'US –China competition may be a win–win for Africa', *The Washington Post*, 20 November 2020.

83 Shu Zhan, 'Thoughts on sustainable Sino-Africa relationship', 24 March 2010, Shanghai.

84 Mzukisi Qobo and Garth le Pere, 'Between resource extraction and industrializing Africa', in Alden and Large, eds, *New Directions in Africa–China Studies*, p. 275.

5 Chinese–African Relations

1 See Monson, *Africa's Freedom Railway*.

2 See Romain Dittgen and Ross Anthony, 'Yellow, red, and black. Fantasies about China and "the Chinese" in contemporary South Africa', in Frank Billé and Sören Urbansky, eds, *Yellow Perils: China Narratives in the Contemporary World* (Honolulu: University of Hawai'i Press, 2018), pp. 108–41.

3 See Juan Cardenal and Herberto Araújo, *China's Silent Army: The Pioneers, Traders, Fixers and Workers Who Are Remaking the World in Beijing's Image* (Allen Lane, 2013); Howard French, *China's Second Continent* (New York: Alfred A. Knopf, 2014).

4 Hannah Postel, 'Moving beyond "China in Africa": Insights from Zambian immigration data', *Journal of Current Chinese Affairs* 46 (2) 2017: 155.

5 Seth Cook, Jixia Lu, Henry Tugendhat and Dawit Alemu, 'Chinese migrants

in Africa: Facts and fictions from the agri-food sector in Ethiopia and Ghana', *World Development* 81, 2016: 61–70.

6 Jonathan Sullivan and Jing Cheng, 'Contextualising Chinese migration to Africa', *Journal of Asian and African Studies* 53 (8) 2018: 1173–87.

7 Between 1995 and 2015, the number of entries into China by nationals of African countries saw a 14-fold increase (to 580,000 in 2015). Heidi Østbø Haugen, 'China–Africa exports: Governance through mobility and sojourning', *Journal of Contemporary Asia* 49 (2) 2019: 301.

8 Gordon Mathews, Linessa Dan Lin and Yang Yang, *The World in Guangzhou: Africans and Other Foreigners in South China's Global Marketplace* (University of Chicago Press, 2017), p. 2.

9 Haugen, 'China–Africa exports'.

10 For context, see Linn Axelsson and Nina Sylvanus, 'Navigating Chinese textile networks: Women traders in Accra and Lomé', in Fantu Cheru and Cyril Obi, eds, *The Rise of China and India in Africa: Challenges, Opportunities and Critical Interventions* (London: Zed Books, 2010), pp. 132–44.

11 Ute Röschenthaler, 'Chinese green tea in Mali, cultural mobility and African agency in the global south', *African and Asian Studies* 19 (1–2) 2020: 152.

12 See Roberto Castillo, *African Transnational Mobility in China: Africans on the Move* (Routledge, 2021).

13 Heidi Østbø Haugen, 'Nigerians in China: A second state of immobility', *International Migration* 50 (2) 2012: 65–80.

14 See Roberto Castillo, '"Homing" Guangzhou: Emplacement, belonging and precarity among Africans in China', *International Journal of Cultural Studies* 19 (3) 2016: 287–306.

15 See the documentary 'Africans in Yiwu' (Zhang Yong, Hodan Abdi and Fu Dong, 2017).

16 See Elaine L. E. Ho, 'The geo-social and global geographies of power: Urban aspirations of "worlding" African students in China', *Geopolitics* 22 (1) 2017: 15–33.

17 Such as Ghanaian software engineer and entrepreneur, Charles Cyril Nettey, who runs an e-commerce business in Shanghai and co-founded the Africa Diaspora Innovation Group. See Heather Li, 'Ghanian entrepreneur in China: Africa Diaspora Innovation Group (ADIG)', 31 December 2020 (https://www.youtube.com/watch?v=aEfq2z-_7pw).

18 There are Gabonese and Zimbabweans of Chinese descent, for example. South Africa has three types of Chinese residents: Chinese South Africans, whose ancestors arrived as far back as the nineteenth century; Chinese from Taiwan and Hong Kong, who immigrated in the 1970s to 1990s; and more recently arrived immigrants from mainland China.

19 See Hannah Postel, 'Moving beyond "China in Africa"'.

20 Su Zhou, 'Number of Chinese immigrants in Africa rapidly increasing', *China Daily*, 14 January 2017.

21 Park, 'One million Chinese in Africa.' Adams Bodomo estimated that 'there are two million Chinese living and working in Africa'. See Adams Bodomo, 'Historical and contemporary perspectives on inequalities and well-being of Africans in China', *Asian Ethnicity*, 21 (4) 2020: 528.

22 According to CARI figures. These include Chinese workers sent to work on Chinese companies' construction contracts in Africa, and Chinese workers sent to work for non-Chinese companies in Africa, but not informal migrants such as traders and shopkeepers.

23 See Carlos Oya and Florian Schaefer, 'Chinese firms and employment dynamics in Africa: A comparative analysis', IDCEA Research Synthesis Report, SOAS, University of London.

24 Tom Hancock, 'Chinese return from Africa as migrant population peaks', *Financial Times*, 28 August 2017.

25 See Miriam Driessen, *Tales of Hope, Tastes of Bitterness: Chinese Road Builders in Ethiopia* (Hong Kong University Press, 2019).

26 The number of Chinese tourists visiting African countries was growing but in 2017, only 0.62% of the 130m foreign trips Chinese made were to African countries. Youyou Zhou, 'Why Chinese are traveling to Africa, and why Africans are traveling to China', *Quartz Africa*, 10 September 2019.

27 Youyou Zhou, 'Beijing is not the most popular Chinese city for passengers flying to or from Africa', *Quartz Africa*, 2 August 2019.

28 Joachim Jarreau, 'Lifting the lid on the black box of informal trade in Africa', *The Conversation*, 24 September 2018 (https://theconversation.com/lifting-the-lid-on-the-black-box-of-informal-trade-in-africa-102867).

29 Edwin Okoth, 'Chinese in Gikomba', *Business Daily*, 10 June 2019 (https://www.businessdailyafrica.com/news/The-Chinese-in-Gikomba/539546-5151338-wj86it/index.html).

30 See Isaac Odoom, 'Dam in, cocoa out; pipes in, oil out: China's engagement in Ghana's energy sector', *Journal of Asian and African Studies*, 52 (5) 2018: 598–620.

31 Gabriel Botchwey, Gordon Crawford, Nicholas Loubere and Jixia Lu, 'South–South irregular migration: The impacts of China's informal gold rush in Ghana', *International Migration*, 57 (4) 2019: 322.

32 Botchwey et al., 'South–South irregular migration', p. 311.

33 Gordon Crawford and Gabriel Botchwey, 'Conflict, collusion and corruption in small-scale gold mining: Chinese miners and the state in Ghana', *Commonwealth and Comparative Politics*, 55 (4) 2017: 444.

34 Richard Aidoo, 'The political economy of Galamsey and anti-Chinese sentiment in Ghana', *African Studies Quarterly* 16 (3/4) 2016: 55.

35 *GhanaWeb*, 'Chinese miners in Ghana becomes contentious issue in presidential campaign', 3 November 2020 (https://www.ghanaweb.com/GhanaHomePage/politics/Small-scale-miners-endorse-Mahama-NDC-1099624).

36 Timothy Ngnenbe, 'Chinese can't engage in illegal mining without local help-Chinese envoy', 13 February 2019, citing Deputy Chief of Mission at the Chinese Embassy, Zhu Jing (https://www.graphic.com.gh/news/general-news/ghananews-no-chinese-can-engage-in-illegal-mining-without-local-collaborators-deputy-chief-of-mission-at-the-chinese-embassy-says.html).

37 Most Chinese in African countries 'are not self-isolated and not more isolated in Africa than are other Asian migrants and whites there'. Hairong Yan, Barry Sautman and Yao Lu, 'Chinese and "self-segregation" in Africa', *Asian Ethnicity* 20 (1) 2019: 40.

38 In 2012, following an attempt by the Tanzania Traders' Union to remove Chinese businesses from Dar es Salaam's Kariakoo commercial area, a Kariakoo Chinese Chamber of Commerce was established with the encouragement of the Chinese embassy.

39 Barry Van Wyk, 'Networking a quiet community: South African Chinese news reporting and networking', *Journal of African Media Studies* 12 (2) 2020: 189–221.

40 Wu and Van Staden, 'Media as a site of contestation'.

41 Paul Wafula and Faith Ngina, 'How the Chinese man ended up calling Kenyans and President Uhuru monkey', *The Standard*, 6 September 2018 (https://www.standardmedia.co.ke/ureport/story/2001294722/how-the-chinese-man-ended-up-calling-kenyans-and-president-uhuru-monkey).

42 Known as the 'Six Don'ts': 'Don't carry large amounts of cash; Don't exchange currency at the airport; Don't show money openly or flaunt wealth; Don't board flights arriving in the evening; Don't reveal travel plans to any unfamiliar people; Don't store passports together with other documents and cash.' See Van Wyk, 'Networking a quiet community'.

43 See Chris Alden and Ross Harvey, 'Chinese transnational criminal organisations and the illegal wildlife trade in Tanzania', *European Review of Organized Crime*, 5 (1) 2021: 10–35.

44 Environmental Investigation Agency, *The Shuidong Connection: Exposing the Global Hub of the Illegal Ivory Trade* (London: EIA, 2017), pp. 1–22.

45 See Stephanie Rupp, 'Ivory trails: Divergent values of ivory elephants in Africa and Asia', in Alden and Large, eds, *New Directions in Africa–China studies*, pp. 225–40.

46 UNODC, *World Wildlife Crime Report: Trafficking in Protected Species.* Vienna (Vienna, 2020), p. 19.

47 Mona Samari, 'Investigation ties foreign-owned trawlers to illegal fishing in Ghana', *China Dialogue Ocean*, 12 September 2019 (https://chinadialogue-ocean.net/10050-investigation-illegal-fishing-in-ghana-pt-1/).

48 Kalima Nkonde, 'How China is slowly colonizing Zambian economy', *Lusaka Times*, 27 July 2018 (https://www.lusakatimes.com/2018/07/27/how-china-slowly-colonizing-zambian-economy/).

49 Arve Ofstand and Elling Tjønneland, 'Zambia's looming debt crisis – is China to blame?' (Bergen: CMI Insight 2019: 01).

50 'China's MFA speaks out on Zambian–Chinese tensions', *Africa Times*, 12 November 2019 (https://africatimes.com/2018/11/23/chinas-mfa-speaks-out-on-zambian-chinese-tensions/).

51 Odyssey, *Zhihu*, 5 October 2018 (https://www.zhihu.com/question/2401 4906/answer/504280572).

52 'Chinese become targets in DR Congo anti-government riots', *AFP*, 25 January 2015.

53 Human Rights Watch, 'DR Congo: Kabila should commit to leave office', 16 December 2016.

54 Lily Kuo, 'Chinese migrants have changed the face of South Africa. Now they're leaving', *Quartz Africa*, 30 April 2017 (https://qz.com/africa/940619/chinese-traderschanged-south-africa-now-theyre-leaving/).

55 Yoon Jung Park, 'Playing the China card or yellow perils? China, "the Chinese", and race in South African politics and society', *Asian Ethnicity* 21 (4) 2020: 13.

56 See Ufrieda Ho, 'Hate speech case: A message about racism, discrimination', *Daily Maverick*, 14 March 2019.

57 Tu T. Huynh, Yoon Jung Park and Anna Ying Chen, 'Faces of China: New Chinese migrants in South Africa, 1980s to present', *African and Asian Studies* 9 (3) 2010: 290.

58 Jinpu Wang and Ning Zhan, 'Nationalism, overseas Chinese state and the construction of "Chineseness" among Chinese migrant entrepreneurs in Ghana', *Asian Ethnicity* 20 (1), 2019: 8–29.

59 Park, 'Playing the China card', p. 6.

60 Tu T. Huynh and Yoon Jung Park, '"Chineseness" through unexplored lenses: Identity-making in China–Africa engagements in the 21st century', *Asian and Pacific Migration Journal* 27 (1) 2018: 5.

61 Haifang Liu, 'Coping with security challenges in African society: The role of overseas Chinese associations in protecting new Chinese migrants in Africa', in Christof Hartmann and Nele Noesselt, eds, *China's New Role in African Politics: From Non-Intervention towards Stabilization?* (Routledge, 2019), p. 73.

62 See Wang and Zhan, 'Nationalism, overseas Chinese state and the construction of "Chineseness"'.

63 See Van Wyk, 'Networking a quiet community'.

64 Li Hangwei and Xuefei Shi, 'Home away from home: The social and political roles of contemporary Chinese associations in Zambia', *Journal of Current Chinese Affairs* 48 (2) 2019: 167, 158.

65 Ibid., p. 153.

66 Ibid., p. 158.

67 Ibid., p. 154.

68 Allen Hai Xiao, 'In the shadow of *the states*: The informalities of Chinese petty entrepreneurship in Nigeria', *Journal of Current Chinese Affairs* 44 (1) 2015: 84.

69 Ibid., p. 86.

70 Ibid., p. 89.

71 Ibid., p. 88.

72 Plus TV Africa, 11 September 2019 (https://www.youtube.com/watch?v=aoYG2YoYS3M).

73 Fauna, 'In Guangzhou, there are about 200,000 Africans, increasing 30–40% every year', *ChinaSmack*, 10 September 2011 (https://www.chinasmack.com/africans-in-guangzhou-opportunities-discrimination).

74 Roberto Castillo and Padmore Adusei Amoah, 'Africans in post-COVID-19 pandemic China: Is there a future for China's "new minority"?', *Asian Ethnicity* 21 (4) 2020: 560–5.

75 Kwaku Opoku Dankwah and Padmore Adusei Amoah, 'Gauging the dispositions between indigenes, Chinese and other immigrant traders in Ghana: Towards a more inclusive society', *Asian Ethnicity* 20 (1) 2019: 1–18.

76 Yan, Sautman, and Yao, 'Chinese and "Self-segregation" in Africa', p. 15.

77 My thanks to Yoon Jung Park for sharing this insight.

78 This section draws on the long-term ethnographic work in Namibia of Gregor Dobler, and his article 'China and Namibia, 1990 to 2015: How a new actor changes the dynamics of political economy', *Review of African Political Economy* 44 (153) 2017: 449–65.

79 Ibid., p. 451.

80 Park, 'Playing the China card'.

6 Security: A New 'Pillar'

1 Shen Dingli, 'Don't shun the idea of setting up overseas military bases', 28 January 2010 (http://www.china.org.cn/opinion/2010-01/28/content_19324522.htm).

2 China has used this position to initiate debates. As rotating president in April 2016, for example, it held a debate on piracy in the Gulf of Guinea.

3 Wang Duanyong and Zhao Pei, 'Security risks facing Chinese actors in sub-Saharan Africa: The case of the Democratic Republic of Congo', in Chris Alden, Abiodun Alao, Zhang Chun and Laura Barber, eds, *China and Africa: Building Peace and Security Cooperation on the Continent* (Palgrave, 2017), p. 263.

4 Speech by Wang Yi, 'Opening of symposium on the international situation and China's foreign relations in 2018', 11 December 2018.

5 *Xinhua*, 'Chinese "blue helmets" safeguard int'l peace, stability', 31 July 2017.

6 'China's military strategy' (Beijing: Information Office of the State Council, 26 May 2015).

7 Xie Yiqiu, '*Bu ganshe nei zheng*' de kunjing (The dilemma of non-interference in domestic affairs)', *Nan feng chuang* (*Southern Review*), 1 January 2010.

8 'President Xi urges new media outlet to "tell China stories well"', *Xinhua*, 31 December 2016.

9 Wang Weixing, '*Quanqiu shiye xia de yidai yilu fengxian yu tiaozhan* (Risks and challenges to the Belt and Road from a global perspective)', 5 June 2015 (http://www.cssn.cn/zzx/gjzzx_zzx/201506/t20150605_2024182. shtml?COLLCC=3527704886&).

10 Lina Benabdallah, 'Explaining attractiveness: Knowledge production and power projection in China's policy for Africa', *Journal of International Relations and Development* 22 (2) 2019: 495–514.

11 Jean-Pierre Cabestan, 'China's military base in Djibouti: A microcosm of China's growing competition with the United States and new bipolarity', *Journal of Contemporary China* 29 (125) 2020: 731–47.

12 State Oceanic Administration and National Development and Reform Commission, 'Vision for maritime cooperation under the Belt and Road Initiative', *Xinhua*, 20 June 2017.

13 'China's national defense in the New Era' (Beijing: Foreign Languages Press Co., 2019).

14 See SIPRI Arms Transfers Database, March 2020; Pieter D. Wezeman et al., 'Trends in international arms transfers, 2019', SIPRI Fact Sheet March 2020.

15 IISS, *The Military Balance 2016* (London: IISS/Routledge, 2016), p. 21.

16 China accounted for some 58% of all of the Sudan government's self-reported arms imports between 2001 and 2012, which retransferred some imported Chinese weapons and ammunition to allied groups in Darfur, a violation of the UN arms embargo on Darfur, and also to rebel groups in South Sudan. See Jonah Leff and Emile LeBrun, 'Following the thread: Arms and

ammunition tracing in Sudan and South Sudan', HSBA Working Paper No. 32. (Geneva: Small Arms Survey, 2014).

17 'Keynote Speech by Assistant Foreign Minister Chen Xiaodong at the Dialogue on the Implementation of China–Africa Peace and Security Initiative', 6 February 2019 (www.fmprc.gov.cn/mfa_eng/wjbxw/t1636100. shtml).

18 China Military Online, 'Defense Ministry's Regular Press Conference on Nov. 29', 30 November 2018 (http://eng.chinamil.com.cn/view/2018-11/30/ content_9360730.htm).

19 Xinhua, 'Spotlight: Chinese "blue helmets" safeguard int'l peace, stability', 31 July 2017 (www.xinhuanet.com/english/2017-07/31/c_136487842.htm).

20 State Council Information Office, 'China's military strategy' (Beijing: May 2015).

21 'Keynote Speech by Assistant Foreign Minister Chen Xiaodong.'

22 See Luke Patey, 'Learning in Africa: China's overseas oil investments in Sudan and South Sudan', Journal of Contemporary China 26 (107) 2017: 756–68.

23 Patey, 'Learning in Africa.'

24 Paul Nantulya, 'Chinese security contractors in Africa', Carnegie-Tsinghua, 8 October 2020.

25 See Alessandro Arduino, China's Private Army: Protecting the New Silk Road (Springer, 2017).

26 See Wang Xuejun, 'Developmental peace: Understanding China's Africa policy in peace and security', in Alden et al., eds, China and Africa: Building Peace and Security Cooperation on the Continent, pp. 67–82.

27 See Lina Benabdallah and Daniel Large, 'Development, security, and China's evolving role in Mali', CARI Working Paper 40 (2020).

28 Devon Curtis, 'China and the insecurity of development in the Democratic Republic of the Congo (DRC)', International Peacekeeping 20 (5) 2013: 551–69.

29 UNSC resolutions on South Sudan contained language supporting China's oil interests, like Resolution 2206 (3 March 2015) calling on belligerents to 'ensure the safety of all personnel and assets of all countries and international entities operating in South Sudan'.

30 For background, see Daniel Large, 'China's Sudan engagement: changing Northern and Southern political trajectories in peace and war', The China Quarterly 199, 2009: 610–26.

31 See AU Constitutive Act, preamble para. 8 (h).

32 See Ricardo Soares de Oliveira and Harry Verhoeven, 'Taming intervention:

sovereignty, statehood and political order in Africa', *Survival* 60 (2) 2018: 7–32.

33 See Liu Mingfu, *The China Dream: Great Power Thinking and Strategic Posture in the Post-American Era* (New York: CN Times Books, 2015).

34 'Additional overseas PLA bases "possible"', *China Daily*, 10 January 2019 (http://www.china.org.cn/china/2019-01/10/content_74358640.htm).

Conclusion

1 Deputy Foreign Minister Zhou Wenzhong, cited in Howard French, 'China in Africa: all trade, with no political baggage', *New York Times*, 8 August 2004.

2 Sakeus Iikela, 'Geingob tells Chinese ambassador "We are not puppets"', *The Namibian*, 22 August 2018 (https://www.namibian.com.na/180733/archive-read/Geingob-tells-Chinese-ambassador-We-are-not-puppets#).

3 William Norris, *Chinese Economic Statecraft: Commercial Actors, State Control and Grand Strategy* (New York: Cornell University Press, 2016).

4 'Xi Jinping's special envoy calls on UN to assist Africa in COVID-19 fight', *CGTN*, 5 December 2020.

5 Carmody and Kragelund, 'Who is in charge?', p. 7.

6 Alex Vines, 'China's Southern Africa debt deals reveal a wider plan', Chatham House Expert Comment, 10 December 2020 (https://www.chathamhouse.org/2020/12/chinas-southern-africa-debt-deals-reveal-wider-plan).

7 George T. Yu, *China's African Policy: A Study of Tanzania* (New York: Praeger, 1975), p. 86.

8 See China's 'Eight principles for economic aid and technical assistance to other countries', 15 January 1964.

9 Scarlett Cornelissen, Fantu Cheru and Timothy M. Shaw, 'Introduction: African and international relations in the 21st century: Still challenging theory?', in Cornelissen, Cheru and Shaw, eds, *Africa and International Relations in the 21st Century* (Palgrave, 2012), p. 7.

10 Benabdallah, 'Power or influence?', p. 95.

11 Macharia Gaitho, 'China threatens to withhold SGR funds over "hostility"', *Daily Nation*, 30 October 2018 (https://nation.africa/kenya/news/china-threatens-to-withhold-sgr-funds-over-hostility--104038).

12 Hannah Ryder, 'African countries want more "win" from the win–win, but China isn't quite ready', *Quartz Africa*, 7 September 2018.

13 See Tom Burgis, *The Looting Machine* (London: William Collins, 2015).

14 Arve Ofstad and Elling Tjonneland, 'Zambia's looming debt crisis: Is China to blame?' (Bergen: CMI Insight, 2019: 01).

15 Alexander Winning and Joe Bavier, 'Ramaphosa is "last hope" for South Africa, Chinese diplomat says', *Reuters*, 29 July 2019 (https://www.reuters.com/article/us-safrica-china-idUSKCN1UO1XG).

16 Mathieu Duchâtel, 'Terror overseas: Understanding China's evolving counter-terror strategy', ECFR Policy Brief, October 2016: 7.

17 Benabdallah, *Shaping the future of power*, p. 16.

18 Emma Mawdsley, 'South–South cooperation 3.0? Managing the consequences of success in the decade ahead', *Oxford Development Studies* 47 (3) 2019: 263.

19 Ibid.

20 Amitav Acharya, *The End of American World Order* (Cambridge: Polity, 2014).

21 See Morten Jerven, *Africa: Why Economists Get It Wrong* (London: Zed, 2015).

22 Jonathan Wheatley and James Kynge, 'China curtails overseas lending in face of geopolitical backlash', *Financial Times*, 8 December 2020.

23 Joseph Cotterill, 'Angola sharpens fight to recover stolen cash as debt pressure mounts', *Financial Times*, 11 November 2020.

24 Ricardo Soares de Oliveira, *Magnificent and Beggar Land: Angola Since the Civil War* (London: Hurst & Co, 2015).

25 Elizabeth Sidiropoulos, 'Options for the lion in the age of the dragon', *South African Journal for International Affairs* 13 (1) 2006: 103.

26 Folashadé Soulé, 'How to negotiate infrastructure deals with China: Four things African governments need to get right', The Conversation.com, 3 January 2019 (https://theconversation.com/how-to-negotiate-infrastructure-deals-with-china-four-things-african-governments-need-to-get-right-109116).

27 David Pilling and Adrienna Klasa, 'Kenya president urges rebalance of China–Africa trade', *Financial Times*, 14 May 2017 (https://www.ft.com/content/947ea960-38b2-11e7-821a-6027b8a20f23).

28 Stephen Chan, 'The middle kingdom and the dark continent: An essay on China, Africa and many fault lines', in Stephen Chan ed., *The Morality of China in Africa* (London: Zed, 2013), p. 33.

29 Alden, *China in Africa*, pp. 128–9.

30 This widely used phrase was invoked by President Xi at the 2018 FOCAC.

31 He Yiting, '*Woguo fazhan huanjing mianlin shenke fuza bianhua* (My country's development environment is facing profound and complex changes)', *Renmin Ribao* (*People's Daily*), 8 December 2020: 9 (http://paper.people.com.cn/rmrb/html/2020-12/08/nw.D110000renmrb_20201208_1-09.htm).

32 W. Gyude Moore, 'A new Cold War is coming. Africa should not pick sides', *Mail and Guardian*, 21 August 2020 (https://mg.co.za/

africa/2020-08-21-a-new-cold-war-is-coming-africa-should-not-pick-sides/).

33 Andrew Small, 'The meaning of systemic rivalry: Europe and China beyond the pandemic', ECFR Policy Brief, 13 May 2020.

34 Rana Mitter, *China's Good War* (Belknap Press, Harvard University Press, 2020), p. 260.

35 Alden and Large, 'Conclusion', in *New Directions in Africa–China Studies*, p. 339.

36 Deng Xiaoping, speech to the UNGA, 1974.

37 Gyude Moore, 'Chinese influence is assured – how should Africa respond?', *African Business*, 16 November 2020.

38 Folashadé Soulé, '"Africa + 1" summit diplomacy and the "new scramble" narrative: Recentering African agency', *African Affairs* 119 (477) 2020: 633–46.

39 Saidong, 'Weilai renkou sibei yu Zhongguo de Feizhou, women gai ruhe miandui (How should China face a new Africa when the population of Africa is four times more than China's in the future?)', *Zhihu*, 5 April 2018 (https://zhuanlan.zhihu.com/p/35181967).

40 China's population is projected to decrease by 31.4m (2.2%), between 2019 and 2050. Jacob Ausubel, 'Populations skew older in some of the countries hit hard by COVID-19', 22 April 2020 (https://www.pewresearch.org/fact-tank/2020/04/22/populations-skew-older-in-some-of-the-countries-hit-hard-by-covid-19/).

41 Saidong, *Weilai renkou sibei yu Zhongguo de Feizhou*.

42 Suisheng Zhao, 'Rhetoric and reality of China's global leadership in the context of COVID-19: Implications for the US-led world order and liberal globalization', *Journal of Contemporary China* 30 (128) 2020: 233–48.

Index